SUPER 10

CBSE Class 10

Social Science

2023 Exam Sample Papers

with 2021-22 Previous Year Solved Papers, CBSE Sample Paper & 2020 Topper Answer Sheet

DISHA™
Publication Inc

DISHA Publications Inc.

45, 2nd Floor, Maharishi Dayanand Marg,
Corner Market, Malviya Nagar, new Delhi -110017
Tel: 49842349/ 49842350

Typeset By
DISHA DTP Team

Buying books from DISHA

Just Got A Lot More Rewarding!!!

We at DISHA Publication, value your feedback immensely and to show our apperciation of our reviewers, we have launched a review contest.

To participate in this reward scheme, just follow these quick and simple steps:
- Write a review of the product you purchase on Amazon/Flipkart.
- Take a screenshot/photo of your review.
- Mail it to *disha-rewards@aiets.co.in*, along with all your details.

Each month, selected reviewers will win exciting gifts from
DISHA Publication. Note that the rewards for each month
will be declared in the first week of next month on our website.

https://bit.ly/review-reward-disha.

Write To
Us At

feedback_disha@aiets.co.in

Contents

Latest Syllabus Issued by CBSE
for Academic Year (2022-2023)

COURSE STRUCTURE
CLASS X
Theory Paper

Time: 03 Hours　　　　　　　　　　　　　　　　　　　　　　　　**Max. Marks: 80**

Unit No.	Unit	No. of Periods	Marks
I	India and the Contemporary World – II	60	25
II	Contemporary India – II	55	25
III	Democratic Politics - II	50	12
IV	Understanding Economic Development	50	13
	Total	**215**	**80**

COURSE CONTENT

Unit 1: India and the Contemporary World – II	60 Periods
Themes	**Learning Objectives**

Themes	Learning Objectives
Section 1: Events and Processes: 1. **The Rise of Nationalism in Europe:** • The French Revolution and the Idea of the Nation • The Making of Nationalism in Europe • The Age of Revolutions: 1830-1848 • The Making of Germany and Italy • Visualizing the Nation • Nationalism and Imperialism 2. **Nationalism in India:** • The First World War, Khilafat and Non - Cooperation • Differing Strands within the Movement • Towards Civil Disobedience • The Sense of Collective Belonging	• Enable the learners to identify and comprehend the forms in which nationalism developed along with the formation of nation states in Europe in the post-1830 period. • Establish the relationship and bring out the difference between European nationalism and anti-colonial nationalisms. • Understand the way the idea of nationalism emerged and led to the formation of nation states in Europe and elsewhere. • Recognize the characteristics of Indian nationalism through a case study of Non-Cooperation and Civil Disobedience Movement. • Analyze the nature of the diverse social movements of the time. • Familiarize with the writings and ideals of different political groups and individuals. • Appreciate the ideas promoting Pan Indian belongingness.

(i)

<table>
<tr><td>

Section 2: Livelihoods, Economies and Societies:

3. The Making of a Global World:
- The Pre-modern world
- The Nineteenth Century (1815-1914)
- The Inter war Economy
- Rebuilding a World Economy: The Post-War Era

4. The Age of Industrialization:
- Before the Industrial Revolution
- Hand Labour and Steam Power
- Industrialization in the Colonies
- Factories Come Up
- The Peculiarities of Industrial Growth
- Market for Goods

Section 3: Everyday Life, Culture and Politics:

5. Print Culture and the Modern World:
- The First Printed Books
- Print Comes to Europe
- The Print Revolution and its Impact
- The Reading Mania
- The Nineteenth Century
- India and the World of Print
- Religious Reform and Public Debates
- New Forms of Publication
- Print and Censorship

</td><td>

- Show that globalization has a long history and point to the shifts within the process.
- Analyze the implication of globalization for local economies.
- Discuss how globalization is experienced differently by different social groups.

- Familiarize with the Pro- to-Industrial phase and Early – factory system.
- Familiarize with the process of industrialization and its impact on labour class.
- Enable them to understand industrialization in the colonies with reference to Textile industries.

- Identify the link between print culture and the circulation of ideas.
- Familiarize with pictures, cartoons, extracts from propaganda literature and newspaper debates on important events and issues in the past.
- Understand that forms of writing have a specific history, and that they reflect historical changes within society and shape the forces of change.

</td></tr>
</table>

Unit 2: Contemporary India – II	55 Periods
Themes	**Learning Objectives**

<table>
<tr><td>

1. Resources and Development:
- Concept
- Development of Resources
- Resource Planning - Resource Planning in India, Conservation of Resources
- Land Resources
- Land Utilization
- Land Use Pattern in India
- Land Degradation and Conservation Measures
- Soil as a Resource - Classification of Soils, Soil Erosion and Soil Conservation (excluding Box Information on State of India's Environment)

2. Forest and Wildlife:
- Conservation of forest and wildlife in India
- Types and distribution of forests and wildlife resources
- Community and Conservation

</td><td>

- Understand the value of resources and the need for their judicious utilization and conservation.
-
-
-
-
-
-
-
- Understand the importance of forests and wild life.
- Understand the ability and knowledge of how forest and wildlife conservation and management relate to the economy and environment, both currently and in the future.

</td></tr>
</table>

3. **Water Resources:**
  • Water Scarcity and The Need for Water Conservation and Management
  • Multi-Purpose River Projects and Integrated Water Resources Management
  • Rainwater Harvesting
	• Comprehend the importance of water as a resource as well as develop awareness towards its judicious use and conservation.

4. **Agriculture:**
  • Types of Farming – Primitive Subsistence, Intensive Subsistence, Commercial
  • Cropping Pattern – Major Crops, Food Crops other than Grains, Non Food Crops, Technological and Institutional Reforms
  • Food Security (excluding impact of globalization on agriculture)
	• Explain the importance of agriculture in national economy
	• Identify various types of farming and discuss the various farming methods; describe the spatial distribution of major crops as well as understand the relationship between rainfall regimes and cropping pattern.
	• Explain various government policies for institutional as well as technological reforms since independence.

5. **Minerals and Energy Resources**
  • What is a mineral?
  • Mode of occurrence of Minerals - Where are these minerals found?, Ferrous Minerals, Non-Ferrous Minerals, Non-Metallic Minerals, Rock Minerals
  • Conservation of Minerals
  • Energy Resources - Conventional Sources of Energy, Non-Conventional Sources of Energy
  • Conservation of Energy Resources
	• Identify different types of minerals and energy resources and places of their availability.
	• Feel the need for their judicious utilization.
	•
	•
	•
	•
	•
	•

6. **Manufacturing Industries:** • Importance of Manufacturing - Industrial Location (excluding Industry Market Linkage), Agro based Industry (excluding Cotton Textiles, Jute Textiles, Sugar Industry), Mineral based Industries (excluding Iron Steel Industry, Cement Industry), Industrial Pollution and Environmental Degradation, Control of Environmental Degradation	• Bring out the importance of industries in the national economy as well as understand the regional disparities which resulted due to concentration of industries in some areas. • Discuss the need for a planned industrial development and debate over the role of government towards sustainable development. • •

7. **Life Lines of National Economy:**
  • Roadways
  • Railways
  • Pipelines
  • Waterways
  • Major Seaports
  • Airways
  • Communication
  • International Trade
  • Tourism as a Trade
	• Explain the importance of transport and communication in the ever-shrinking world.
	• Understand the role of trade and tourism in the economic development of a country.

Unit 3: Democratic Politics – II	50 Periods
Themes	**Learning Objectives**
1. Power Sharing: • Belgium and Sri Lanka • Majoritarianism in Sri Lanka • Accommodation in Belgium • Why power sharing is desirable? • Forms of Power Sharing	• Familiarize with the centrality of power sharing in a democracy. • Understand the working of spatial and social power sharing mechanisms.
2. Federalism: • What is Federalism? • What make India a Federal Country? • How is Federalism practiced? • Decentralization in India	• Analyze federal provisions and institutions. • Explain decentralization in rural and urban areas.
4. Gender, Religion and Caste: • Gender and Politics - Public/Private division, Women's political representation • Religion, Communalism and Politics – Communalism, Secular State (excluding image on page 46, 48, 49 of NCERT Textbook – Democratic Politics –II - reprinted edition 2021) • Caste and Politics - Caste inequalities, Caste in politics, Politics in caste	• Identify and analyze the challenges posed by communalism to Indian democracy. • Recognize the enabling and disabling effects of caste and ethnicity in politics. • Develop a gender perspective on politics.
6. Political Parties: • Why do we need Political Parties? – Meaning, Functions, Necessity • How many parties should we have? • National Parties • State Parties • Challenges to Political Parties • How can Parties be reformed?	• Analyze party systems in democracies. • Introduction to major political parties, challenges faced by them and reforms in the country.
7. Outcomes of Democracy: • How do we assess democracy's outcomes? • Accountable, responsive and legitimate government • Economic growth and development • Reduction of inequality and poverty • Accommodation of social diversity • Dignity and freedom of the citizens	• Evaluate the functioning of democracies in comparison to alternative forms of governments. • Understand the causes for continuation of democracy in India. • Distinguish between sources of strengths and weaknesses of Indian democracy.

<table>
<tr><td colspan="2">Unit 4: Understanding Economic Development</td><td>50 Periods</td></tr>
<tr><td colspan="2" align="center">Themes</td><td align="center">Learning Objectives</td></tr>
<tr>
<td colspan="2">

1. Development:
- What Development Promises - Different People, Different Goals
- Income and Other Goals
- National Development
- How to compare different countries or states?
- Income and other criteria
- Public Facilities
- Sustainability of Development

</td>
<td>

- Familiarize with concepts of macroeconomics.
- Understand the rationale for overall human development in our country, which includes the rise of income, improvements in health and education rather than income.
- Understand the importance of quality of life and sustainable development.

</td>
</tr>
<tr>
<td colspan="2">

2. Sectors of the Indian Economy:
- Sectors of Economic Activities
- Comparing the three sectors
- Primary, Secondary and Tertiary Sectors in India
- Division of sectors as organized and unorganized
- Sectors in terms of ownership: Public and Private Sectors

</td>
<td>

- Identify major employment generating sectors.
- Reason out the government investment in different sectors of economy.

</td>
</tr>
<tr>
<td colspan="2">

3. Money and Credit:
- Money as a medium of exchange
- Modern forms of Money
- Loan activities of Banks
- Two different Credit situations
- Terms of Credit
- Formal Sector Credit in India
- Self Help Groups for the Poor

</td>
<td>

- Understand money as an economic concept.
- Understand the role of financial institutions from the point of view of day-to- day life.

</td>
</tr>
<tr>
<td colspan="2">

4. Globalization and the Indian Economy:
- Production across countries
- Interlinking production across countries
- Foreign Trade and integration of markets
- What is Globalization?
- Factors that have enabled Globalization
- World Trade Organization
- Impact of Globalization in India
- The Struggle for a fair Globalization

</td>
<td>

- Explain the working of the Global Economic phenomenon.

</td>
</tr>
<tr>
<td colspan="2">

5. Consumer Rights:

To be used only for Project Work

</td>
<td>

- Gets familiarized with the rights and duties as a consumer; and legal measures available to protect from being exploited in markets.

</td>
</tr>
</table>

CBSE SAMPLE QUESTION PAPER (THEORY)
SESSION : 2022-2023

Time Allowed : 3 Hours **Max. Marks : 80**

General Instructions

1. Question paper comprises Six Sections – A, B, C, D, E and F. There are 37 questions in the question paper. All questions are compulsory.
2. **Section A** – From question 1 to 20 are MCQs of 1 mark each.
3. **Section B** – Question no. 21 to 24 are Very Short Answer Type Questions, carrying 2 marks each. Answer to each question should not exceed 40 words.
4. **Section C** – contains Q.25to Q.29 are Short Answer Type Questions, carrying 3 marks each. Answer to each question should not exceed 60 words
5. **Section D** – Question no. 30 to 33 are long answer type questions, carrying 5 marks each. Answer to each question should not exceed 120 words.
6. **Section-E** – Questions no from 34 to 36 are case based questions with three sub questions and are of 4 marks each
7. **Section F** – Question no. 37 is map based, carrying 5 marks with two parts, 37a from History (2 marks) and 37b from Geography (3 marks).
8. There is no overall choice in the question paper. However, an internal choice has been provided in few questions. Only one of the choices in such questions have to be attempted.
9. In addition to this, separate instructions are given with each section and question, wherever necessary.

SECTION A (MCQS) (1 × 20 = 20)

1. What helped in the colonisation of Asian and African countries?
   Identify the correct statement from the following options.
   (a) Intergovernmental policies for the expansion of trade
   (b) Governmental invite to the mother countries for expansion
   (c) Technology, investments and improvement in transport
   (d) Capitalists of these regions wanted trade with colonial powers

2. Which of the following newspaper was started by Bal Gangadhar Tilak?
   (a) Hindu   (b) Kesari   (c) Sudharak   (d) Pratap

3. Look at the picture given below. Identify the name of the painter of this painting from the following options.
   (a) Abindra Nath Tagore (b) Rabindra Nath Tagore (c) Raja Ravi Verma (d) Samant Das Gupta
   Note : The following question is for Visually Impaired Candidates only in lieu of Q. No. 3
   Who among the following was the author of the book 'Gita Govind'?
   (a) Tulsidas   (b) Surdas   (c) Jayadev   (d) Raidas

4. Arrange the following in chronological order:
   I. Print culture created the conditions for the French Revolution
   II. Martin Luther's writings led to beginning of the Protestant Reformation
   III. Menocchio reinterpreted the message of the Bible
   IV. Johann Gutenberg invented Printing press
   (a) III, II, I & IV   (b) I, II, III & IV   (c) IV, III, II & I   (d) IV, II, III & I

5. Identify the crop with the help of the following information
   • It is a crop which is used both as food and fodder.
   • It is a kharif crop which requires temperature between 21°C to 27°C.
   • It grows well in old alluvial soil.
   • Use of modern inputs have contributed to the increasing production of this crop.
   (a) Wheat   (b) Maize   (c) Rice   (d) Sugarcane

6. Which of the following description of forest is NOT correct?
   (a) Reserved Forest -Reservation of more than half of forests
   (b) Protected Forest- Reservation of 1/3 of the forests
   (c) Unclassed Forest-Reservation of forest under govt. and private individuals
   (d) Permanent Forest-Reserved and unclassed forest for the production of timber

7. Match the following :

RESOURCES	EXAMPLES
a. Renewable Resources:	I. Forests and wildlife
b. Non -Renewable Resources:	II. The oceanic resources
c. National Resources:	III. Roads, canals and railway
d. International Resources:	IV. Minerals and fossil fuels

   (a) a-I, b-IV, c-III, d-II   (b) a-II, b-I, c-IV, d-III   (c) a-IV, b-I , c-IV, d-II   (d)   a-I, b-IV, c-II, d-III

8. Consider the following statements regarding power sharing arrangements in Belgium and identify the incorrect one from the following:
   (a) Equal number of members from Dutch and French community in the central government
   (b) Separate government for Brussels with equal representation of communities
   (c) The state government to be subordinate to the central government
   (d) Community government elected by people belonging to one language community

9. Which one of the following subjects comes under the legislation of Centre and State in India?
   (a) Education   (b) Forests   (c) Banking   (d) Trade

10. Which of the following statement is true regarding Feminist Movements?
    (a) A group which favours giving more power to working women at rural and urban level.
    (b) A movement that believes in giving exclusive rights to female in urban areas.
    (c) Radical women's movements aimed at equality in personal and family life as well.
    (d) It is the practice of placing a feminine and masculine point of view in decision making.

11. Which one among the following pairs is correctly matched?

LIST I	LIST II
A. Bharatiya Janata Party	National Democratic Alliance
B. Congress Party	Left front
C. Communist Party of India	Regional Party
D. Mizo National Front	United Progressive Alliance

12. In the question given below, there are two statements marked as **Assertion (A)** and **Reason (R)**.
    Read the statements and choose the correct option.
    Assertion (A): Democracy is an accountable, responsive and legitimate government
    Reason (R): Democracies have regular, free and fair elections and decision-making is based on norms and procedures
    (a) Both A and R are true and R is the correct explanation of A.
    (b) Both A and R are true but R is not the correct explanation of A.
    (c) A is true but R is false. (d)   A is false but R is true.

13. Which one of the following religions was protected and fostered by Sri Lankans in their constitution?
    (a) Christianity   (b) Hinduism   (c) Buddhism   (d) Islam

14. Read the given data and find out children of which state has attained maximum elementary school education?

States	Per Capita Income For 2018– 19 (in Rs)	Infant Mortality Rate per 1,000 live births (2018)	Literac y Rate % 2017–18	Net Attendance Ratio (per 100 persons) secondary stage (age 14 and 15 years) 2017–18
HARYANA	2,36,147	30	82	61
KERALA	2,04,105	7	94	83
BIHAR	40,982	32	62	43

Sources: Economic Survey 2020–21, P.A 157, National Sample Survey Organisation (Report No. 585), National statistical office, Government of India.

    (a) Haryana   (b) Bihar   (c) Haryana and Kerala both   (d)   Kerala

15. Read the following data and select the appropriate option from the following.

Educational Achievement of Rural Population of Uttar Pradesh		
Category	**Male**	**Female**
Literacy rate for rural population	76%	54%
Literacy rate for rural children in age group 10-14 years	90%	87%
Percentage of rural children aged 10-14 attending school	85%	82%

How much percentage of girls are not attending school?

  (a) 81%   (b) 61%   (c) 69%   (d) 18%

16. Find the odd one out from the following options:

  (a) Tourist Guide, Barber, Tailor, and Potter

  (b) Teacher, Doctor, Vegetable Vendor and Lawyer

  (c) Postman, Cobbler, Soldier and Police Constable

  (d) Indian Railways, Jet Airways, Doordarshan and Metro

17. Fill in the blank:

Sector	Criteria Used
Primary, Secondary & Tertiary	Nature of economic activity
Organized & Unorganized	?

  (a) Nature of Employment activities

  (b) Nature of Social activities

  (c) Nature of Production activities

  (d) Nature of Political activities

18. Read the information given below and select the correct option

Rohan has taken a loan of Rs.5 lakhs from the bank to purchase a house on 12% rate of interest. He has to submit papers of new house and salary record to the bank. What is this process called as?

  (a) Interest Rate   (b) Collateral   (c) Principal Amount (d) Instalments

19. Which of the following international agencies allow free trade and work on mutual trade between countries?

  (a) WTO   (b) IMF   (c) UPU   (d) FAO

20. Identify the correct statements about globalization.

  I.   Removal of barriers by the government

  II.   Foreign companies are allowed to set up factories

  III. Has enabled all companies to increase their investments

  IV. Has lessened foreign investment and foreign trade

  (a) I &II   (b) II & III   (c) I & III   (d) II & IV

SECTION B (VERY SHORT ANSWER QUESTIONS)   (2 × 4 =8)

21. Analyse any two factors that were responsible for the Great Depression in America during 1929.

22. Mention the provisions that constitute India into a secular country.

23. Suggest any two ways to conserve energy resources in India.

OR

Suggest any two ways to improve the usage of Solar energy.

24. In what ways Government can increase employment in the rural sector?

SECTION C (SHORT ANSWER BASED QUESTIONS)   (5 × 3 =15)

25. How was the social and political situation of India affected by the First World War? Explain.

OR

How did the Indian merchants and industrialists relate themselves to the Civil Disobedience Movement? Explain.

26. Examine the factors that influence the distribution pattern of the railway network in India.

27. In what ways Multi National Corporation (MNC) different from other companies? Explain with an example.

28. Differentiate between democratic and non-democratic government.

29. 'Tertiary sector is different from other sectors.' Justify the statement with suitable arguments.

SECTION D (LONG ANSWER BASED QUESTIONS)   (5 × 4 =20)

30 Highlight the various measures and practices that French revolutionaries introduced to create a sense of collective identity amongst the French people.

OR

Highlight the role of Otto Von Bismarck in making of Germany.

31. 'Manufacturing sector is considered as the backbone of general and economic development.' Examine the statement in the context of India.

OR

Examine the multi-pronged aspects of Information Technology and Electronics Industry.

32. Describe the role of political parties in India.

OR

Describe the necessity or utility of political parties in democratic countries.

33. Explain the role of Self-Help Groups (SHGs) in the rural society.

OR

Explain the significance of The Reserve Bank of India in the Indian economy.

SECTION E (CASE BASED QUESTIONS)   (4 × 3 =12)

34. Read the source given below and answer the question that follows:

Will Thorne is one of those who went in search of seasonal work, loading bricks and doing odd jobs. He describes how job-seekers walked to London in search of work:

'I had always wanted to go to London, and my desire … was stimulated by letters from an old workmate … who was now working at the Old Kent Road Gas Works … I finally decided to go

… in November, 1881. With two friends I started out to walk the journey, filled with the hope that we would be able to obtain employment, when we get there, with the kind assistance of my friend … we had little money when we started, not enough to pay for our food and lodgings each night until we arrived in London. Some days we walked as much as twenty miles, and other days less. Our money was gone at the end of the third day … For two nights we slept out – once under a haystack, and once in an old farm shed … On arrival in London we tried to find … my friend

… but … were unsuccessful. Our money was gone, so there was nothing for us to do but to walk around until late at night, and then try to find some place to sleep. We found an old building and slept in it that night. The next day, Sunday, late in the afternoon, we got to the Old Kent Gas Works, and applied for work. To my great surprise, the man we had been looking for was working at the time. He spoke to the foreman and I was given a job.'

Quoted in Raphael Samuel, 'Comers and Goers', in H.J. Dyos and Michael Wolff, eds, The Victorian City: Images and Realities, 1973.

34. (1) Analyse the major factor which led London become an attractive place for the job seekers.

34. (2) Analyse the reason for the appointment of Will Thorne by the Old Kent Gas works.

34. (3) Examine the preference of hand labour over machines by the industrialists of the Victorian Britain.

35. Read the given extract and answer following questions

Narmada Bachao Andolan or Save Narmada Movement is a Non-Governmental Organisation (NGO) that mobilized tribal people, farmers, environmentalists and human rights activists against the Sardar Sarovar Dam being built across the Narmada river in Gujarat. It originally focused on the environmental issues related to trees that would be submerged under the dam water. Recently it has re-focused the aim to enable poor citizens, especially the oustees (displaced people) to get full rehabilitation facilities from the government.

People felt that their suffering would not be in vain… accepted the trauma of displacement believing in the promise of irrigated fields and plentiful harvests. So, often the survivors of Rihand told us that they accepted their sufferings as sacrifice for the sake of their nation. But now, after thirty bitter years of being adrift, their livelihood having even being more precarious, they keep asking: "Are we the only ones chosen to make sacrifices for the nation?"

Source: S. Sharma, quoted in In the Belly of the River. Tribal conflicts over development in Narmada valley. A. Baviskar. 1995.

35. (1) With what objective 'Sardar Sarovar Dam' was built?

35. (2) Analyse the reason of protest by the tribal people.

35. (3) Highlight the issues on which 'Save Narmada Movement' worked on.

36. Read the given extract and answer following questions.

Power sharing arrangements can also be seen in the way political parties, pressure groups and movements control or influence those in power. In a democracy, the citizens must have freedom to choose among various contenders for power. In contemporary democracies, this takes the form of competition among different parties. Such competition ensures that power does not remain in one hand. In the long run, power is shared among different political parties that represent different ideologies and social groups. Sometimes this kind of sharing can be direct, when two or more parties form an alliance to contest elections. If their alliance is elected, they form a coalition government and thus share power. In a democracy, we find interest groups such as those of traders, businessmen, industrialists, farmers and industrial workers. They also will have share in governmental power, either through participation in governmental committees or bringing influence on the decision-making process.

36. (1) 'Power sharing is an essential component of democracy.' Give one example to prove the statement.

36. (2) How is alliance building an example of power sharing?

36. (3) How Political parties, pressure groups and movements help in controlling or influencing those who are in power?

SECTION F (MAP SKILL BASED QUESTIONS) $(2 + 3 = 5)$

37. (a) Two places A and B have been marked on the given outline map of India.
Identify them and write their correct names on the lines drawn near them.
A. Indian National Congress session at this place in 1920
B. The place where Mahatma Gandhi broke Salt Law.

(b) On the same outline map of India locate and label any THREE of the following with suitable Symbols.
(a) Hirakud Dam
(b) Tarapur Atomic Power Station
(c) Noida Software Technology Park
(d) Kochi Port

Note: The following questions are for Visually Impaired Candidates only in lieu of Q. No.37.
Attempt any FIVE questions.

37.1 Name the Place where the session of Indian National Congress was held in September 1920.

37.2 Name the place where Mahatma Gandhi broke Salt Law.

37.3 Name the State where Hirakud Dam is located.

37.4 Name the State where Tarapur nuclear plant is located.

37.5 Name the State where Noida Software Technology Park is located.

37.6 Name the State where Kochi 'Sea Port' is located.

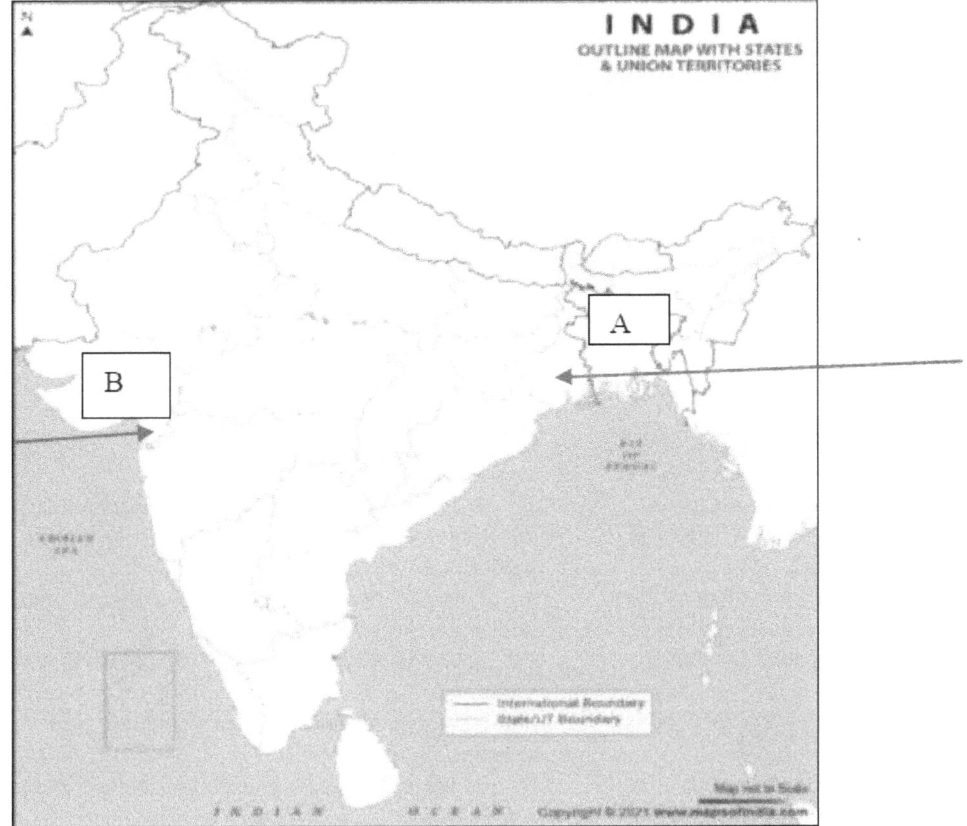

SOLUTIONS

1. (c) Technology, investments and improvement in transport Page 83
2. (b) Kesari Page 175
3. (c) Raja Ravi Verma Page 171
   Note : The following question is for Visually Impaired Candidates only in lieu of Q. No. 3
   (c) Jayadev Page-167
4. (d) IV, II, III & I Page 107-113
5. (b) Maize Page 38
6. (d) Permanent Forest-Reserved and unclassed forest for the production of timber Page 20
7. (a) a-I, b-IV, c-III, d-II Page 2
8. (c) The State government to be subordinate to the Central government Page 4
9. (a) Education - Page 16, 17
10. (c) Radical women's movements aimed at equality in personal and family life as well. Page 41
11. (a) Bharatiya Janta Party – National Democratic Alliance Page 81
12. (a) Both A and R are true and R is the correct explanation of A. Page 90
13. (c) Buddhism Page 2
14. (d) Kerala Page 7
15. (d) 18% - Page 12
16. (d) Indian Railways, Jet Airways, Doordarshan and Metro Page 14-29
17. (a) Nature of employment activities Page 32
18. (b) Collateral Page 44
19. (a) WTO Page 65
20. (a) I & II Page 64
21. i. Agricultural overproduction remained a problem and it was made worse by falling agricultural prices.
   ii. As prices slumped and agricultural incomes declined, farmers tried to expand production and bring a larger volume of produce to the market but it pushed down prices.
   iii. In the mid-1920s, many countries financed their investments through loans from the US, it was extremely easy to raise loans in the US when the going was good.
   iv. But in the first half of 1928 countries that depended crucially on US loan faced an acute crisis.
   v. The withdrawal of US loans affected the rest of the world in different ways In Europe it led to the failure of small major banks and the collapse of currencies such as the British pound sterling.
   vi. Any other relevant point (ANY TWO POINTS) Page 94
22. i. There is no official religion for the Indian state. Our Constitution does not give a special status to any religion.
   ii. The Constitution provides to all individuals and communities freedom to profess, practice and propagate any religion, or not to follow any.
   iii. The Constitution prohibits discrimination on grounds of religion.
   iv. Secularism is an idea constitutes one of the foundations of our country.
   v. At the same time the Constitution allows the state to intervene in the matters of religion in order to ensure equality within religious communities.
   vi. Any other relevant point (ANY TWO POINTS) Page 49
23. i. Promotion of energy conservation and increased use of renewable energy sources
   ii. Have to adopt a cautious approach for the judicious use of our limited energy resources.
   iii. Use public transport systems instead of individual vehicles
   iv. Switch off electricity when not in use
   v. Using power-saving devices
   vi. Use non-conventional sources of energy.
   vii. Any other relevant point (ANY TWO POINTS) Page 63

OR

   i. Reducing the cost of solar panels
   ii. Use of efficient solar panel models.
   iii. Rising awareness about the importance of renewable energy
   iv. Easy installation process
   v. Buy panels with High Concentrated Photovoltaic (CPV) Cells.
   vi. Avoid installing solar panels in shaded areas.
   vii. Any other relevant point (ANY TWO POINTS) Page 62
24. i. by introducing mega projects-new dam is constructed and canals
   ii. by introducing tertiary facilities in an area
   iii. to identify, promote and locate industries and services in semi-rural areas
   iv. It is also possible to set up industries that process vegetables and agricultural produce like potato, sweet potato,
   v. by promoting tourism, or regional craft industry, or new services like IT.
   vi. Any other relevant point (ANY TWO POINTS) Page 27
25. i. The war created a new economic and political situation.
   ii. It led to a huge increase in defence expenditure which was financed by war loans and increasing taxes: customs duties were raised and income tax introduced.

iii. Through the war years prices increased – doubling between 1913 and 1918 –leading to extreme hardship for the common people.

iv. Villages were called upon to supply soldiers, and the forced recruitment in rural areas caused widespread anger.

v. Crops failed in many parts of India, resulting in acute shortages of food.

vi. This was accompanied by an influenza epidemic. Million people perished as a result of famines and the epidemic.

vii. Any other relevant point (ANY THREE POINTS) Page 54

OR

i. Indian merchants and industrialists were keen on expanding their business, and reacted against colonial policies that restricted business activities.

ii. They wanted protection against imports of foreign goods, and a rupee-sterling foreign exchange ratio that would discourage imports.

iii. To organise business interests, they formed the Indian Industrial and Commercial Congress in 1920 and the Federation of the Indian Chamber of Commerce and Industries (FICCI) in 1927.

iv. Led by prominent industrialists like Purshottamdas Thakurdas and G. D. Birla, the industrialists attacked colonial control over the Indian economy, and supported the Civil Disobedience Movement

v. They gave financial assistance and refused to buy or sell imported goods.

vi. Most businessmen wanted to flourish trade without constraints.

vi. Any other relevant point (ANY THREE POINTS) Page 66

26. Physical and economic factors have influenced the distribution pattern of the Indian Railways network in the following ways:

i. Northern Plain: Level land, high population density and rich agricultural resources have favoured development of railways in these plains. However, a large number of river requiring construction of bridges across their wide river beds posed some obstacles.

ii. Peninsular region and the Himalayan region: it is a hilly terrain. The railway tracks are laid through low hills, gaps or tunnels. So, it is very difficult to lay the railway lines. The Himalayan mountainous regions too are not favourable for the construction of railway line due to high relief, sparse population and lack of economic opportunities.

iii. Desert of Rajasthan: on the sandy plain of western Rajasthan too, it is very difficult to lay railway lines which has hindered the development of railways.

iv. Swamps of Gujarat, forested tracts of Madhya Pradesh, Chhattisgarh, Orissa and Jharkhand; these are also not suitable for the development of railways.

v. The contiguous stretch of Sahyadri could be crossed only through gaps or passes. Although the Konkan railway along the west coast has been developed but it has also faced a number of problems such as sinking of track in some stretches and landslides

vi. Any other relevant point (ANY THREE POINTS) Page 82

27. i. Domestic companies tend to restrict their operations to the country of origin, while multinational corporations operate in more than two countries. Ex- Infosys

ii. Companies (Infosys) expand globally for many reasons, mostly to obtain new markets, cheaper resources and reduction in operational costs, all of which significantly affect financial management. These benefits also increase the risks faced by multinational corporations.

iii. Multinational (Infosys) financial management differs from domestic financial management in six essential ways

iv. Unlike their domestic financial management counterparts, multinationals are subject to exchange rates that differ based on the prevailing inflation rate in the foreign countries where they operate.

v. Any other point (ANY THREE POINTS) Page 57

28. i. Democratic govts. are transparent, legitimate and accountable whereas nondemocratic govt are selected and formed at their own discretion

ii. Democratic govt. provides dignity and freedom to all without any discrimination

iii. Conflicts are resolved through debate, discussions and negotiation rather than discretion

iv. Minority and majority cooperation are the common phenomenon in the democratic govt.

v. Enhances dignity of all without any discrimination

vi. Any other relevant point (ANY THREE POINTS) Page 90-96

29. i. Tertiary sector is basic service sector whereas primary and secondary are the sectors that produce goods

ii. Tertiary sector support and help in the development of the primary and secondary sectors

iii. Tertiary activities are an assistance for the production process.

iv. Tertiary s sector provides services like transport, banking, communication, etc

v. It generates more employment then other sectors.

vi. Any other relevant point (ANY THREE POINTS) Page 20

30. i. The ideas of la patrie (the fatherland) and le citoyen (the citizen) emphasised the notion of a united community enjoying equal rights under a constitution.

ii. A new French flag, the tricolour, was chosen to replace the former royal standard.

iii. The Estates General was elected by the body of active citizens and renamed the National Assembly.

iv. New hymns were composed, oaths taken and martyrs commemorated

v. A centralized administrative system was put in place

and it formulated uniform laws for all citizens within its territory.

vi. Internal customs duties and dues were abolished and a uniform system of weights and measures was adopted.

vii. Regional dialects were discouraged and French, as it was spoken and written in Paris, became the common language of the nation.

viii. Any other relevant point (ANY FIVE POINTS) Page 5

OR

i. Prussia took on the leadership of the movement for national unification.

ii. Its chief minister, Otto von Bismarck, was the architect of this process carried out with thehelp of the Prussian army and bureaucracy.

iii. Three wars over seven years – with Austria, Denmark and France – ended in Prussian victory and completed the process of unification.

iv. In January 1871, the Prussian king, William I, was proclaimed German Emperor in a ceremony held at Versailles.

v. On January 1871, an assembly comprising the princes of the German states, representatives of the army, important Prussian ministers including the chief minister Otto von Bismarck gathered in the Hall of Mirrors in the Palace of Versailles to proclaim the new German Empire headed by Kaiser William I of Prussia.

vi. Any other relevant point (ANY FIVE POINTS) Page 16

31. i. Manufacturing industries help in modernising agriculture.

ii. It helps in reducing the heavy dependence of people on agricultural income by providing them jobs in secondary and tertiary sectors.

iii. It helps in eradication of unemployment and poverty from our country.

iv. It helps in reducing regional disparities by establishing industries in tribal and backward areas.

v. Export of manufactured goods expands trade and commerce.

vi. It helps in bringing foreign exchange.

vii. Any other relevant point (ANY FIVE POINTS) Page 64

OR

i. The electronics industry covers a wide range of products from transistor sets to television, telephones, cellular telecom, pagers, telephone exchange, radars, computers and many other equipment required by the telecommunication industry.

ii. Bangalore has emerged as the electronic capital of India. Other important centres for electronic goods are Mumbai, Delhi, Hyderabad, Pune, Chennai, Kolkata, Lucknow and Coimbatore.

iii. 18 software technology parks provide single window service and high data communication facility to software experts.

iv. A major impact of this industry has been on employment generation.

v. It is encouraging to know that 30 per cent of the people employed in this sector are women.

vi. This industry has been a major foreign exchange earner in the last two or three years because of its fast growing Business Processes Outsourcing (BPO) sector.

vii. The continuing growth in the hardware and software is the key to the success of IT industry in India.

ix. Any other relevant point (ANY FIVE POINTS) Page 76

32. i. Parties contest elections.

ii. Parties put forward different policies and programmes and the voters choose from them.

iii. Parties play a decisive role in making laws for a country.

iv. Parties form and run governments.

v. Those parties that lose in the elections play the role of opposition to the parties in power, by voicing different views and criticising government for its failures or wrong policies.

vi. Parties shape public opinion.

vii. Parties provide people access to government machinery and welfare schemes implemented by governments.

viii Any other relevant point (ANY FIVE POINTS) Page 74

OR

i. Elected representative will be accountable to their constituency for what they do in the locality. The rise of political parties is directly linked to the emergence of representative democracies. 5 large scale societies need representative democracy.

ii. As societies became large and complex, they also needed some agency to gather different views on various issues and to present these to the government.

iii. They needed some way to bring various representatives together so that a responsible government could be formed.

iv. They needed a mechanism to support or restrain the government, make policies, justify or oppose them.

v. Political parties fulfil these needs that every representative government has. We can say that parties are a necessary condition for a democracy

vii. Any other relevant point (ANY FIVE POINTS) Page 75

33. i. The idea is to organize rural poor, in particular women, into small Self Help Groups (SHGs) and pool (collect) their savings.

ii. A typical SHG has 15-20 members, usually belonging to one neighbourhood, who meet and save regularly. Saving per member varies from Rs 25 to Rs 100 or more, depending on the ability of the people to save.

iii. Members can take small loans from the group itself to meet their needs.

iv. The group charges interest on these loans but this is still less than what the moneylender charges.

v. After a year or two, if the group is regular in savings, it becomes eligible for availing loan from the bank.

vi. Loan is sanctioned in the name of the group and is meant to create self-employment opportunities for the members.

vii. Small loans are provided to the members for releasing mortgaged land, for meeting working capital needs

viii. Most of the important decisions regarding the savings and loan activities are taken by the group members.

ix. The group decides as regards the loans to be granted – the purpose, amount, interest to be charged, repayment schedule etc. Also, it is the group which is responsible for the repayment of the loan.

x. Any case of non-repayment of loan by any one member is followed up seriously by other members in the group.

xi. Any other relevant point (ANY FIVE POINTS) Page 51

OR

i. It supervises the functioning of formal sources of loans.

ii. The banks maintain a minimum cash balance out of the deposits they receive.

iii. The RBI monitors that the banks actually maintain the cash balance.

iv. The RBI sees that the banks give loans not just to profit-making businesses and traders but also to small cultivators, small scale industries, to small borrowers etc.

v. Periodically, banks have to submit information to the RBI on how much they are lending, to whom, at what interest rate, etc.

vi. Any other relevant point (ANY FIVE POINTS) Page 75

34.(1) Due to the industrial revolution and availability of job opportunities in factories of London.

34.(2) Gas work was the seasonal industry and they were in need to low wage workers.

34.(3)
   i. Machines needed huge capital investments
   ii. Machines were costly, ineffective, difficult to repair.

iii. Labour was available at low wages.

iv. In seasonal industries only seasonal labour was required.

v. Any other relevant point (ANY TWO POINTS) Page 109

35.(1)
   i. To secure power
   ii. Irrigation
   iii. Drinking water for the drought-prone region.
   iv. Any other relevant point (ANY ONE POINT)

35.(2)
   i. Huge displacement of people
   ii. Demand for rehabilitation
   iii. Harm of harvest
   iv. Loss of livelihood
   v. Any other relevant point (ANY ONE POINT)

35.(3)
   i. Against huge displacement of people
   ii. Environmental issue
   iii. Demand for rehabilitation of tribal
   iv. To provide tribal the source of livelihood
   v. Any other relevant point (ANY TWO POINTS) Page 27

36.(1)
   i. It helps in reducing the possibility of conflict between the social groups.
   ii. power sharing is a good way to ensure the stability of political order
   iii. Any other relevant point (ANY ONE POINT)

36.(2)
   i. When two or more parties form an alliance to contest elections or to form a government is called as sharing of power.
   ii. Alliance could be between regional and national parties which is again an example of power sharing
   iii. Political ideas are shared
   iv. Any other relevant point (ANY ONE POINT)

36.(3)
   i. Freedom of choice entails competition among the different parties.
   ii. Such competition ensures that power does not remain in one hand, but is shared among different political parties representing different ideologies and social groups.
   iii. Any other relevant point (ANY TWO POINTS) Page 9

37.(a)
   A. Calcutta
   B. Dandi

37.(b)

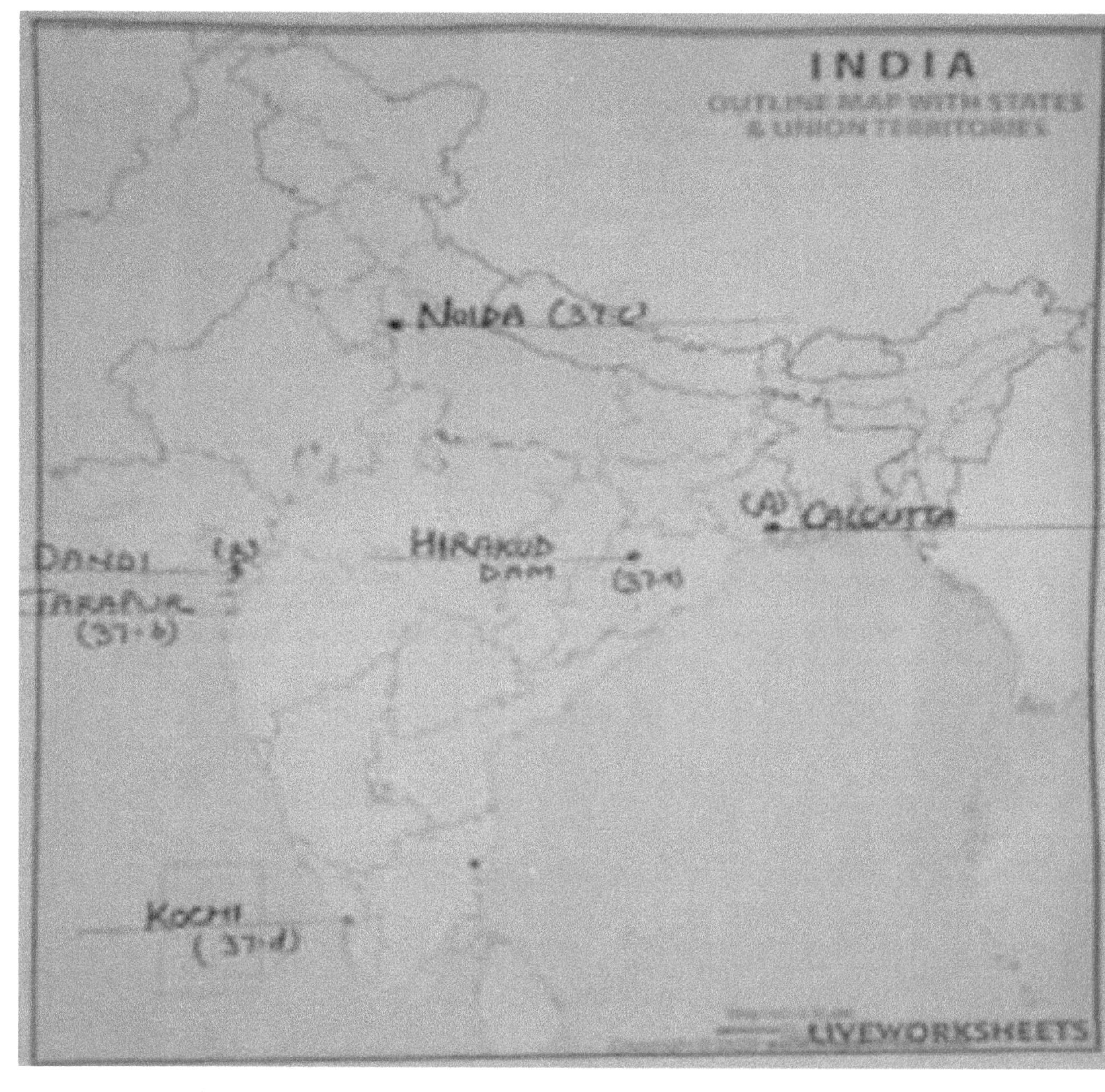

INDIA
OUTLINE MAP WITH STATES
& UNION TERRITORIES
NOIDA (37-c)
CALCUTTA (A)
DANDI (B)
HIRAKUD DAM (37-a)
TARAPUR (37-b)
KOCHI (37-d)
LIVEWORKSHEETS

All India 2022
CBSE Board Solved Paper
Term-II

1. Why did Indian merchants and industrialists support the Civil Disobedience Movement? Explain.

2. Examine the significance of pipelines as a means of transportation in the country.

3. Why has India adopted a multi-party system? Explain.

4. How is 'Demand Deposit 'an essential feature of money?

5. Study the given flow chart and answer the questions that follow:

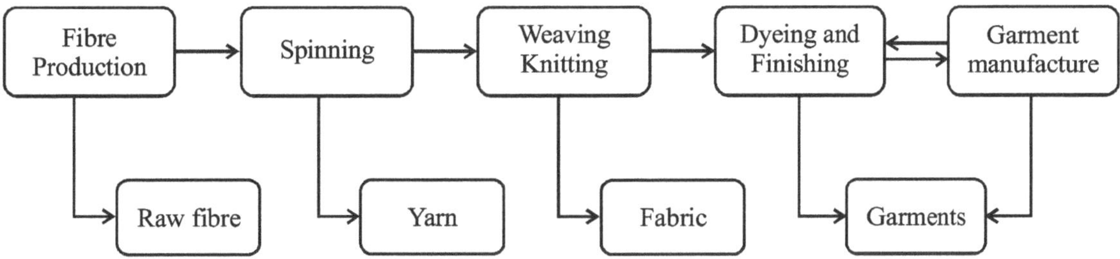

   5.1 Which is the basic material required for garment manufacturing ?

   5.2 Give one example of value addition in the textile industry.

6. (a) Differentiate between formal and informal sources of Credit

OR

   (b) How does a bank work as a key component of the financial system? Explain

7. "It was essential to preserve folk tradition in order to discover one's national identity and restore a sense of pride in one's past." Support the statement in reference to India.

8. Explain the role of the Election Commission in the registration and recognition of political parties in India.

9. (a) "Democracy is a better form of government than any other alternative." Analyse the statement.

OR

   (b) Analyse the reasons for the overwhelming support for the idea of democracy all over the world.

10. (a) Examine the factors which facilitate globalization in India.

OR

   (b) Assess, how globalization has touched the lives of the larger society.

"We believe that it is the inalienable right of the Indian people, as of any other people, to have freedom and to enjoy the fruits of their toil and have the necessities of life, so that they may have opportunities for growth. We believe also that if any government deprive people of these rights and oppresses them, the people have a further right to alter it or to abolish it.

The British Government in India has not only deprived the Indian people of their freedom but has based itself on the exploitation of the masses, and has ruined India economically, politically, culturally, and spiritually.

11. Why was freedom considered an inalienable right of the Indianpeople?

12. Why was Purna Swaraj considered essential by the people of India?

13. Explain the significance of the Lahore Session of Congress (1930).

For a long time, trade and transport were restricted to a limited space. With the development in science and technology, the area of influence of trade and transport expanded far and wide. Today, the world has been converted into a large village with the help of efficient and fast moving transport. Transport has been able to achieve this with the help of equally developed communication system. Therefore, transport, communication and trade are complementary to each other. Today, India is well-linked with the rest of the world despite its vast size, diversity and linguistic and socio-cultural plurality. Railways, airways, waterways, newspapers, radio, television, cinema and internet, etc. have been contributing to its socio-economic progress in many ways. The trades from local to international levels have added to the vitality of its economy. It has enriched our life and added substantially to growing amenities and facilities for the comforts of life.

14. How is science an important factor in the development of transport?

15. How does transport integrate social and cultural plurality? Explain.

16. Analyze the importance of communication for a nation.

17. On the given political outline map of India (on page)

(a) Identify the place marked as 'A' with the help of the following information and write its correct name on the line marked near it.

(b) On the same given map of India, locate and label the following:

(a) (i) Narora Nuclear Power Plant

OR

Bengaluru Software Technology Park

(b) Indira Gandhi International Airport

1. The industrialists and the merchants supported the Civil Disobedience Movement initially to protect their own business interests. They gave monetary help and refused to buy and sell imported and foreign goods. They demand to remove restrictions or trade barriers imposed on them.

2. The pipeline transport network is a new arrival in the transportation of India. Transport of crude oil, petroleum products, and natural gas from oil and natural gas fields to refineries, fertilizer factories, and big thermal power plants. ' Even solids can be transported through pipelines when converted into a slurry.

3. India is a democratic country and India adopted a multi-party system because of the social and geographical diversity of the nation. Through this system, different and diverse parties could represent the sections of the society and power does not absorb into the hands of one single party.

4. Demand deposits share the essential features of money in following ways:-
   (i) The facility of cheques against demand deposits makes it possible to directly settle payments without the use of cash.
   (ii) Since demand deposits are accepted widely as a means of payment, along with currency, they constitute money in the modern economy.

5. 5.1 Raw Fibre
   5.2 Garments

6. (a) Formal sources follow the sources of credit that are registered by the govt. and have to follow its rules and regulations whereas informal sources include those small and scattered units which are largely outside the control of the government.

   The main motive of formal sources is social welfare whereas the main motive of informal sources is profit-making.

   Formal sources usually charge lower rates of interest whereas in informal sources they charge much higher rates of interest.

   RBI dominates the functions of formal sources of credit but in informal sources, there is no organisation that dominates the credit activities.

   Banks and cooperatives are examples of formal sources and moneylenders, traders, employees, friends and relatives etc are example of informal sources.

OR

(b) A financial system is an economic arrangement wherein financial institutions facilitate the transfer of funds and assets between borrowers, lenders, and investors. Its goal is to efficiently distribute economic resources to promote economic growth and generate a return on investment (ROI) for market participants.

7. Nationalism spreads when people begin to believe that they are all part of the same nation when they discover some unity that binds them together. History, fiction, folklore and songs, popular prints and symbols, all played a part in the making of nationalism. We should not forget our old folk tradition infact we should also accept new traditions and carry forward both at same pace.

8. The Election Commission is regarded as the guardian of elections in the country. In every election, it issues a Model Code of Conduct for political parties and candidates to conduct elections in a free and fair manner. The Election Commission implements the Code of Conduct and punishes any candidate or party that violates it. During the election period, the EC can order the government to follow some guidelines, to prevent the use and misuse of governmental power to enhance its chances to win elections, or to transfer some government officials.

9. (a) Democracy is a better form of government than any other alternative because of the following factors:

Democracy promotes equality among citizens.

Democracy provides a method in order to resolve conflicts.

Democracy allows room to correct mistakes.

Democracy enhances the dignity of the individual.

Democracy also improves the quality of decision making.

OR

(b) Despite any shortcomings that we might witness in a democratic model of governance, it is still the most preferred form of government all over the world including in South Asia. Some reasons for this are given below:

People have the right to choose who governs them through regular elections.

The elected government is answerable to the people and to ensure its stability, has to deliver on its promises.

Democracy ensures transparency.

It accommodates diversity and promotes inclusion and equality.

It gives an equal chance of participation to all the citizens. An important pillar of democracy is ensuring the dignity and freedom of people.

The true power lies with people.

Lastly, democracy has proven to be a better model than dictatorship, aristocracy, or any other form of governance.

10. The important factors are:

(i) Historical: The trade routes were made over the years so that goods from one kingdom or country moved to another. The well known silk-route from east to west is an example of historical factor.

(ii) Economy: The cost of goods and values to the end-user determine the movement of goods and value addition. The overall economics of a particular industry or trade is an important factor in globalisation.

(iii) Resources and Markets: Natural resources like minerals, coal, oil, gas, human resources, water, etc. make an important contribution in globalisation.

(iv) Production Issues: Utilisation of built-up capacities of production, sluggishness in domestic market and over production makes a manufacturing company look outward and go global. The development of overseas markets and manufacturing plants in autos, four-wheelers and two-wheelers is a classical example.

(v) Political: The political issues of a country make globalisation channelised as per political bosses. The regional trade understandings or agreements determine the scope of globalization. Trading in European Union and special agreement in the erstwhile Soviet block and SAARC are examples.

(vi) Industrial Organisation: Technological development in the areas of production, product mix and firms are helping organisations to expand their operations. The hiring of services and procurement of sub-assemblies and components have a strong influence in the globalisation process.

(vii) Technologies: The stage of technology in a particular field gives rise to the import or export of products or services from or to the country. European countries like England and Germany exported their chemical, electrical, and mechanical plants in the 50s and 60s and exported high tech (then) goods to underdeveloped countries. Today India is exporting computer/software-related services to advanced counties like the UK, USA, etc.

OR

(b) Globalization is associated with rapid and significant human changes. The movements of people from rural to urban areas have accelerated, and the growth of cities in the developing world especially is linked to substandard living for many. Concepts of national identity, and family, job and tradition are changing rapidly and significantly.

Globalization indicates that the world today is more interconnected than before.

Globalization in its basic economic sense refers to the adoption of open and unfettered trading markets (through lowering of trade barriers, removal of capital controls, and liberalization of foreign exchange restrictions).

Large volumes of money movement increased volumes of trade, and changes in information technology and communication are all integral to a global world.

There is also a significant movement of people from one country to another for trade and work. Such increases in the movement of goods, labour, and services have weakened national barriers and restrictions that are imposed by a nation-state.

"Global interaction, rather than insulated isolation, has been the basis of economic progress in the world. Trade, along with migration, communication, and dissemination of scientific and technical knowledge, has helped to break the dominance of rampant poverty and the pervasiveness of 'nasty, brutish and short lives that characterized the world. And yet, despite all the progress, life is still severely nasty, brutish and short for a large part of the world population.

11. It was the inalienable right of the Indian people to have freedom and to enjoy the fruits of their hard labour and have the necessities of life so that they might have full opportunities of growth.

12. Purna Swaraj is considered essential by the people of India because the Poorna Swaraj is about the declaration of complete independence in India.

13. This session was very significant because in this Lahore session the prominent party Indian National Congress, took the resolution of Poorna Swaraj or complete independence. In this, the Indian tricolour flag was hoisted by Pandit Jawahar Lal Nehru on the bank of the Ravi river.

14. Science and technology could beneficially target the field of intermediate transport technologies to suit the needs of developing countries and the field of energy where reduced consumption, cheaper energy and cheaper transport techniques should be sought.

15. Transport has been able to achieve this with the help of an equally developed communication system. Therefore, transport, communication, and trade are complementary to each other. Today, India is well-linked with the rest of the world despite its vast size, diversity, and linguistic and socio-cultural plurality.

16. Communication has a major role to play in that. It has brought all regions in a nation close and all nations in the world closer . Without a well developed communication infrastructure, no nation can assume an important position on the globe

Communication not only helps to facilitate the process of sharing information and knowledge with others, but also helps people to develop relationships with others

17. (a) The place where the Non-Cooperation Movement was called off due to violence.

    (b) (i) A- Chauri Chaura

        (ii)

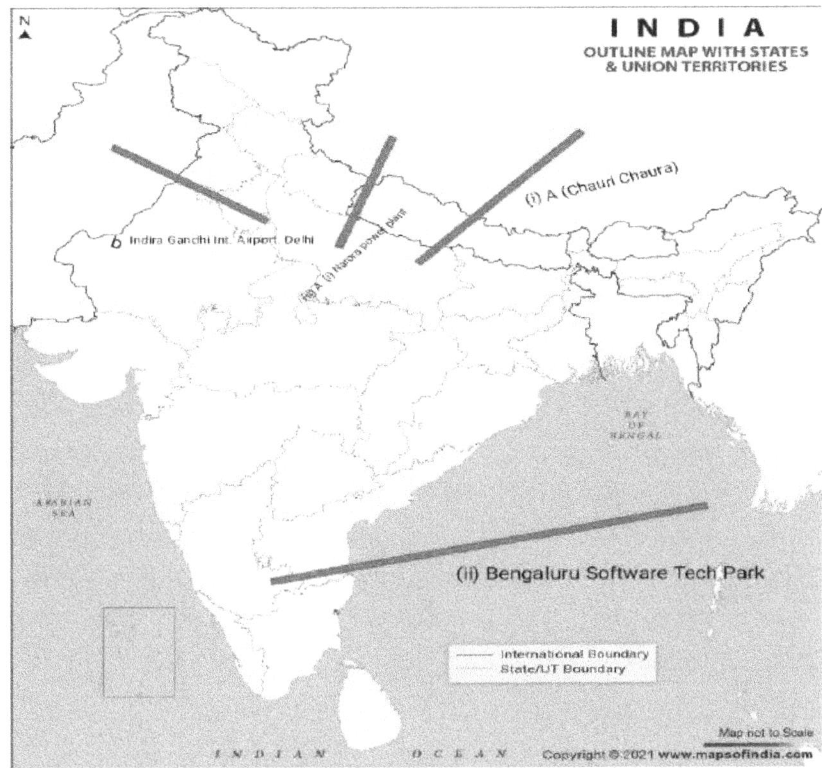

All India 2022
CBSE Board Solved Paper
Term-I

1. Industrialisation began in which one of the following European countries in the second half of the eighteenth century?

    (a) Germany   (b) France   (c) Italy   (d) England

2. Which type of governments were mainly driven in Europe after the defeat of Napoleon in 1815 ?

    (a) Conservative   (b) Liberal   (c) Federal   (d) Feudal

3. Which one of the following group of countries collectively defeated Napoleon in 1815?

    (a) Britain, Russin, Prussia and Austria   (b) Britain, Russian, Prussia and Australia

    (c) Britain, Russia, Netherlands and Germany   (d) Britain, Luxembourg, Germany and Italy

4. In which one of the following countries did the first liberalist-nationalist upheaval take place in July 1830 ?

    (a) France   (b) Germany   (c) England   (d) Italy

5. Who among the following remarked "When France sneezes, the rest of Europe catches cold"?

    (a) Lord Byron   (b) Metternich   (c) Johann Herder   (d) Napoleon

6. Who among the following was the architect for the unification of Germany

    (a) Otto von Bismarck   (b) William 1   (c) Frederick III   (d) William II

7. Who among the following had sought to put together a coherent programme for a unitary Italian Republic during the 1830s?

    (a) Victor Emmanuel I   (b) Victor Emmanuel II   (c) Giuseppe Mazzini   (d) Count Cavour

8. In which one of the following states is overgrazing the main reason for land degradation ?

    (a) Maharashtra   (b) Punjab   (c) Haryana   (d) Uttar Pradesh

9. Identify the soil which ranges from red to brown in colour and saline in nature:

    (a) Red soil   (b) Laterite soil   (c) Arid soil   (d) Alluvial soil

10. Which one of the following forces leads to maximum soil erosion in plains ?

    (a) Wind   (b) Glacier   (c) Running water   (d) Earthquake

11. Deforestation due to mining has caused severe land degradation in which one of the following states ?

    (a) Odisha   (b) Tamil Nadu   (c) Kerala   (d) Gujarat

12. Who among the following was proclaimed King of united Italy in 1861?

    (a) Charles 1   (b) Victor Emmanuel II   (c) Giuseppe Garibaldi   (d) Nero

13. Which one of the following subjects is included in the Union list?

    (a) Communication   (b) Trade   (c) Commerce   (d) Irrigation

14. Which one of the following elements is not included in the Belgium model?

    (a) Dutch and French speaking ministers shall be equal in the government.

    (b) Many powers of the central government have been given to state governmental

    (c) Brussels has a separate government in which both the communities have equal representation

    (d) There is a community government which has special powers of administration

15. Which one of the following countries is the example of 'Holding together federation'?

   (a) Australia   (b) India   (c) U.S.A.   (d) Switzerland

16. Which one of the following ethnic communities is in majority in Sri Lanka?

   (a) Sri Lankan Tamils   (b) Indian Tamils   (c) Muslims   (d) Sinhalese

17. Which one of the following subjects is included in the State list?

   (a) Banking   (b) Business   (c) Currency   (d) Communication

18. Activities that help in the development of Primary and Secondary sectors come under which one of the following sectors ?

   (a) Primary   (b) Secondary   (c) Tertiary   (d) Quaternary

19. Identify the correct feature of Unitary form of government from the following options:

   (a) There are two or more levels of government.   (b) Different tiers of government govern the same citizens.

   (c) Each tier of government has its own jurisdiction.   (d) The sub-units are subordinate to the central government.

20. At the initial stages of development, which one of the following sectors was the most important of economic activity?

   (a) Primary   (b) Secondary   (c) Tertiary   (d) Quaternary

21. Activities in which natural products are changed into other forms come under which one of the following sectors ?

   (a) Primary   (b) Secondary   (c) Tertiary   (d) Quaternary

22. The products received by exploiting natural resources come under which one of the following sectors ?

   (a) Quaternary   (b) Tertiary   (c) Secondary   (d)Primary

23. Which one of the following factors is mainly responsible for declining water level in India ?

   (a) Irrigation   (b) Industrialisation   (c) Urbanisation   (d) Over-utilization

24. Which one of the following subjects is included in the Concurrent List ?

   (a) Trade   (b) Commerce   (c) Agriculture   (d) Marriage

25. Two statements are given below as Assertion (A) and Reasoning (R). Read the statement and choose the most appropriate option.

   Assertion (A): After Russian occupation in Poland, the Russian language was imposed on its people.

   Reason (R): The use of Polish soon came to be a symbol of struggle against Russian dominance.

   (a) Both Assertion (A) and Reason (R) are true and Reason (R) is the correct explanation of Assertion (A).

   (b) Both Assertion (A) and Renson (R) are true, but Reason (R) is not the correct explanation of Assertion (A).

   (c) Assertion (A) is true but Reason (R) is false.

   (d) Assertion (A) is false but Reason (R) is true.

26. Read the facts regarding the Revolution of the Liberals in Europe during 1848 and choose the correct option:

   1. Abdication of the monarch

   2. Universal male suffrage had been proclaimed

   3. Political Rights to women were given

   4. Freedom of the press had been asked for

   (a) Only 1 and 2 are correct.   (b) Only 1, 2 and 3 are correct.

   (c) Only 1 and 4 are correct.   (d) only 1, 2 and 4 are correct

27. Two statements are given below as Assertion (A) and Reasoning (R). Read the statement and choose the most appropriate option.

   Assertion (A): Weavers in Silesia had led a revolt against contractors in 1845.

   Reason (R): Contractors had drastically reduced their payments

   (a) Both Assertion (A) and Reason (R) are true and Reason (R) is the correct explanation of Assertion (A).

(b)   Both Assertion (A) and Reason (R) are true but Reason (R) is not the correct explanation of Assertion (A).

(c)   Assertion (A) is true but Ronson (R) is false.

(d)   Assertion (A) is false but Reason (R) is true.

28.   On which of the following modern aspects did the new Germany place a strong emphasis?

1   Currency   2.   Banking   3.   Legal system   4.   Demography

(a)   Only 1 and 2 are correct.   (b)   Only 2 and 3 are correct.

(c)   Only 3 and 4 are correct.   (d)   Only 1, 2 and 3 are correct.

29.   Which one of the following Italian states was ruled by an Italian princely house?

(a)   Papal State   (b)   Lombardy   (c)   Venetia   (d)   Sardinia-Piedmont

30.   Identify the characteristics of Cavour among the following and choose the correct option:

1.   He was an Italian statesman.   2.   He spoke French much better than Italian

3.   He was a tactful diplomat.   4.   He belonged to a Royal family.

(a)   Only 1 and 2 are correct.   (b)   Only 1, 2 and 3 are correct.

(c)   Only 2, 3 and 4 are correct.   (d)   Only 1, 2 and 4 are correct.

31.   Two statements are given below as Assertion (A) and Reasoning (R). Read the statement and choose the most appropriate option

Assertion (A): In Britain, the formation of the nation-state was not the result of a sudden upheaval.

Reason (R): Ethnic groups of Britain extended its influence

(a)   Both Assertion (A) and Reason (R) are true and Reason (R) is the correct explanation of Assertion (A)

(b)   Both Assertion (A) and Reason (R) are true but Reason (R) is not the correct explanation of Assertion (A).

(c)   Assertion (A) is true but Reason (R) is false.

(d)   Assertion (A) is false but Reason (R) is true.

32.   Which among the following is not a problem of resource development?

(a)   Depletion of resources for satisfying the greed of few individuals

(b)   Accumulation of resources in few hands

(c)   Indiscriminate exploitation of resources

(d)   An equitable distribution of resources

33.   Which one of the following human activities have contributed most in land degradation?

(a)   Deforestation   (b)   Overgrazing   (c)   Mining   (d)   Over-irrigation

34.   Two statements are given below as Assertion (A) and Reasoning (R).

Read the statement and choose the most appropriate option:

Assertion (A): Indian farmers should diversify their cropping pattern from cereals to high value crops.

Reason (R): This will increase income and reduce environmental degradation simultaneously.

(a)   Both Assertion (A) and Ronson (R) are true and Reason (R) is the correct explanation of Assertion (A)

(b)   Both Assertion (A) and Reason (R) are true but Reason (R) is not the correct explanation of Assertion (A)

(c)   Assertion (A) is true but Ronson (R) is false,

(d)   Assertion (A) is false but Reason (R) is true

35.   Two statements are given below as Assertion (A) and Reasoning (R). Read the statement and choose the most appropriate

option:

Assertion (A): Majority community is dominant in a few democratic states

Reason (R) : Dominance can undermine the unity of the country,

(a)　Both Assertion (A) and Ronson (R) are true and Reason (R) is the correct explanation of Assertion (A)

(b)　Both Assertion (A) and Reason (R) are true but Reason (R) is not the correct explanation of Assertion (A)

(c)　Assertion (A) is true but Ronson (R) is false,

(d)　Assertion (A) is false but Reason (R) is true

36.　Two statements are given below as Assertion (A) and Reasoning (R). Read the statement and choose the most appropriate option:

Assertion (A): Power sharing is good.

Reason (R): It helps to reduce the possibility of conflicts between social groups.

(a)　Both Assertion (A) and Ronson (R) are true and Reason (R) is the correct explanation of Assertion (A)

(b)　Both Assertion (A) and Reason (R) are true but Reason (R) is not the correct explanation of Assertion (A)

(c)　Assertion (A) is true but Ronson (R) is false,

(d)　Assertion (A) is false but Reason (R) is true

37.　Choose the correct pair among the following:

(Country) - (Administration)

(a)　Russia - Unitary　　　　(b)　China - Federal　　　　(c)　Canada - Unitary　　　　(d)　Argentina - Federal

38.　Two statements are given below as Assertion (A) and Reasoning (R). Read the statement and choose the most appropriate option:

Assertion (A): The distrust between Sinhalese and Tamil communities turned into widespread conflict in Sri Lanka

Reason (R): 1956 Act recognized Sinhala as the only official language.

(a)　Both Assertion (A) and Ronson (R) are true and Reason (R) is the correct explanation of Assertion (A)

(b)　Both Assertion (A) and Reason (R) are true but Reason (R) is not the correct explanation of Assertion (A)

(c)　Assertion (A) is true but Ronson (R) is false,

(d)　Assertion (A) is false but Reason (R) is true

39.　Identify 'Horizontal power sharing' arrangements among the following in modern democracies:

(a)　Different organs of government　　　　　　　(b)　Governments at different levels

(c)　Different social groups　　　　　　　　　　　(d)　Different parties, pressure groups and movements

40.　Match Column I with Column II and choose the correct option:

Column I:	**Column II**
I.　Union List:	A.　Computer-related matter
II.　State List:	B.　Forest
III.　Concurrent List	C.　Police
IV.　Subsidiary Matters	D.　Defence

(a)　I-D II-C III-B IV-A　　　(b)　I-A II-B III-C IV-D　　　(c)　I-D II-C II-B IV-A　　　(d)　I-B II-A III-C IV-D

41.　Which of the following countries is an example of 'coming together' federation ?

(a)　United States of America　　　　　　　(b)　India

(c)　Spain　　　　　　　　　　　　　　　　(d)　Belgium

42. What is not an integral part of the government?

    (a) Office of the Prime Minister
    (b) Legislature
    (c) Executive
    (d) Judiciary

43. Two statements are given below as Assertion (A) and Reasoning (R). Read the statement and choose the most appropriate option:

    Assertion (A): Kerala has low Infant Mortality Rate.

    Reason (R): Kerala has adequate provision of basic health and education facilities.

    (a) Both Assertion (A) and Ronson (R) are true and Reason (R) is the correct explanation of Assertion (A)

    (b) Both Assertion (A) and Reason (R) are true but Reason (R) is not the correct explanation of Assertion (A)

    (c) Assertion (A) is true but Ronson (R) is false,

    (d) Assertion (A) is false but Reason (R) is true

44. Suppose there are four families in your locality, the average per capita income of whom is 10,000. If the income of three families is 6,000 8,000 and 14,000 respectively, what would be the income of the fourth family?

    (a) 5,000
    (b) 10,000
    (c) 12,000
    (d) 15,000

45. Which one of the following sectors shows the highest share in Gross Domestic Product (GDP) in India ?

    (a) Primary
    (b) Secondary
    (c) Tertiary
    (d) Quaternary

46. Which one of the following sectors shows the highest share in employment in 2017-18, in India?

    (a) Primary
    (b) Secondary
    (c) Tertiary
    (d) Quaternary

Case A: Read the source given below. Attempt any 5 questions out of 6 (Q. No. 47-52) questions.

Jhumming: The 'slash and burn' agriculture is known as 'Milps' in Mexicon and Central America, 'Conuco' in Vanexuela, 'Roca' in Brazil, 'Masole' in Central Africa, 'Ladang' in Indonesia, 'Ray' in Vietnam.

In India, this primitive form of cultivation is called 'Bewar' or 'Dahiya' in Madhya Pradesh, 'Pody' or 'Penda' in Andhra Pradesh, 'Pama Dabi' 'Koman' or 'Bringa' in Odisha' 'Kumari' in Western Ghats' 'Vaire' or 'Waltre' in South eastern Rajasthan. 'Khil' in the Himalayan belt, 'Kuruw' in Jharkhand, and 'Jhumming' in the North-eastern region.

47. How is Primitive Subsistence Agriculture related to Jhumming?

    (a) It is based on shifting cultivation
    (b) It is intensive in nature
    (c) It is based on plantation cultivation
    (d) It depends upon cash crop

48. The 'slash and burn' agriculture is known as' Conuco' in which one of the following countries?

    (a) Venezuela
    (b) Brazil
    (c) Indonesia
    (d) Mexico

49. The slash and burn agriculture is known as "Roca' in which one of the following countries?

    (a) Mexico
    (b) Indonesia
    (c) Brazil
    (d) Venezuela

50. Identify the major problem of Jhumming cultivation.

    (a) Single crop dominance
    (b) Modern inputs
    (c) High cost
    (d) Low production

51. In India 'slash and burn agriculture is known as 'Bewar', in which one of the following States?

    (a) Andhra Pradesh
    (b) Madhya Pradesh
    (c) Rajasthan
    (d) Jharkhand

52. Match Column I with Column II and choose the correct options:

Column I:	Column II
(I) Andhra Pradesh:	(A) Kuruwa
(II) Odisha:	(B) Valre
(III) Rajasthan:	(C) Penda
(IV) Jharkhand:	(D) Pama Dabi

(a)   1-C 11-D III -B IV-A   (b)   I-A 1-B III-C IV-D   (c)   1-B II-A III-D IV-C   (d)   1-D 1-C III-A IV-B

Case B: Read the source given below. Attempt any 5 questions out of 6 (Q. No. 53 - 58) questions.

Take the case of Laxmi with her two-hectare plot of unirrigated land. The government can spend some money or banks can provide a loan, to construct a well for her family to irrigate the land. Laxmi will then be able to irrigate her land and take a second crop. wheat, during the rabi season. Let us suppose that one hectare of wheat can provide employment to two people for 50 days (including sowing, watering, fertiliser application and harvesting). So two more members of the family can be employed in her own field. Now suppose a new dam is constructed and anals are due to irrigate many such firms. This could lead to a lot of employment generation within the agriculture sector to reduce the problem of underemployment.

53. Which one of the following economic sectors is Laxmi related to ?

    (a)   Primary   (b)   Secondary.   (c)   Tertiary   (d)   Quaternary

54. Which one of the following categories of farmers is Laxmi related to?

    (a)   Big   (b)   Medium   (c)   Marginal   (d)   Agricultural labourer

55. In which one of the following sectors is underemployment seen at the maximum?

    (a)   Industry   (b)   Agriculture   (c)   Trade   (d)   Commerce

56. How does construction of dams and canals create employment in large numbers in rural areas

    (a)   Large number of engineers are needed   (b)   Large number of technicians are also required

    (c)   Adjustment of large number of unalolled labourers   (d)   Executives and administrators can easily be adjusted

57. Which one of the following is the main result of increasing irrigation facilities in the field of agriculture ?

    (a)   Increase in production

    (b)   Increase in productivity

    (c)   Change in cropping pattern

    (d)   Promote high yielding of crops

58. Which one of the following means of irrigation generally comes under the Public Sector?

    (a)   Well   (b)   Tubewall   (c)   Tank   (d)   Canal

Map-Based Questions - 59 and 60 are Mandatory

59. On the outline political map of India (on page 24) 'A' is marked as a Dam. Identify it! from the following options:

    (a)   Tehri   (b)   Sardar Sarovar   (c)   Hirakud   (d)   Nagarjuna Sagar

60. On the same map 'B' is also marked as the largest Jute producer state. Identify it from the following options in

    (a)   West Bengal   (b)   Bihar   (c)   Assam   (d)   Odisha

Solutions

1. **(d)** Industrialisation began in England in the second half of the eighteenth century. Rapid industrialization first began in Britain, starting with mechanized spinning in the 1780s, with high rates of growth in steam power and iron production occurring after 1800.

2. **(a)** Following the defeat of Napoleon in 1815, European governments were driven by a spirit of conservatism. Conservatives believed that established, traditional institutions of state and society – like the monarchy, the Church, social hierarchies, property and the family – should be preserved.

3. **(a)** In 1815, representatives of the European powers Britain, Russia, Prussia and Austria who had collectively defeated Napoleon, met at Vienna to draw up a settlement for Europe.

4. **(a)** The first upheaval took place in France in July 1830. During the first upheaval of France in July 1830, the Bourbon monarch Charles X was overthrown and replaced by his cousin, Louis Philippe, Duke of Orleans.

5. **(b)** because events in France had consequences beyond France. They influenced the events in the rest of Europe. For example, the July Revolution of 1830 in France sparked an uprising in Brussels which led to Belgium breaking away from the United Kingdom of the Netherlands.

6. **(a)** Otto Von Bismarck is regarded as the architect of German unification.

7. **(c)** During the 1830s, Giuseppe Mazzini had sought to put together a coherent programme for the unitary Italian Republic. He had also formed a secret society called Young Italy for the dissemination of his goals.

8. **(a)** Some human activities such as deforestation, over grazing, mining and quarrying have contributed significantly to land degradation. In states like Gujarat, Rajasthan, Madhya Pradesh and Maharashtra overgrazing is one of the main reasons for land degradation.

9. **(c)** Arid soil is red to brown in colour. Its texture is sandy and saline in nature. It lacks humidity and moisture.

10. **(c)** Running water is primary causes of land degradation; it is responsible for about 84% of the global extent of degraded land, making excessive erosion one of the most significant environmental problems worldwide

11. **(a)** In Odisha, large scale deforestation for mining has badly affected the quality of land. Mining is one of the most important reasons for land degradation in this state.

12. **(b)** In 1861 King Victor Emmanuel II of Sardinia was proclaimed King of united Italy.

13. **(a)** The Union List includes subjects of national importance such as defence of the country, foreign affairs, banking, communications and currency.

14. **(d)** Statement d is not included in the Belgium model. These community governments are elected by people belonging to one language community – Dutch, French and German speaking – no matter where they live. This government has the power to take decisions regarding matters relating to culture, education and language-related issues of that community only.

15. **(b)** India is an example of 'Holding together federation'. 'Holding together federation' is a federation in which the powers of the country are divided between the central government and constituent states. The central government has greater authority when compared to states.

16. **(d)** The Sinhala community forms the majority group in Sri Lanka. They speak a distinctive language (Sinhala) related to the Indo-Aryan tongues of north India, and are mainly Buddhist.

17. **(b)** Business is included in the State list. Subjects like police, local governments, trade and commerce, agriculture within the state are included in the State List.

18. **(c)** Activities that help in the development of Primary and Secondary sectors come under Tertiary sector. The tertiary sector covers a wide range of activities from commerce to administration, transport, financial and real estate activities, business and personal services, education, health and social work.

19. **(d)** It is a form of power division as it divides the responsibilities and power between the National and State governments.

    It is the government system where ultimate authority is properly distributed between the federal government and regional governments.

    The power division theory reflects the government's executive, legislative, and judicial powers to be split into different sections and not consolidated into one Regardless of the corrupting influence of direct control, the divisions should be independent and distinct.

20. **(a)** At the initial stages of development, the primary sector was the most important economic activity.

21. **(b)** Activities in which natural products are changed into other forms come under the Secondary sector. The secondary sector covers all those activities consisting in varying degrees of processing of raw materials (manufacturing, construction industries).

22. **(d)** It comes under the primary sector of the economy since these economic activities involve the extraction of resources directly from the earth.

23. **(d)** Over-utilization is mainly responsible for declining water levels in India. As a result of increasing population, all the facilities such as houses, shops, roads, offices, pavements etc. increases to fulfill the increasing demands. This, in turn, decreases the open area for seepage of water into the ground.

24. **(d)** The Concurrent List contains subjects of common interest to both the Union as well as the States. These include education, forest, trade unions, marriage, adoption, and succession.

25. **(a)** Language too played an important role in developing nationalist sentiments. After Russian occupation, the Polish language was forced out of schools and the Russian language was imposed everywhere. In 1831, an armed rebellion against Russian rule took place which was ultimately crushed. Following this, many members of the clergy in Poland began to use language as a weapon of national resistance. Polish was used for church gathering and all religious instructions. As a result, a large number of priests and bishops were put in jail or sent to Siberia by the Russian authorities as punishment for their refusal to preach in Russia. The use of Polish came to be seen as a symbol of the struggle against Russian dominance.

26. **(d)** All the statements are correct except statement 3. This is because Political Rights to women were not given in Europe during the revolution of 1848.

27. **(a)** Silesia is a province in southwestern Poland. The weavers in Silesia held a revolt against the contractors in 1845. The reason for the revolt was the unacceptable behaviour of the contractors. The contractor had asked the weavers to finish the assigned task in a very short span of time and had reduced their wages drastically. The angry weavers attacked the warehouses and even the residences of some contractors. They damaged the machinery and the raw material. The Prussian army had to mediate in order to control the situation.

28. **(d)** The new state Germany placed a strong emphasis on modernising the currency, banking, legal and judicial systems in Germany.

29. **(d)** Only Sardinia-Piedmont was under the rule of an Italian princely household. The Italian language also had not acquired a common form and had many regional and local variations.

So people living in these regions, except Sardinia - Piedmont, would not have thought of themselves as Italians.

30. **(b)** Count Camillo de Cavour was born during Napoleon's rule in a wealthy family in Italy. He, later on, grew up to become a tactful diplomat who believed in realistic politics. Although born in Italy, he had an excellent command of the French language. He allied with both France and Prussia when it was needed, even though the two nations were enemies to one another. Cavour is often regarded as the 'brain' behind the unification of Italy.

31. **(a)** In Britain the formation of the nation-state was not the result of a sudden upheaval or revolution It was the result of a long-drawn-out process. The primary identities of the people who inhabited the British Isles were ethnic ones-such as English Welsh Scot or Irish.

32. **(d)** the major problems in development of resource:
(i) Most of the resources are limited in supply.
(ii) Most of the resources are unevenly distributed over the country.
(iii) Over-utilisation of the resources may lead to pollution of the environment.

33. **(a)** Deforestation have contributed most in land degradation. Deforestation in agriculture accounts for 60% of global land degradation as well as about 30% of all man-made carbon emissions. With increasing human population, trees around the world are cleared everyday to make way for agriculture in fertile lands to meet the increasing food demand.

34. **(a)** Indian farmers should diversify their cropping pattern from cereals to high-value crops. This will increase incomes and reduce environmental degradation simultaneously. Because fruits, medicinal herbs, flowers, vegetables, bio-diesel crops like jatropha and jojoba need much less irrigation than rice or sugarcane.

35. **(a)** Both Assertion (A) and Reason (R) are true and Reason (R) is the correct explanation of Assertion (A).
Imposing the will of the majority community over others may look like an attractive option in the short run, but in the long run, it undermines the unity of the nation.

36. **(a)** Power sharing is good because it helps to reduce the possibility of conflict between social groups. Since social conflict often leads to violence and political instability, power sharing is a good way to ensure the stability of political order.

37. **(d)** The government of Argentina, within the framework of a federal system, is a presidential representative democratic republic. The President of Argentina is both head of state and head of government. Executive power is exercised by the President. Legislative power is vested in the National Congress.

38. **(a)** A specific act to recognize Sinhala as the only official language was passed in the year 1956, thus neglecting Tamil.

The government only followed the preferential policies favouring the Sinhala candidates for multiple positions in government jobs, army and educational institutions.

A new constitution proclaimed that the State will also preserve and encourage Buddhism, the religion of the Sinhala's majority nation.

The people felt that the Government does not respect their language and culture and felt alienated.

39. **(a)** Power is shared among different organs of government, such as the legislature, executive and judiciary. This horizontal distribution of power allows different organs of government placed at the same level to exercise different powers.

40. **(c)** A. Union List - Defence

B. State List - Police

C. Concurrent List - Forest

D. Residuary powers- Computer-related matter

41. **(a)** The United States of America is an example of 'coming together' federation. Coming Together' refers to the form of federalism where small individual states come together to form a Union or Nation. In this type of federalism the states have individual identity and have majority of control over their governance.

42. **(a)** The Prime Minister's Office is not an Integral Part of the government. The Union government is mainly composed of the executive, the legislature, and the judiciary, and powers are vested by the constitution in the prime minister, parliament, and the supreme court, respectively.

43. **(a)** Kerala has low infant mortality rate because of adequate facilities of basic health and education. It mainly concentrate on human resources development. Human development ranking of Kerala is much higher than punjab because of combinations of factors like health, education and income.

44. **(c)** Per capita income is the total income of the country/ state divided by the number of people in that country/ state.

There are four families here. The average per capita income (10000) is equal to (6000+8000+14000+x) / 4

Income of the fourth family is Rs. 40000 - Rs. 28,000 = Rs. 12000.

45. **(c)** Tertiary sectors show the highest share in Gross Domestic Product (GDP) in India. The services sector is the largest sector of India. Gross Value Added (GVA) at current prices for the services sector is estimated at 96.54 lakh crore INR in 2020-21. The services sector accounts for 53.89% of India's GVA of 179.15 lakh crore Indian rupees.

46. **(a)** Primary sectors show the highest share in employment in 2017-18, in India. The primary sector in India is known as the agriculture and related sectors of fishing, dairying farming and forestry. it has the highest number of people employed under this section.

47. **(a)** Jhumming is practiced in hilly areas of North Eastern States with use of primitive tools and without application of modern technology and modern input and it only provides basic food grains for subsistence level, so called primitive farming.

48. **(a)** Slash and Burn agriculture is known as Roca in Brazil, Milpa in Central America, Conuco in Venezuela and Ray in Vietnam.

49. **(c)** Slash and Burn agriculture is known as Roca in Brazil, Milpa in Central America, Conuco in Venezuela and Ray in Vietnam.

50. **(d)** Low production is the major problem of Jhumming cultivation. Decrease in the span of jhum cycle because of populace pressure doesn't permit adequate time for the land to recuperate bringing about diminishing yields and land debasement.

51. **(b)** In India, this primitive form of cultivation(slash and burn) is called Bewar or Dahiya in Madhya Pradesh.

52. **(a)** In Andhra Pradesh slash and burn agriculture is known as Penda.

In Odisha slash and burn agriculture is known as Pama Dabi

In Rajasthan slash and burn agriculture is known as Valre

In Jharkhand slash and burn agriculture is known as Kuruwa

53. **(a)** Laxmi related to the Primary sector of economy as she was engaged in farming and agriculture.

54. **(c)** Laxmi is related to the category of Marginal farmers. Farmers having less than two hectares (five acres) of land are called small farmers and those having less than one hectare (2.5 acres) are called marginal farmers.

55. **(b)** In the agriculture sector underemployment is seen at the maximum. There are more people in agriculture than is necessary. So, even if a few people are moved out , production will not be affected. In other words, workers in the agricultural sector are underemployed. Each one is doing some work but no one is fully employed.

56. **(c)** Large scale projects like the construction of dams and canals open up a large space for work. -These projects need workers from different kinds of fields, hence opening up an opportunity for each kind. -These projects open up employment in transport, labour, tourism, food and lodgings and many more.

57. **(a)** Increase in production is the main result of increasing irrigation facilities in the field of agriculture. Irrigation helps to grow agricultural crops, maintain landscapes, and revegetate disturbed soils in dry areas and during periods of less than average rainfall. Irrigation also has other uses in crop production, including frost protection, suppressing weed growth in grain fields and preventing soil consolidation.

58. **(d)** Canal generally comes under the Public Sector. Canal is the artificial waterway that brings water from the water source to the area of irrigated. it is one of the essential form of irrigation used in agriculture

59. **(c)** The A marked dam is Hirakud Dam. Hirakud Dam is built across the Mahanadi River, about 15 kilometres from Sambalpur in the state of Odisha in India. It is the longest earthen dam in the world

60. **(a)** The B marked location is West Bengal.

West Bengal is the largest Jute producer state.

Approximately 60 percent of the total world produce of jute is cultivated in India with an annual estimated production of 10.14 million tonnes of jute. Jute is a bio-degradable crop grown mainly in the Ganges delta.

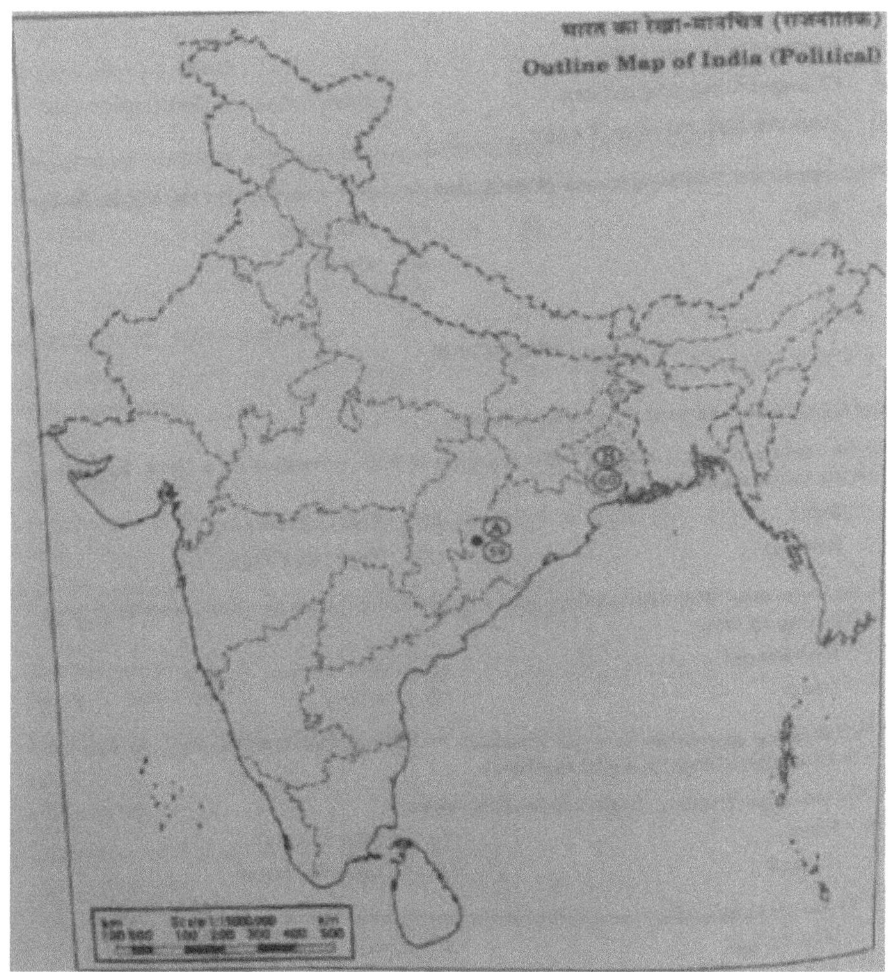

CBSE TOPPER-2020
Answer Sheet

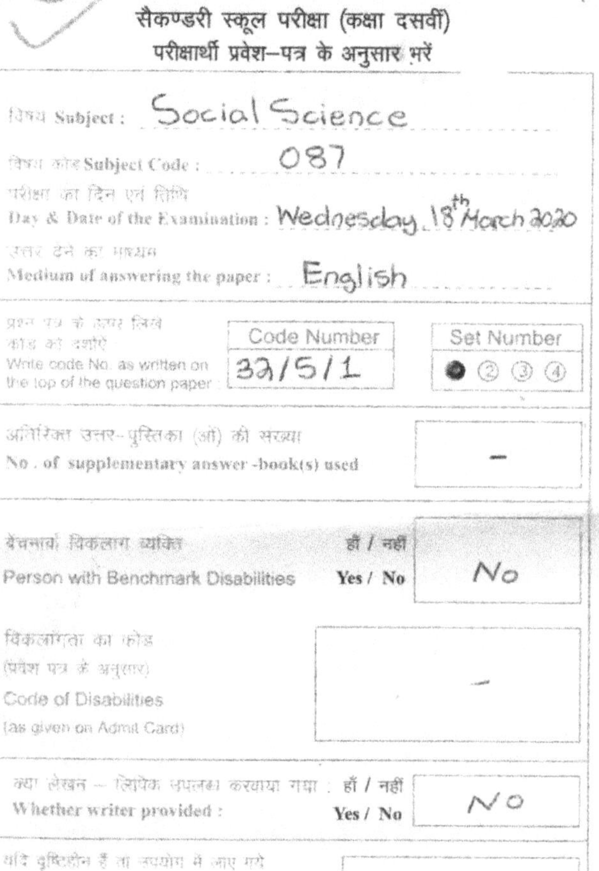

केन्द्रीय माध्यमिक शिक्षा बोर्ड, दिल्ली
सैकण्डरी स्कूल परीक्षा (कक्षा दसवीं)
परीक्षार्थी प्रवेश–पत्र के अनुसार भरें

विषय Subject : Social Science

विषय कोड Subject Code : 087

परीक्षा का दिन एवं तिथि
Day & Date of the Examination : Wednesday 18th March 2020

उत्तर देने का माध्यम
Medium of answering the paper : English

प्रश्न पत्र के ऊपर लिखे
कोड को दर्शाएँ
Write code No. as written on
the top of the question paper

Code Number	Set Number
32/5/1	● ② ③ ④

अतिरिक्त उत्तर–पुस्तिका (ओं) की संख्या
No. of supplementary answer -book(s) used : —

बेन्चमार्क विकलांग व्यक्ति
Person with Benchmark Disabilities | हाँ / नहीं Yes / No : No

विकलांगता का कोड
(प्रवेश पत्र के अनुसार)
Code of Disabilities
(as given on Admit Card) : —

क्या लेखन – लिपिक उपलब्ध करवाया गया : हाँ / नहीं
Whether writer provided : Yes / No : NO

यदि दृष्टिहीन हैं तो उपयोग में लाए गए
सॉफ्टवेयर का नाम
If Visually challenged, name of software used : —

*एक खाने में एक अक्षर लिखें। नाम के प्रत्येक भाग के बीच एक खाना रिक्त छोड़ दें। यदि परीक्षार्थी का नाम 24 अक्षरों से अधिक है, तो केवल नाम के प्रथम 24 अक्षर ही लिखें।

Each letter be written in one box and one box be left blank between each part of the name. In case Candidate's Name exceeds 24 letters, write first 24 letters.

कार्यालय उपयोग के लिए
Space for office use

प्रश्न सं. 35 के लिए

For question no. 35

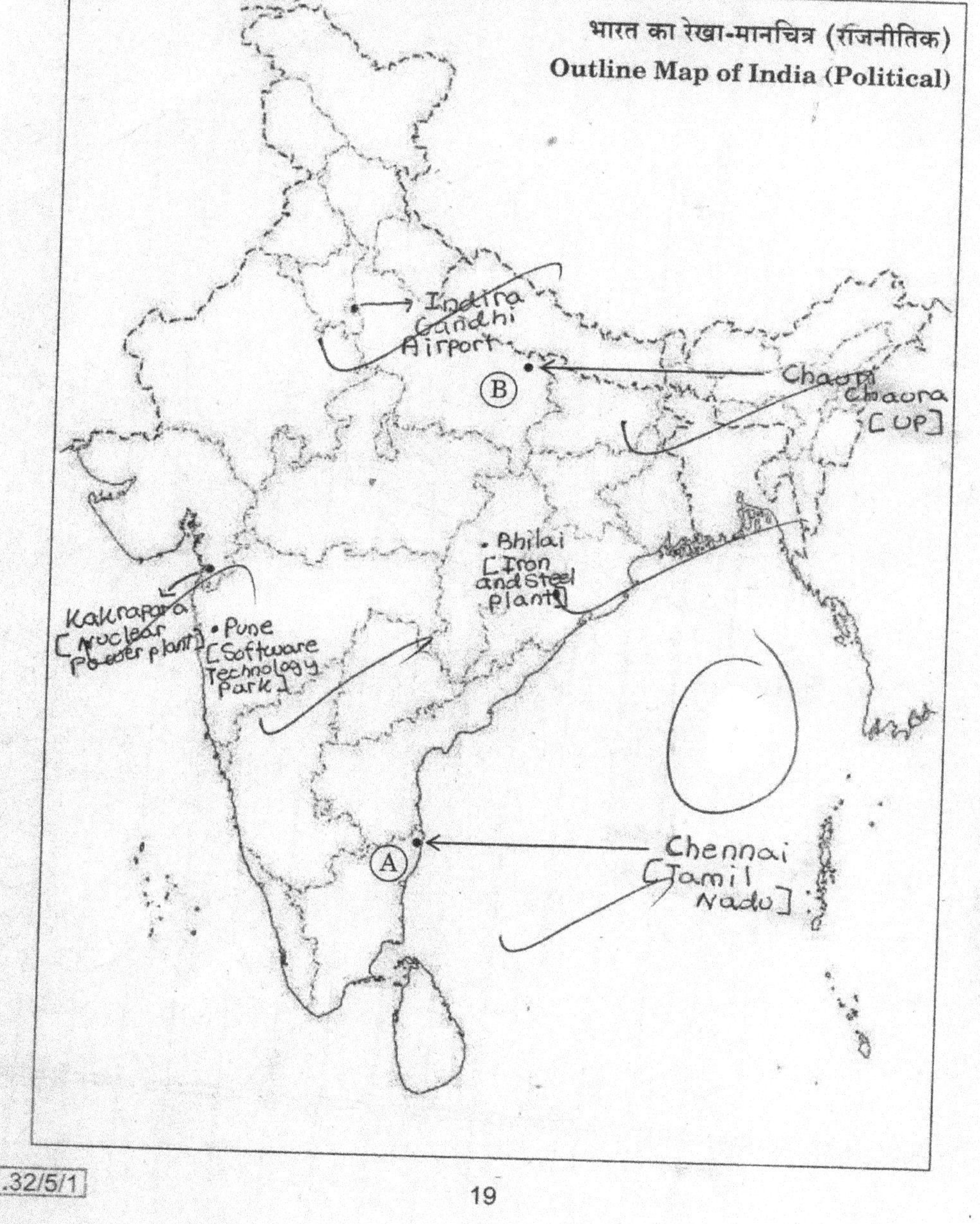

34.3) People can play an important role in the struggle for fair globalisation:

-> Massive campaigns and representation by people's organisations have influenced important decisions relating to trade and investments at the WTO world trade organisation.

-> People can pressurize the government to ensure that labour laws are being properly implemented and that workers get their rights.

-> People can support small-scale industries by providing the raw materials at low costs.

18 19

° Money or material things are important, but other factors are hence important too.

34) 34.1) Globalisation has made a large number of goods available. Consumers have a wide choice of goods and services. It is visible as today, consumers have the latest models of digital cameras, mobile phones, televisions and new autombbiles made by the leading manufacturers.

34.2)

-> Foreign trade connects two or more countries. Producers can sell not only in their own country but In markets of other countries too.

-> Buyers also have a wide choice of goods beyond what is domestically produced. Producers thousands of miles away compete with each other as prices of the similar goods tend to be the same in different markets.

Thus foreign trade results in integration of markets.

33)
- It is indeed true that money cannot buy all the goods and services that one must need to live well.

- For example, money cannot ensure that we live in a pollution-free environment or get unadulterated medicine. It can also not prevent infectious diseases if the whole community does not take steps.

- It is cheaper to have collective security for the entire community than security for each house. Similarly, if only one child is interested in studying, that child may not be able to go to school unless his or her parents are financially capable.

- Hence, it is cheaper to provide collective services. The quality of our life also depends on security, equal treatment, respect, no discrimination and friendship.

17

- It is not a simple matter to realize all people are equal, especially in societies that have been built on the basis of subordination and oppression, since centuries.

- For example, the dignity of women. Women all around the world have started several campaigns to be treated with respect. It has become easier for them to wage a struggle in democracy as disrespect of women lacks its legal and its moral foundations.

- Similarly, democracy has helped strengthen the claims of various disadvantaged and discriminated against castes. It has helped them, as in democratic India today, untouchability is unexpectable, legally and morally as well.

-> The emergence of political parties can be linked to representative democracy, as societies become large and complex.

-> People need some ways to elect representatives, bring people together to form a responsible government, form policies, support, reject them, and make laws for the country.

Hence there is a need for political parties in India.

3a) ° All people want to be treated with dignity and respect. Conflicts arise when people feel that they are not being treated with respect.

° However, the passion for dignity and respect is the basis of democracy. Democracies all over the world have realized this, at least in principle.

of the country. But this has faced problems of sinking of tracks in some areas, and landslides too.

31) A political party is a group of people that come together to contest elections and hold power in the government. They agree on some policies and programmes for the society to promote the collective good.

Necessity of political parties:
-> The need for political parties can be seen in a situation where no political parties exist. Then, every candidate will be independant and will not be able to make a promise for any policies. They will be responsible for their own constituency but no one will be responsible for how the country is run.

-> For example, though no political parties exist officially in Panchayat elections, it can be seen that villages split up into some factions and each puts up its panel of candidates. This is what a political party does.

of the country. But this has faced problems of sinking of tracks in some areas, and landslides too.

31) A political party is a group of people that come together to contest elections and hold power in the government. They agree on some policies and programmes for the society to promote the collective good.

Necessity of political parties:
-> The need for political parties can be seen in a situation where no political parties exist. Then, every candidate will be independant and will not be able to make a promise for any policies. They will be responsible for their own constituency but no one will be responsible for how the country is run.

-> For example, though no political parties exist officially in Panchayat elections, it can be seen that villages split up into some factions and each puts up its panel of candidates.
This is what a political party does.

30)
- The distribution pattern of the Indian Railways was influenced by physical, economic and administrative factors.
- The Northern Plains provided the most favourable conditions for its growth, because of vast level land, high population density, and rich agricultural resources. However there were large number of rivers here were required construction of bridges across their wide beds.
- In the hilly terrains of the peninsular regions, tracks had to be laid in the low hills, gaps, or passes.
- The Himalayan regions were unfavourable for its growth as it had high relief, sparse population and lack of economic opportunities.
- It was also difficult to lay tracks in the swamps of Gujarat, sandy plains of Rajasthan, and forested areas of Madhya Pradesh, Chhatisgarh, Orissa, and Jharkhand.
- The continous stretch of the Sahadryls could only be crossed through gaps or passes.
- The development of the Konkan railway along the western coast helped in access in the most important economic region

Section C

29)
- The aim of post-war institution was to generate full employment in the industrial world and economic reconstruction.
- In 1944, in the Bretton Woods Conference in New Hampshire, the IMF and World Bank were set up.
- IMF or international monetary fund looks into the external surpluses and deficits of its member nations. The World Bank or International Bank for Reconstruction and Development was set up for post-war economic restructions.
- These were known as Bretton Woods Twins. They commenced operations in 1947. The USA has effective right of veto.
- The following years saw an unprecedented rise of trade and incomes. Between 1950-1970, world trade grew from 5% - 8%. Incomes grew by 5% and unemployment ranged below 5%.

=> Small-scale industries can be set up in semirural areas. Cold storages, honey collection centres and industries processing vegetables can be set up.

=> Even if some people move out of the land, production will not be affected. Thus, some money of the family can take a loan from cooperative societies and buy land, and can start cultivation there. These family members can take help from their relatives as and when needed.

=> Thus, all the members in the family will be fully employed, and the family income can increase. Labour effort will not be divided.

202

27) -> Workers who receive their salary often open a bank account in their name and deposit their extra money. This amount earns some interest and remains safe with the bank.

-> Since these can be withdrawn, these are known as demand deposits. These share the essential features of money.

-> Demand deposits enable the payment by cheque. A cheque is a piece of paper Instructing the bank to pay a certain amount from the person's bank account to the person in whose name the cheque has been issued.

-> Thus demand deposit as well as paper money constitute currency in the modern economy.

28) ○ Underemployment occurs when people are working less than what they are capable of. It can be minimized by:

=) Some members of family can be employed in jobs set up by the government, eg. MGNREGA 2005 provides 100 days wage employment too.

26)
- The central government prescribes that the number of Dutch and French speaking ministers shall be equal in the central government. Some laws require support of majority of members in both groups, thus no one group can take decisions unilaterally.

- Many powers of the central government have been given to the State governments in both the regions which are not Subordinate to the central government

- Brussels has a separate government in which both the communities have equal representation. French agreed to equal representation in Brussels because Dutch agreed to equal representation in the central government.

- The Community government is elected by members of one language group no matter where they live. Dutch, German or French. It has power related to the educational, language and cultural issues.

25) • Every village or group of villages has a gram panchayat which consists of several ward members [panch] and a president [sarpanch]. It is elected by all the adult ward members living in that ward.

• It is under the supervision of the gram sabha which consists of the adult members of that population who meet a few times a year to discuss the performance of the gram sabha and the annual budget.

• A few Gram Sabhas form a Panchayat Samiti or Block or Mandal elected by all the Panchayat members in that area.

• A few Panchayat Samitis constitute the Zilla Parishad which is consists of MLAs, members of legislative assemblies, and other ministers.

• Zilla Parishad chairperson is the political head of Zilla Parishad.

° Gold and silver are found as placer deposits in the sands of valley floors and base of hills.

° Seawater contains magnesium and bromine salts. Manganese nodules are also found in the seabeds.

24) 1) Green revolution [package technology] and white revolution [operation flood] were set up by the government, but this led to development in concentrated areas.

2) Farmers were given crop insurance against failure of crops in case of droughts, floods, fires, etc. Establishment of grameen banks, cooperatives and banks that provided loans at reasonable rates of interest.

3) Kisan Credit Card, PAIS [Personal accident insurance scheme], renumerative prices, special weather bulletins, special programmes on TV and radio channels were also set up to reduce the exploitation by middlemen and speculators.

23)
- In igneous and metamorphic rocks, minerals occur in the cracks, crevices, faults and joints. Zinc is mined in this way. They are formed when minerals in their liquid/gaseous forms are forced upwards to the Earth's surface through cavities. They cool and solidify as they rise. Major metallic minerals are formed in this way.

- In sedimentary rocks, they occur in beds and layers as a result of decomposition, accumulation and concentration in horizontal strata. Coal and iron ore are formed in this way. Gypsum, potash and sodium salt are another class of ~~sodiu~~ sedimentary salts which are obtained through evaporation in arid areas.

- Bauxite is formed by the decomposition of surface rocks and removal of soluble constituents leaving a residual mass of weathered material containing ores.

public property.
-> Thus ideas of national unity were allied to the ideology of liberalism.
-> In the economic sphere, it stood for freedom of markets and abolition of State-imposed restrictions on movement of goods.

22) 22.1) There was intense debate over the issue of widow immolation between Hindu orthodoxy and social and religious reformers. Reformers spoke about how age-old traditions must be changed.

22.2)
-> Printed tracts and newspapers not only spread the new ideas but they shaped the nature of the debate.
-> They circulated a variety of arguments and were printed in the everyday spoken language of ordinary people in order to reach a wider audience.

20) Credit arrangements: Rate of interest per ~~common~~ month is five percent.

Rate of Interest	Five Percent per month
Present amount to be repaid	₹5000
Purpose of availing loan	Expenses on sudden illnesses or even functions in the family.

This is an example of informal credit.

Section B

21) -› Industrialization began in early nineteenth century Europe and brought with it new social classes like the middle class.

—› The men and women of the middle class were businessmen and professionals and had ideas of national unity and developed liberalism.

-› Liberalism is derived from the Latin word 'liber' which means free. For the new middle classes this stood for freedom of the individual and equality before the law.

-› Since the end of the French Revolution, liberalism stood for the end of autocracy and clerical privileges

-› Politically it stood for the concept of government by consent.

—› Nineteenth century liberals also stressed the inviolability of

13) Bahujan Samaj Party [BSP] was formed under the leadership of Kanshi Ram.

14) An example of economic development in dictatorial regimes is high per capita income, high literacy rate, low infant mortality rate, etc.

15) India is a secular country

16) State Election Commission is set up to conduct Panchayat and Municipal elections.

17) Investment in public facilities like healthcare and education.

18) (A) Only I and II

19) (B) Both (A) and (R) are true but (R) is not the correct explanation of (A)

7) The Printing Press was invented by Johann Gutenberg.

8) (B) TISCO

9) Burial grounds are an example of community owned resources.

10) A - 75 - 100cm

B - About 21° - 27° above 25°

11) The railways can make various stops in pilgrimage sites in India and can advertise the same. This will enable passengers to conduct multi-farious activities. It is a great integrating force.

12) People can be educated of the traditional cottage industries in India, awareness can be spread about the national movement.

This will cause people to buy the handspun khadi which will help increase production of traditional handloom mills.

Section A

1) (A) Otto Von Bismarck - Germany

2) (A) Industrialists were close to the Congress.

3) Raja Ram Mohan Roy published Sambad Kaumudi.

4) The Statue of Liberty held the torch of liberty in one hand and the charter of the rights of man for the others. All the countries payed homage to the statue as they passed by. The countries past the Statue had already become nation-states.
It represented the struggle for freedom, to become independant Nation-states.

5) The leaders were Muhammed Ali and Shaukat Ali.

6) (O) To suggest changes in the functioning of the constitutional system in India.

केन्द्रीय माध्यमिक शिक्षा बोर्ड, दिल्ली
सैकण्डरी स्कूल परीक्षा (कक्षा दसवीं)
परीक्षार्थी प्रवेश–पत्र के अनुसार भरें

विषय Subject : **Social Science**

विषय कोड Subject Code : **087**

परीक्षा का दिन एव तिथि
Day & Date of the Examination : **Wednesday, 18th March 2020**

उत्तर देने का माध्यम
Medium of answering the paper : **English**

प्रश्न पत्र के ऊपर लिखे
कोड की संख्या
Write code No. as written on
the top of the question paper :

Code Number	Set Number
32/5/1	● ② ③ ④

अतिरिक्त उत्तर–पुस्तिका (ओं) की संख्या
No. of supplementary answer -book(s) used : **–**

बेंचमार्क विकलांग व्यक्ति — हाँ / नहीं
Person with Benchmark Disabilities — Yes / No : **No**

विकलांगता का कोड
(प्रवेश पत्र के अनुसार)
Code of Disabilities
(as given on Admit Card) : **–**

क्या लेखन – लिपिक उपलब्ध करवाया गया : हाँ / नहीं
Whether writer provided : Yes / No : **NO**

यदि दृष्टिहीन हैं तो उपयोग में लाए गये
सॉफ्टवेयर का नाम
If Visually challenged, name of software used : **–**

*एक खाने में एक अक्षर लिखें। नाम के प्रत्येक भाग के बीच एक खाना रिक्त छोड़ दें। यदि परीक्षार्थी का
नाम 24 अक्षरों से अधिक है, तो केवल नाम के प्रथम 24 अक्षर ही लिखें।
**Each letter be written in one box and one box be left blank between each part of the
name. In case Candidate's Name exceeds 24 letters, write first 24 letters.**

कार्यालय उपयोग के लिए
Space for office use

1 Sample Paper
LATEST PATTERN

BLUE PRINT

SR NO	CHAPTER NAME	PER UNIT MARKS	MCQ	VSATQ	SATQ	LATQ	CBQ	MBQ	TOTAL MARKS
	UNIT-1 : HISTORY								
1	The rise of nationalism in Europe		Q (2, 4)	Q (1)					4
2	Nationalism in India		Q (3)			Q (1)		Q (2)	15
3	The making of a global world	20							
4	The age of industrialization				Q (2)				
5	Print Culture and the modern world		Q (1, 5)						2
	Unit-2 : GEOGRAPHY								
1	Resources and development		Q (1)						1
2	Forest and Wildlife resources				Q (4)				3
3	Water resources		Q (8)				Q (3)	Q (1b-ii)	6
4	Agriculture	20	Q (6, 9)						
5	Minerals and energy resources								
6	Manufacturing Industries							Q (1b-I, iii)	2
7	Lifelines of national economy			Q (2)		Q (4)		Q (1b-IV)	1
	UNIT – 3 : POLITICAL SCIENCE								
1	Power sharing		Q (11)						1
2	Federalism		Q (10, 12, 14)						3
3	Gender, religion and caste	20			Q (3, 5)				6
4	Political parties		Q (13)	Q (3)					3
5	Outcomes of Democracy					Q (3)			5
	UNIT-4 : ECONOMICS								
1	Development		Q (15, 16, 20)						3
2	Sectors of Indian Economy		Q (19)						1
3	Money and Credit	20				Q (2)	Q (1)		9
4	Globalization of the Indian economy		Q (17)	Q (4)	Q (1)				6
	TOTAL MARKS		20(20)	8(4)	15(5)	20(4)	12(3)	5	80

Time Allowed : 3 Hours | **Max. Marks : 80**

General Instructions

1. Question paper comprises Six Sections – A, B, C, D, E and F. There are 37 questions in the question paper. All questions are compulsory.
2. **Section A** – From question 1 to 20 are MCQs of 1 mark each.
3. **Section B** – Question no. 21 to 24 are Very Short Answer Type Questions, carrying 2 marks each. Answer to each question should not exceed 40 words.
4. **Section C** – contains Q.25to Q.29 are Short Answer Type Questions, carrying 3 marks each. Answer to each question should not exceed 60 words
5. **Section D** – Question no. 30 to 33 are long answer type questions, carrying 5 marks each. Answer to each question should not exceed 120 words.
6. **Section-E** – Questions no from 34 to 36 are case based questions with three sub questions and are of 4 marks each
7. **Section F** – Question no. 37 is map based, carrying 5 marks with two parts, 37a from History (2 marks) and 37b from Geography (3 marks).
8. There is no overall choice in the question paper. However, an internal choice has been provided in few questions. Only one of the choices in such questions have to be attempted.
9. In addition to this, separate instructions are given with each section and question, wherever necessary.

SECTION A (MCQS) (1 × 20 = 20)

1. In which of the following years, Buddhist missionaries from China introduced hand-printing technology?
   (a) 758-760 AD   (b) 768-770 AD   (c) 772-774 AD   (d) 776-778 AD
2. In the question given below, there are two statements marked as **Assertion (A)** and **Reason (R)**.
   Read the statements and choose the correct option.
   Assertion (A): Serfdom and bonded labour were abolished in Habsburg dominion and Russia.
   Reason (R): Monarchs had realised that revolution could be resisted only by granting concessions to the liberal nationalist rebels.
   (a) Both A and R are true and R is the correct explanation of A.
   (b) Both A and R are true, but R is not the correct explanation of A.
   (c) A is true, but R is false.
   (d) A is false, but R is true
3. Identify the appropriate reason for the formation of the Swaraj Party from the option given below.
   (a) It wanted members of Congress to return to Council Politics.
   (b) It wanted members of Congress to ask for Poorna Swaraj for Indians.
   (c) It wanted members of Congress to oppose the Simon Commission.
   (d) It wanted members of Congress to ask the Dominion State for India.
4. In the given image, the courier of Rhineland loses all that he has on his way home from Leipzig. Study the picture and answer the question that follows.

   Who is represented as a postman?
   Identify from the given options.
   (a) Napoleon Bonaparte   (b) Giuseppe Garibaldi   (c) Otto von Bismarck   (d) Giuseppe Mazzini
5. Consider the following events related to Print culture and identify the correct chronological response from the options given thereafter :
   (i) Buddhist missionaries from China introduced hand printing technology into Japan around 768-770 AD.
   (ii) Gutenberg perfected the system of Olive Press.
   (iii) Marco Polo brought wood block printing technology to Italy.
   (iv) The earliest kind of print technology was developed in China.
   (a) (ii), (iii), (iv), (i)   (b) (iv), (i), (iii), (ii)   (c) (i), (iii), (iv), (ii)   (d) (ii), (iv), (i), (iii)

6. Identify the major producer state of Rubber from the given options.
    (a) Kerala   (b) Maharashtra   (c) Assam   (d) Jammu and Kashmir

7. What percentage of land in India consists of fertile plains?
    (a) 38%   (b) 43%   (c) 46%   (d) 61%

8. Which among the following statements is/are correct about plantations?
    (i) The plantations have a large area and they are usually found in areas of low population density.
    (ii) It is capital intensive.
    (iii) The plantation farming has been an agricultural practice primarily in tropical and sub-tropical regions.
    Select the correct codes from the options given below.
    (a) Only (i)   (b) Only (ii)   (c) Both (ii) and (iii)   (d) All of these

9. In commercial farming, a single crop is grown on a large area. Identify which state the given crops belong to

	Crops		States
A.	Sugarcane	1.	Assam
B.	Coffee	2.	Uttar Pradesh
C.	Tea	3.	Kerala
D.	Rubber	4.	Karnataka

    (a) 1, 3, 4, 2   (b) 2, 4, 1, 3   (c) 3, 1, 2, 4   (d) 4, 2, 3, 1

10. Identify the region/area of India with the help of the following information.
- The Central Government has special powers in running these areas.
- These areas are too small to become an independent state.

    Select the appropriate option from the following.
    (a) Towns   (b) Union Territories   (c) District   (d) City

11. Which of the following statements is not an advantage of Power Sharing?
    (a) It helps to reduce the possibility of conflicts between social groups.
    (b) It helps to ensure the stability of the political order.
    (c) It creates problems for the majority class of the population.
    (d) It increases the participation among citizens in the formation of government.

12. Consider the following statements about the Holding-Together Federation.
    (i) A large country divides its power between constituent states and the national government.
    (ii) The Central government tends to be more powerful vis-a-vis the states.
    (iii) The Central government and the state always seem to have equal powers.
    (iv) Constituent states have unequal powers.
    (a) (i) and (ii)   (b) (ii) and (iii)   (c) (i), (ii) and (iv)   (d) Only (iv)

13. Fill in the blanks

Subject	List I	List II
Defense		Union List
Hospitals and Dispensaries	....	

    (a) Union List   (b) State list   (c) Concurrent list   (d) None of the above

14. Identify the administrative body of Indian Federal system with the help of the following information.
- It is a forum to discuss local governance and development.
- All the decisions are taken through this and no decision is official and valid without the consent of this body at the village level.

    Select the appropriate option from the following.
    (a) Block Samiti   (b) Gram Sabha   (c) Zila Parishad   (d) Municipality

15. According to the Human Development Report of UNDP, 2018, the HDI ranking of countries are mentioned below.

Column-A	Column-B
Sri Lanka	76
India	130
Pakistan	150
Nepal	149

Why does Sri Lanka have a better rank than India in the Human Development Report for 2018?
Choose the correct option from the following.

(a) The per capita income of Sri Lanka is higher than in India.
(b) Sri Lanka has a low population as compared to India.
(c) The literacy ratio i.e. enrolment ratio in all levels of schools in Sri Lanka is comparatively better than India.
(d) Both (a) and (c)

16. Read the given data and calculate the average income of the family
   (a) 7000   (b) 16000   (c) 10000   (d) 12000

17. Which of the following term is defined as the average expected length of life of a person at the time of the birth?
   (a) Maternity Rate   (b) Life Expectancy   (c) Life Span   (d) Mortality Rate

18. If BMI is less than 18.5 then the person would be considered as which of the following?
   (a) Overweight   (b) Under nourished   (c) Underweight   (d) Malnourished

19. Under which economic sector does the production of a community through the natural process come?
   (a) Public sector   (b) Primary sector   (c) Secondary sector   (d) Tertiary sector

20. What is the purpose of publishing the HDR for the UNDP?
   (a) To tell how to adjust inequalities
   (b) To measure how development has improved human life.
   (c) To emphasise the importance of individuals and their ability to unleash their maximum potential.
   (d) All of the above

SECTION B (VERY SHORT ANSWER QUESTIONS)   (2 × 4 =8)

21. What is meant by Absolutist?
22. Write a precise note on Airways in India.
23. Name the national political party which espouses secularism and welfare of weaker sections and minorities. Mention any two features of that party.
24. State any two negative effects of Globalisation?

OR

State any two positive effects of Globalisation?

SECTION C (SHORT ANSWER BASED QUESTIONS)   (5 × 3 =15)

25. Enlist few facilities available in SEZ that are developed by Central and State governments to attract foreign Investment.

OR

How is stability in jobs for the workers affected due to globalisation?

26. Mention the main contents of Indian National Congress in December 1929 held under the leadership of Jawaharlal Nehru.
27. Briefly explain how caste inequalities are still prevailing in India.
28. Give a brief description of the forest cover in India.
29. Name the national political party which gets inspiration from India fs ancient culture and values. Mention four features of that party.

SECTION D (LONG ANSWER BASED QUESTIONS)   (5 × 4 =20)

30. Write a precise note on the following.
   (i) Peasant movement in Awadh
   (ii) Tribal movements in Gudem Hills region

OR

   (i) Highlight the role of poor peasantry in the Civil Disobedience Movement.
   (ii) Comment on the role of merchants and industrialists in the Civil Disobedience Movement.

31. How can the formal sector loans be made beneficial for poor farmers and workers? Suggest any five measures.

OR

Answer the following.
   (i) Why do lenders ask for collateral while lending? Mention any four items that can be kept as collateral against the loan.
   (ii) How will the terms of credit become difficult for the small and marginal farmers?

32. How is democracy a better form of government in comparison with other forms of governments? Explain.

OR

Give an example of why the democratic government is known as a responsive government.

33. Roadways still have an edge over railways in India h. Give reasons.

OR

Write a note on the improvements made by the Indian Railways.

SECTION E (CASE BASED QUESTIONS) (4 × 3 = 12)

34. Read the given extract and answer the following questions.

Ever since humans appeared on the earth, they have used different means of communication. But, the pace of change has been rapid in modern times. Long distance communication is far easier without physical movement of the communicator or receiver. Personal communication and mass communication including television, radio, press, films, etc. are the major means of communication in the country. The Indian postal network is the largest in the world. It handles parcels as well as personal written communications. Cards and envelopes are considered first-class mail and are airlifted between stations covering both land and air. The second-class mail includes book packets, registered newspapers and periodicals. They are carried by surface mail, covering land and water transport. To facilitate quick delivery of mail in large towns and cities, six mail channels have been introduced recently. They are called Rajdhani Channel, Metro Channel, Green Channel, Business Channel, Bulk Mail Channel and Periodical Channel.

34.(1) Examine the role of the Indian postal network.

34.(2) Differentiate between mass communication and personal communication.

34.(3) Analyse the significance of communication for a nation.

35. Read the given extract and answer the following questions.

'To the altar of this revolution we have brought our youth as incense'. Many nationalists thought that the struggle against the British could not be won through non-violence. In 1928, the Hindustan Socialist Republican Army (HSRA) was founded at a meeting in Feroz Shah Kotla ground in Delhi. Amongst its leaders were Bhagat Singh, Jatin Das and Ajoy Ghosh. In a series of dramatic actions in different parts of India, the HSRA targeted some of the symbols of British power. In April 1929, Bhagat Singh and Batukeshwar Dutt threw a bomb in the Legislative Assembly. In the same year there was an attempt to blow up the train that Lord Irwin was travelling in. Bhagat Singh was 23 when he was tried and executed by the colonial government. During his trial, Bhagat Singh stated that he did not wish to glorify the cult of the bomb and pistol' but wanted a revolution in society: 'Revolution is the inalienable right of mankind. Freedom is the imprescriptible birthright of all. The labourer is the real sustainer of society. To the altar of this revolution we have brought our youth as incense, for no sacrifice is too great for so magnificent a cause. We are content. We await the advent of revolution. Inquilab Zindabad!

35.(1) When was HSRA founded?

35.(2) Why was Bhagat Singh put on trial?

35.(3) Why was the Hindustan Socialist Republican Army (HSRA), founded?

36. Read the given extract and answer the following questions.

Many thought that given the disadvantages and rising resistance against the multi-purpose projects, a water harvesting system was a viable alternative, both socio-economically and environmentally. In ancient India, along with the sophisticated hydraulic structures, there existed an extraordinary tradition of water-harvesting systems. People had in-depth knowledge of rainfall regimes and soil types and developed wide-ranging techniques to harvest rainwater, groundwater, river water, and floodwater in keeping with the local ecological conditions and their water needs. In hill and mountainous regions, people built diversion channels like the 'guls' or 'kuls' of the Western Himalayas for agriculture. 'Rooftop rainwater harvesting' was commonly practised to store drinking water, particularly in Rajasthan. In the flood plains of Bengal, people developed inundation channels to irrigate their fields. In arid and semi-arid regions, agricultural fields were converted into rain-fed storage structures that allowed the water to stand and moisten the soil like the 'khadins' in Jaisalmer and 'Johads' in other parts of Rajasthan.

36.(1) What were Guls or Kuls?

36.(2) What do you understand about rainwater harvesting?

36.(3) State any two benefits of rooftop rainwater harvesting?

SECTION F (MAP SKILL BASED QUESTIONS) (2 + 3 = 5)

37.(1) Two places A and B have been marked on the given outline map of India. Identify them and write their correct names on the lines drawn near them.

    A. The place where the Indian National Congress Session was held in September 1920.

    B. The place where the Jallianwala Bagh incident took place.

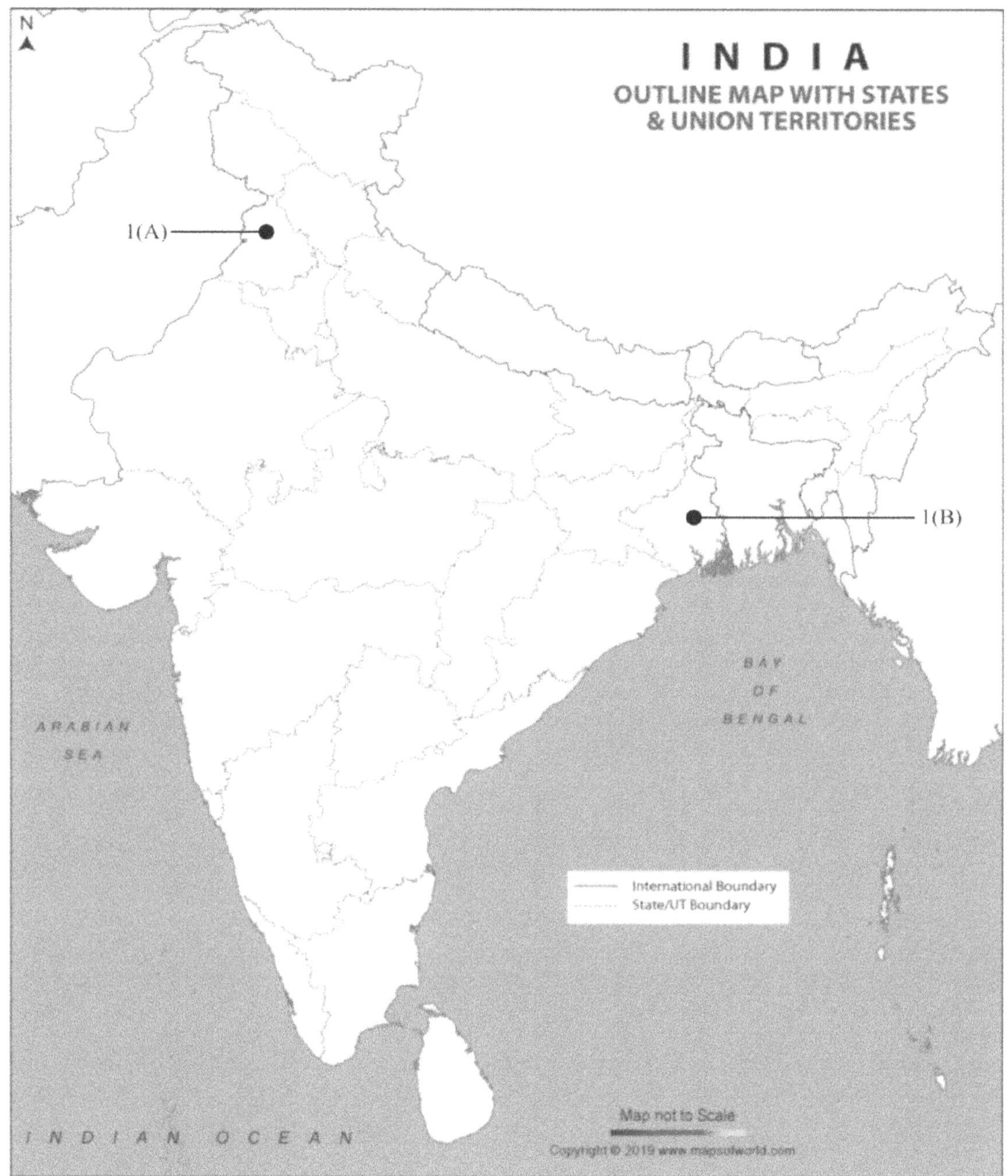

(b). On the same outline map of India locate and label any THREE of the following with suitable Symbols.

    (i)   A nuclear power plant in Uttar Pradesh

    (ii) A major port in Andhra Pradesh

    (iii) A nuclear power plant

    (iv) A software technology park

2 Sample Paper

LATEST PATTERN

BLUE PRINT

SR NO	CHAPTER NAME	PER UNIT MARKS	MCQ	VSATQ	SATQ	LATQ	CBQ	MBQ	TOTAL MARKS
	UNIT-1 : HISTORY								
1	The rise of nationalism in Europe		Q (2,4)		Q (2)		Q (3)	Q (1a)	11
2	Nationalism in India		Q (1)			Q (1)			6
3	The making of a global world	20							
4	The age of industrialization		Q (3)						1
5	Print Culture and the modern world		Q (5)	Q (2)					3
	Unit-2 : GEOGRAPHY								
1	Resources and development		Q (7)			Q (3)			6
2	Forest and Wildlife resources			Q (3)					2
3	Water resources		Q (8,9)						2
4	Agriculture	20	Q (6)						1
5	Minerals and energy resources								
6	Manufacturing Industries				Q (1)		Q (2)	Q (1b iii, iv)	9
7	Lifelines of national economy							Q (1b I, ii)	2
	UNIT – 3 : POLITICAL SCIENCE								
1	Power sharing		Q (10						1
2	Federalism		Q (11, 13, 14)						3
3	Gender, religion and caste	20			Q (3)				3
4	Political parties		Q (12)	Q (4)	Q (4)	Q (2)			11
5	Outcomes of Democracy		Q (15)						1
	UNIT-4 : ECONOMICS								
1	Development								
2	Sectors of Indian Economy		Q (16, 18, 19, 20)						4
3	Money and Credit	20	Q (17)		Q (5)	Q (4)	Q (1)		13
4	Globalization of the Indian economy			Q (1)					2
	TOTAL MARKS		20(20)	8(4)	15(5)	20(4)	12(3)	5	80

Time Allowed : 3 Hours   **Max. Marks : 80**

General Instructions

1. Question paper comprises Six Sections – A, B, C, D, E and F. There are 37 questions in the question paper. All questions are compulsory.
2. **Section A** – From question 1 to 20 are MCQs of 1 mark each.
3. **Section B** – Question no. 21 to 24 are Very Short Answer Type Questions, carrying 2 marks each. Answer to each question should not exceed 40 words.
4. **Section C** – contains Q.25to Q.29 are Short Answer Type Questions, carrying 3 marks each. Answer to each question should not exceed 60 words
5. **Section D** – Question no. 30 to 33 are long answer type questions, carrying 5 marks each. Answer to each question should not exceed 120 words.
6. **Section-E** – Questions no from 34 to 36 are case based questions with three sub questions and are of 4 marks each
7. **Section F** – Question no. 37 is map based, carrying 5 marks with two parts, 37a from History (2 marks) and 37b from Geography (3 marks).
8. There is no overall choice in the question paper. However, an internal choice has been provided in few questions. Only one of the choices in such questions have to be attempted.
9. In addition to this, separate instructions are given with each section and question, wherever necessary.

SECTION-A (MCQS)   (1 × 20 = 20)

1. Choose the correctly matched pair about the incidents with their year of occurrence from the given options.
   (a) Indian Industrial and Commerce Congress was formed-1927
   (b) Federation of the Indian Chamber of Commerce and Industries- 1920
   (c) Poona Pact- 1932
   (d) Mohammad Iqbal demanded Separate Electorates for Muslims- 1928
2. Which of the following option/s is/are correct about the Female allegory of France?
   (i) She was named Marianne.
   (ii) She took part in the French Revolution.
   (iii) She was a symbol of National Unity.
   (iv) Her characteristics were drawn from those of liberty and the Republic.
   (a) Only (i)   (b) Only (ii)   (c) (i), (iii) and (iv)   (d) (iii) and (iv)
3. Arrange the following events in a chronological order-
   I.   First spinning and weaving mill of Madras began production.
   II. First jute mill comes up in Bengal
   III. James Watt patents the steam engine
   IV. Earliest factories start in England.
   (A) I, II, IV, III   (B) IV, I, II, III   (C) IV, III, II, I   (D) III, IV, II, I
4. The given image depicts the 'Planting of Tree of Liberty' painted by Karl Fritz.

   In Which country is the scene taking place? Identify from the given options.
   (a) Leipzig, Germany   (b) Frankfurt, Germany   (c) Paris, France   (d) Zweibrücken, Germany
5. In the question given below, there are two statements marked as **Assertion (A)** and **Reason (R)**.
   Read the statements and choose the correct option.
   Assertion (A) : After the mid 19th century women's schools were set up in the cities and towns.
   Reason (R) : Many journals begans carrying the writings of women and explained why women should be educated.
   (a) Both A and R are true and R is the correct explanation of A
   (b) Both A and R are true, but R is not the correct explanation of A
   (c) A is true, but R is false
   (d) A is false, but R is true

6. Identify the crop with the help of clues given below
- High temperature is required during the time of growth.
- Grows well on well-drained fertile soils in the flood plains where soils are renewed every year.

  (a) Rubber   (b) Cotton   (c) Jute   (d) Coffee

7. Choose the correctly matched pair about the soil and their areas.
  (a) Red Laterite Soil - West Bengal
  (b) Arid Soil- Kerala
  (c) Yellow and Red Soil- Chhattisgarh
  (d) Alluvial Soil -Madhya Pradesh

8. With people being made the decision-makers by the Madhya Pradesh government, 2.9 million hectares or about 1 percent of India's land area are being greened across the state through which of the following methods?
  (a) Waste Management
  (b) Watershed Management
  (c) Rainwater Harvesting
  (d) None of these

9. Which of the following port was planned with a view to decongest the Mumbai port and serve as a hub port to this region?
  (a) Kandla port   (b) Mormugao port   (c) Jawaharlal Nehru port   (d) None of these

10. Match the following.

List I	List II
A. Brussels has a separate government in which	1. Accepted equal representations in Brussels
B. Belgian leaders between 1970 and 1993	2. In a legitimate government
C. French-speaking people	3. Dutch and French speaking people have equal representation
D. Citizens acquire a stake in the system through participation	4. Amended their constitution four times

	A	B	C	D
(a)	1	3	4	2
(b)	3	4	1	2
(c)	4	2	3	1
(d)	2	1	4	3

11. Which of the following can be considered a form of sharing of powers between the governments?
  (i) Division of Powers between the Chief Minister and Governor.
  (ii) Division of Powers between Central and State legislatures.
  (iii) Power sharing between the Union and the States through lists of subjects.
  (iv) Power division between Bureaucracy and Executive.
  (a) Only (i)   (b) Only (ii)   (c) Both (ii) and (iv)   (d) Both (ii) and (iii)

12. Who said that religion can never be separated from politics?
  (a) Mahatma Gandhi   (b) Dr BR Ambedkar   (c) PR Naicker   (d) None of them

13. Fill in the blanks

Subject	List
Education	. . . . .
Police	State List

  (a) Concurrent List   (b) Union List   (c) State List   (d) None of the above

14. Arrange in sequence according to the occurrence of the events
  I. States on the basis of language created
  II. Rise of regional political parties leading to coalitions.
  III. India's journey as a democracy begins.
  IV. Central government agrees to continue the use of English. CODES-
  (a) II, III, IV, II   (b) III, I, IV, II   (c) IV, II, III, I   (d) I, II, III, IV

15. In the question given below, there are two statements marked as **Assertion (A)** and **Reason (R)**.
Read the statements and choose the correct option.
Assertion (A) : Democracy transforms people from the status of a subject into that of a citizen.
Reason (R) : Most individuals believe that their vote makes a difference to the way the government is run and to their own self-interest.

(a) Both A and R are true and R is the correct explanation of A

(b) Both A and R are true, but R is not the correct explanation of A

(c) A is true, but R is false

(d) A is false, but R is true

16. Analyse the table given below and answer the question that follows.

The source shows a database of workers employed in different sectors (in millions)

Sector	Unorganised	Organised	Total
Primary	240	2	242
Secondary	54	9	63
Tertiary	76	17	93
Total	370	28	398
Total in%			**100%**

Reena is working as an accountant in a company where she receives poor working conditions especially in terms of wages which is much below than in the formal sector. What percentage of Tertiary sector workers in India is employed in Unorganised Sector according to the table?

(a) 71.2% (b) 80% (c) 81.7% (d) 91.7%

17. Sunil works in a private company, Anil works as a daily wage earner. Both want a credit of Rs 30,000.
The Bank is more likely to give credit to whom?

(a) Anil as he is more needy.

(b) Sunil as he has regular employment.

(c) Neither Sunil nor Anil will be provided credit from the bank.

(d) Both Anil and Sunil will be provided credit from the bank.

18. Anubha has taken a loan of 10 Lakh at an interest of 5 percent, from the bank in which
She is working. Anubha works in which sector of the economy?

(a) Primary (b) Secondary (c) Tertiary (d) All of these

19. Identify the system where goods were exchanged without using money from the given options.

(a) Goods system (b) Exchange system (c) Barter system (d) Both (a) and (b)

20. Which of the following will be the aspiration of a working woman?

(a) To have a safe and secure work environment at the office.

(b) To have better technologies that can store data easily.

(c) To have good job opportunities where her education can be made use of.

(d) To have fully functioning day care facilities in the office premises.

SECTION B (Very Short Answer Questions) (2 × 4 =8)

21. List two factors that encourage the MNCs to set up their production units at a place.

22. Define the Vernacular Press Act.

23. State the main effect of the Chipko Movement in India.

24. State any two conditions as laid down by the Election Commission to recognise a 'State Party' and 'National Party'.

OR

State the merits of Two-party system

SECTION C (Short Answer Based Questions) (5 × 3 =15)

25. Write a short note on

(i) Automobile Industry

(ii) IT and Electronics Industry

OR

How do industries create thermal and noise pollution? Mention their consequences.

26. Write a detailed note on Giuseppe Mazzini.

27. Mention any three aspects of life in which women are discriminated against in our country.

28. Discuss any two reasons which indicates that caste alone cannot determine election results in India

29. State the role of credit for development in an economy.

SECTION D (Long Answer Based Questions)   (5 × 4 =20)

30. Some of the political organisations in India were lukewarm in their response to the 'Civil Disobedience Movement'. Examine the statement.

OR

Sketch out a precise narrative of the genesis of Gandhi's idea of non-cooperation with the British and the circumstantial significance of launching the first mass movement of India in 1920.

31. Dynastic succession is one of the most serious challenges before the political parties."
Examine the statement.

OR

"Political parties are rightly called the government in disguise." Justify the statement in reference to democratic politics by giving five arguments (P)

32. "Planning is the widely accepted strategy for judicious use of resources in a country like India". Justify this statement with two relevant points and an example.

OR

Mention any four institutional efforts made at global level for 'resource conservation'.

33. What could be the possible reason when the banks might not be willing to lend credit to certain borrowers?

OR

Explain with an example how the terms of credit can be unfavourable for the small farmer. Also Suggest some ways by which small farmers can get cheap credit.

SECTION E (Case Based Questions)   (4 × 3 =12)

34. **Read the given extract and answer the following questions.**

Money is a fascinating subject and full of curiosities. The history of money and how various forms were used at different times is an interesting story. Modern forms of money are linked to the banking system. The present situation in India, where newer forms of money are slowly spreading with computerisation of the banking system, offers many opportunities to students to explore on their own. We need not get into a formal discussion of the 'functions of money' but let it come up as questions.

The stock of money consists of currency held by the public and the demand deposits that they hold with the banks. This is the money that people can use as they wish and the government has to ensure that the system works smoothly.

What would happen when the government declares that some of the currency notes used by people would be made invalid and would be replaced by new currency? In India, during November 2016, currency notes in the denomination of ₹ 500 and ₹ 1,000 were declared invalid. People were asked to surrender these notes to the bank by a specific period and receive new ₹ 500, ₹ 2,000 or other currency notes. This is known as 'Demonetisation'.

Since then, people were also encouraged to use their bank deposits rather than cash for transactions. Hence, digital transactions started by using bank-to-bank transfer through the internet or mobile phones, cheques, ATM cards, credit cards and Point of Sale (POS) swipe machines at shops. This is promoted to reduce the requirement of cash for transactions and also control corruption.

34.(1) What can be counted as a modern form of money?

34.(2) Which factor according to the given case primarily facilitates the expansion of newer currency?

34.(3) State the benefits of demonetisation.

35. **Read the given extract and answer the following questions.**

The Chemical industry in India is fast growing and diversifying. It contributes approximately 3 per cent of the GDP. It is the third largest in Asia and occupies the twelfth place in the world in term of its size. It comprises both large and small scale manufacturing units. Rapid growth has been recorded in both inorganic and organic sectors. Inorganic chemicals include sulphuric acid (used to manufacture fertilizers, synthetic fibres, plastics, adhesives, paints, dyes stuffs), nitric acid, alkalis, soda ash (used to make glass, soaps and detergents, paper) and caustic soda. These industries are widely spread over the country.

Organic chemicals include petrochemicals, which are used for manufacturing of synthetic fibers, synthetic rubber, plastics, dye-stuffs, drugs and pharmaceuticals. Organic chemical plants are located near oil refineries or petrochemical plants. The chemical industry is its own largest consumer. Basic chemicals undergo processing to further produce other chemicals that are used for industrial application, agriculture or directly for consumer markets.

35.(1) State one difference between organic and inorganic chemicals.

35.(2) Where organic chemical plants are generally located?

35.(3) State the features of chemical industries.

36. **Read the given extract and answer the following questions.**

Another important feature of the Civil Disobedience Movement was the large-scale participation of women. During Gandhi's Salt March, thousands of women came out of their homes to listen to him. They participated in protest-marches, manufactured salt and picketed foreign cloth and liquor shops. Many went to jail. In urban areas, these women were from high caste families. In rural areas, they came from rich peasant households. Moved by Gandhiji's call, they began to see service to the nation as a sacred duty of women.

36.(1) When did Gandhiji initiate a movement in Champaran in Bihar against the oppressive indigo plantation system?

36.(2) What was the reason behind launching the civil disobedience movement?

36.(3) State any two impacts of the civil disobedience movement.

SECTION F (Map Skill Based Questions) (2 + 3 = 5)

37. (a) On the given political map of India, two places are marked as A and B. Identify them with the help of the following information.

A   The place where the Indian National Congress was held in 1927.

B   The place where the Cotton Mill Workers Satyagraha took place.

(b) On the same outline map of India locate and label any THREE of the following with suitable Symbols.

(A) Netaji Subhash Chandra Bose International Airport

(B) Kochi Sea Port

(C) Kakrapar Nuclear Power Plant

(D) Tarapur Nuclear Power Plant

3 Sample Paper

BLUE PRINT

SR NO	CHAPTER NAME	PER UNIT MARKS	MCQ	VSATQ	SATQ	LATQ	CBQ	MBQ	TOTAL MARKS
	UNIT-1 : HISTORY								
1	The rise of nationalism in Europe	20	Q (1)				Q (3)		5
2	Nationalism in India		Q (2)	Q (1)		Q (1		Q (1A)	8
3	The making of a global world		Q (4)						1
4	The age of industrialization		Q (3)						1
5	Print Culture and the modern world		Q (5)			Q (3)			6
	Unit-2 : GEOGRAPHY								
1	Resources and development	20				Q (1)			
2	Forest and Wildlife resources					Q (2)			3
3	Water resources			Q (9)					4
4	Agriculture			Q (7)					1
5	Minerals and energy resources			Q (8)					1
6	Manufacturing Industries							Q (2)	4
7	Lifelines of national economy				Q (2)				3
	UNIT – 3 : POLITICAL SCIENCE								
1	Power sharing	20	Q (11, 12)						2
2	Federalism		Q (6, 13, 14)	Q (3)		Q (2)	Q (1)		14
3	Gender, religion and caste								
4	Political parties			Q (4)					2
5	Outcomes of Democracy		Q (10)						1
	UNIT-4 : ECONOMICS								
1	Development	20	Q (15, 17, 19)						3
2	Sectors of Indian Economy		Q (18)						1
3	Money and Credit		Q (20)		Q (3)				4
4	Globalization of the Indian economy		Q (16)	Q (4)	Q (5)	Q (4)			11
	TOTAL MARKS		20(20)	8(4)	15(5)	20(4)	12(3)	5	80

Time Allowed : 3 Hours   **Max. Marks : 80**

General Instructions

1. Question paper comprises Six Sections – A, B, C, D, E and F. There are 37 questions in the question paper. All questions are compulsory.
2. **Section A** – From question 1 to 20 are MCQs of 1 mark each.
3. **Section B** – Question no. 21 to 24 are Very Short Answer Type Questions, carrying 2 marks each. Answer to each question should not exceed 40 words.
4. **Section C** – contains Q.25 to Q.29 are Short Answer Type Questions, carrying 3 marks each. Answer to each question should not exceed 60 words
5. **Section D** – Question no. 30 to 33 are long answer type questions, carrying 5 marks each. Answer to each question should not exceed 120 words.
6. **Section-E** – Questions no from 34 to 36 are case based questions with three sub questions and are of 4 marks each
7. **Section F** – Question no. 37 is map based, carrying 5 marks with two parts, 37a from History (2 marks) and 37b from Geography (3 marks).
8. There is no overall choice in the question paper. However, an internal choice has been provided in few questions. Only one of the choices in such questions have to be attempted.
9. In addition to this, separate instructions are given with each section and question, wherever necessary.

SECTION A (MCQS)   (1 × 20 = 20)

1. The Vienna Congress was convened in 1815 for what purpose?
   (a) To declare completion of German Unification.
   (b) To restore conservative regime in Europe.
   (c) To declare war against France.
   (d) To start the process of Italian unification.
2. Find the incorrect option.
   (a) Jyotiba Phule wrote about the injustices of the caste system in his book 'Gulamgiri
   (b) In 1877, The Statesman' newspaper was founded
   (c) Gutenberg invented the printing press
   (d) Vernacular Press Act was passed in 1872
3. Which of the following two pairs of cities grew after the European companies gained power in trade?
   (a) Surat and Hooghly
   (b) Madras and Masulipatnam
   (c) Bombay and Calcutta
   (d) Kandla and Visakhapatnam
4. Which of the following option(s) is/are correct about the features of the economic situation which existed in Europe in nineteen century?
   (i) Migration of population from rural to urban regions.
   (ii) Small producers had to face stiff competition from England.
   (iii) Industrial Revolution became more advanced in most countries of Europe.
   (iv) Number of job seekers exceeded the employment opportunities.
   (a) Both (i) and (ii)   (b) Both (ii) and (iii)   (c) (i), (ii) and (iv))   (d) Both (iii) and (iv)
5. Arrange the following in sequence.
   1. Martin Luther 'Ninety Five Theses'
   2. The first Tamil Book Printed
   3. The first Malayalam book was printed
   4. Vernacular Press Act passed.
   (a) 4, 3, 2, 1   (b) 1, 4, 3, 2   (c) 1, 2, 3, 4   (d) 3, 2, 4, 1

6. Coalition Government is formed by the two or more Political Parties. Which of the following options best signifies this image related to coalition?

(a) Coalition government is a new form of Government in India.

(b) The ruling party and the opposition party form the coalition government.

(c) In the coalition government the leader decides every rule.

(d) The leader of the coalition keeps the partners of the government satisfied.

7. In the question given below, there are two statements marked as **Assertion (A)** and **Reason (R)**.

Read the statements and choose the correct option.

Assertion (A) Rubber is grown in tropical and subtropical areas.

Reason (R) It requires a moist and humid climate with rainfall of more than 100cm and temperature above 50°C.

(a) Both A and R are true and R is the correct explanation of A.

(b) Both A and R are true, but R is not the correct explanation of A.

(c) A is true, but R is false

(d) A is false, but R is true.

8. Consider the following statement about Bauxite.

I. From bauxite, a clay like substance alumina is extracted.

II. Jharkhand is the largest bauxite producer of India.

III. Bellary-Chitradurga belt is famous for bauxite reserves in India.

Which of the following is true?

(a) Only I   (b) II and III   (c) I and III   (d) All of these

9. Fill in the blanks-

Methods	Area
Khadins	Jaisalmer
Inundation Channel	… … … …

(a) Uttar Pradesh   (b) Gujarat   (c) West Bengal   (d) Chhattisgarh

10. In dealing with power sharing, which one of the following statements is not correct about democracy?

(a) People are the source of all political power.

(b) In a democracy, due respect is given to diverse groups and views that exist in a society.

(c) In a democracy, if the power to decide is dispersed, it is not possible to take quick decisions and enforce them.

(d) In a democracy, people rule themselves through institutions of self-governance.

11. Identify the political reason/s behind the conflicts in Sri Lanka.

(a) Failure of non-government organisations

(b) policies of the government

(c) Absence of representation for weaker sections

(d) Unwillingness of political parties to resolve conflicts

12. Match the following-

List 1	List 2
A. Sri Lanka got independence	1. 1956
B. Sinhala became official language	2. 2009
C. Civil war ended in Sri Lanka	3. 1948
D. LTTE formed	4. 1976

(a) 2, 1, 4, 3   (b) 3, 1, 2, 4   (c) 2, 4, 3, 1   (d) 4, 1, 2, 3

13. find the correct option from the given codes.
    (i)   In a Federal government, the constitution is supreme.
    (ii) In a Federal government, the constitution may be written or unwritten.
    (iii) In a Unitary government, there is no division of powers between centre and states.
    (iv) Legislature may be bicameral or unicameral in unitary government.
    (a) Only (ii)　　　(b) Both (i) and (ii)　　　(c) (i), (iii) and (iv)　　(d) All of these

14. In Unitary form of government
    (a) all the power is divided between the centre/union and the state provincial government.
    (b) all the power is with the citizens.
    (c) The State Government has all the powers.
    (d) power is concentrated with the Central Government.

15. The sum of the total production of all goods and services in the three sectors are combinedly called as
    (a) NDP　　　(b) GNI　　　(c) GDP　　　(d) NI

16. Identify the correct meaning of 'custom barrier' from the given options.
    (i)   It is a measure of limiting trade across borders of different cities and principalities
    (ii) It is a tax collected at airports to boost exports.
    (iii) It is a physical barrier between two cities.
    (iv) It helps to decrease the price of the products.
    (a) (i) and (ii)　　　(b) Only (i)　　　(c) Both (ii) and (iii)　(d) Both (iii) and (iv)

17. According to the Human Development Report of UNDP, 2018, the HDI ranking of countries are mentioned below.

List A	List B
A. Sri Lanka	1. 76
B. India	2. 130
C. Pakistan	3. 150
D. Nepal	4. 149

Why does India rank low in the Human Development Index despite its huge size and population? Select the most suitable options from the following
    (a) Less investment in social infrastructure.
    (b) Gender Inequality is still prevalent.
    (c) Increasing Income Inequalities among different sections of the society.
    (d) All of the above

18. In the question given below, there are two statements marked as **Assertion (A)** and **Reason (R)**. Read the statements and choose the correct option.
    Assertion (A) There is a need for protection and support of the workers in the unorganised sector.
    Reason (R) Workers in an unorganised sector get paid really less and are heavily exploited.
    (a) Both A and R are true and R is the correct explanation of A.
    (b) Both A and R are true, but R is not the correct explanation of A.
    (c) A is true, but R is false.
    (d) A is false, but R is true.

19. If the Body Mass Index (BMI) is ____________ then the adult person would be considered underweight.
    (a) less than 18.5　　　(b) less than 10.5　　　(c) less than 25.5　　　(d) less than 28.5

20. Which among the following is not a feature of informal source of credit?
    (a) It is supervised by the Reserve Bank of India
    (b) Rate of interest is not fixed.
    (c) Terms of credit are very flexible.
    (d) Traders, employers, friends, relatives, etc provide informal credit sources.

SECTION B (VERY SHORT ANSWER QUESTIONS)　　(2 × 4 =8)

21. How the Rowlatt Act affected the National Movement?
22. What do you understand about Border Roads?
23. What is meant by the system of 'checks and balances'?

24. Give one characteristic feature of a 'Special Economic Zone'?

OR

What do you understand by the term 'Foreign Direct Investment'?

SECTION C (SHORT ANSWER BASED QUESTIONS) (5 × 3 =15)

25. Explain the effects of worldwide economic depression on India, towards the late 1920's.

OR

Why did Mahatma Gandhi start the Civil Disobedience Movement? How did this movement unite the country? Explain.

26. Describe how humans are dependent on the ecological system for their existence?

27. What is money? Why is modern money currency accepted as a medium of exchange?

28. Explain the status of women's representation in India's legislative bodies.

29. How can we say that globalisation has been advantageous to consumers as well as producers? Give reasons.

SECTION D (LONG ANSWER BASED QUESTIONS) (5 × 4 =20)

30. Explain the anthropogenic factors of land degradation.

OR

Explain with the Gandhian point of view that why conservation of resources is necessary?

31. State the various merits of decentralization.

OR

Which policies led to the success of federalism in India?

32. Briefly Explain various stages of development of printing technology in China.

OR

Write a detailed note on-

A. The Gutenberg Press

B. Erasmus Idea of the printed books

33. How the rapid improvement in technology has been playing a key role in encouraging the process of globalisation.

OR

How are local companies benefited by collaborating with multinational companies? Explain with examples.

SECTION E (CASE BASED QUESTIONS) (4 × 3 =12)

34. Read the given text and answer the following questions given below.

A major step towards decentralisation was taken in 1992. The Constitution was amended to make the third-tier of democracy more powerful and effective. Now, it is constitutionally mandatory to hold regular elections to local government bodies. Seats are reserved in the elected bodies and the executive heads of these institutions for the Scheduled Castes, Scheduled Tribes and Other Backward Classes. At least one-third of all positions are reserved for women. An independent institution called the State Election Commission has been created in each state to conduct panchayat and municipal elections.

The state governments are required to share some powers and revenue with local government bodies. The nature of sharing varies from state to state. Rural local government is popularly known by the name Panchayati Raj. Each village, or a group of villages in some states, has a gram panchayat. This is a council consisting of several ward members, often called panch, and a president or sarpanch. They are directly elected by all the adult population living in that ward or village. It is the decision-making body for the entire village. The panchayat works under the overall supervision of the gram sabha. All the voters in the village are its members. It has to meet at least twice or thrice in a year to approve the annual budget of the gram panchayat and to review the performance of the gram panchayat.

34.(1) What do you understand by the term decentralization in democracy?

34.(2) When did one third of total seats were reserved for women in rural local government in India?

34.(3) State any two advantages of rural local government.

35. Read the given text and answer the following questions given below.

NTPC is a major power providing corporation in India. It has ISO certification for EMS (Environment Management System) 14001. The corporation has a proactive approach for preserving the natural environment and resources like water, oil and gas and fuels in places where it is setting up power plants. This has been possible through the following ways.

- Optimum utilization of equipment adopting latest techniques and upgrading existing equipment.
- Minimizing waste generation by maximizing ash utilization.
- Providing green belts for nurturing ecological balance and addressing the question of special purpose vehicles for afforestation.
- Reducing environmental pollution through ash pond management, ash water recycling system and liquid waste management.

35.(1) What does NTPC refer to?

35.(2) State the approach adopted by NTPC.

35.(3) List out the ways adopted by the NTPC towards the preservation of the natural environment.

36. **Read the given text and answer the following questions given below.**

Like Germany, Italy too had a long history of political fragmentation. Italians were scattered over several dynastic states as well as the multi-national Habsburg Empire. During the middle of the nineteenth century, Italy was divided into seven states, of which only one, Sardinia-Piedmont, was ruled by an Italian princely house. The North was under Austrian Habsburgs, the centre was ruled by the Pope and the Southern regions were under the

domination of the Bourbon kings of Spain. Even the Italian language had not acquired one common form and still had many regional and local variations.

During the 1830s, Giuseppe Mazzini had sought to put together a coherent programme for a unitary Italian Republic. He had also formed a secret society called Young Italy for the dissemination of his goals. The failure of revolutionary uprisings both in 1831 and 1848 meant that the mantle now fell to Sardinia-Piedmont under its ruler King Victor Emmanuel II to unify the Italian states through war. In the eyes of the ruling elites of this region, a unified Italy offered them the possibility of economic development and political dominance.

Chief Minister Cavour who led the movement to unify the regions of Italy was neither a revolutionary nor a democrat. Like many other wealthy and educated members of the Italian elite, he spoke French much better than he did Italian. Through a tactful diplomatic alliance with France engineered by Cavour, Sardinia-Piedmont succeeded in defeating the Austrian forces in 1859. Apart from regular troops, a large number of armed volunteers under the leadership of Giuseppe Garibaldi joined the fray. In 1860, they marched into South Italy and the Kingdom of the Two Sicilies and succeeded in winning the support of the local peasants in order to drive out the Spanish rulers. In 1861, Victor Emmanuel II was proclaimed king of united Italy.

36.(1) Describe the political fragmentary of Italy.

36.(2) What was Young Italy Society?

36.(3) Write a note on Count Camillo de Cavour.

SECTION F (MAP SKILL BASED QUESTIONS) (2 + 3 =5)

37.(a) On the outline map of India, Identify them and write their correct names on the lines drawn near them.

(A) The location of the Indian National Congress Session of 1927.

(B) A place where Gandhiji ceremonially violated the Salt Law and manufactured salt by boiling salt sea water.

(b) On the same outline map of India locate and label any three of the following with suitable symbols.

I. A major port on the southeast coast of India.

II. Mumbai sea port

III. A software technology park

IV. A major dam in Odisha.

4 Sample Paper

LATEST PATTERN

BLUE PRINT

SR NO	CHAPTER NAME	PER UNIT MARKS	MCQ	VSATQ	SATQ	LATQ	CBQ	MBQ	TOTAL MARKS
	UNIT-1 : HISTORY								
1	The rise of nationalism in Europe	20	Q ((1, 3, 4)					Q (1a)	5
2	Nationalism in India		Q (2, 5)						2
3	The making of a global world						Q (1)		4
4	The age of industrialization			Q (2)		Q (1)			7
5	Print Culture and the modern world				Q (2)				3
	Unit-2 : GEOGRAPHY								
1	Resources and development	20					Q (3)		4
2	Forest and Wildlife resources								
3	Water resources		Q (9)		Q (5)	Q (3)		Q (1b-I, IV)	10
4	Agriculture		Q (6, 7)						2
5	Minerals and energy resources		Q (8)						1
6	Manufacturing Industries								
7	Lifelines of national economy			Q (1)				Q (1b-II, III)	4
	UNIT – 3 : POLITICAL SCIENCE								
1	Power sharing	20	Q (18, 19)			Q (4)			7
2	Federalism		Q (17, 20)						2
3	Gender, religion and caste				Q (1)				3
4	Political parties			Q (4)			Q (2)		6
5	Outcomes of Democracy								
	UNIT-4 : ECONOMICS								
1	Development	20	Q (11, 12, 14, 16)	Q (3)					6
2	Sectors of Indian Economy		Q (10, 13, 15)						3
3	Money and Credit				Q (3, 4)	Q (2)			11
4	Globalization of the Indian economy								
	TOTAL MARKS		20(20)	8(4)	15(5)	20(4)	12(3)	5	80

Time Allowed : 3 Hours   **Max. Marks : 80**

General Instructions

1. Question paper comprises Six Sections – A, B, C, D, E and F. There are 37 questions in the question paper. All questions are compulsory.
2. **Section A** – From question 1 to 20 are MCQs of 1 mark each.
3. **Section B** – Question no. 21 to 24 are Very Short Answer Type Questions, carrying 2 marks each. Answer to each question should not exceed 40 words.
4. **Section C** – contains Q.25to Q.29 are Short Answer Type Questions, carrying 3 marks each. Answer to each question should not exceed 60 words
5. **Section D** – Question no. 30 to 33 are long answer type questions, carrying 5 marks each. Answer to each question should not exceed 120 words.
6. **Section-E** – Questions no from 34 to 36 are case based questions with three sub questions and are of 4 marks each
7. **Section F** – Question no. 37 is map based, carrying 5 marks with two parts, 37a from History (2 marks) and 37b from Geography (3 marks).
8. There is no overall choice in the question paper. However, an internal choice has been provided in few questions. Only one of the choices in such questions have to be attempted.
9. In addition to this, separate instructions are given with each section and question, wherever necessary.

SECTION-A (MCQS)   (1 × 20 = 20)

1. Why did women and non-propertied men organise opposition movements through the 18th and early 19th century in Europe?
   (a) Demanding for property
   (b) Demanding equal political rights
   (c) Demanding membership in Jacobian club
   (d) Demanding equal distribution of wealth
2. When did the Non-cooperation Khilafat Movement begin in India?
   (a) January 1919   (b) January 1921   (c) February 1920   (d) February 1922
3. Which of the following statements about the French Revolution' are correct?
   (i) After the end of the French Revolution it was proclaimed that it was the people who would henceforth constitute the nation and shape its destiny.
   (ii) France will have a constitutional monarchy and the new republic will be headed by a member of the royal family.
   (iii) A centralised administrative system will be put in place to formulate uniforms laws for all citizens.
   (iv) Imposition of internal custom duties and dues will continue to exist in France.
   (a) (ii) and (iii)   (b) (ii) and (iv)   (c) (i) and (iii)   (d) (iii) and (iv)
4. Which of the following aspects best signifies this image in 1848 in France?
   (a) Peasant uprising, 1848
   (b) Massacre at Chios
   (c) Hall of Versailles
   (d) Frankfurt Parliament
5. Arrange the following events in a chronological order-
   I.   Distressed Uttar Pradesh peasants organised by Baba Ramchandra.
   II. Incident of Chauri Chaura;
   III Mahatma Gandhi returned to India.
   IV   Khilafat Committee was formed in Bombay
   (a) III, II, I, IV   (b) III, I, IV, II   (c) IV, II, I, III   (d) IV, I, II, III
6. Identify the crop with the help of given clues
   • It is a tropical as well as a sub-tropical crop.
   • It grows well in hot and humid climates.
   • A temperature of 21°C to 27°C and an annual rainfall between 75cm and 100cm.
   (a) Oil seeds   (b) Sugarcane   (c) Tea   (d) Coffee
7. Aus, Aman and Boro are types of which crop?
   (a) Maize   (b) Paddy   (c) Jowar   (d) Bajra

8. Match the following-

List I	List II
A. Ferrous minerals	1. Potash
B. Non-ferrous minerals	2. Uranium
C. Non-metallic minerals	3. Nickel
D. Energy minerals	4. Bauxite

	A	**B**	**C**	**D**
(a)	3	4	1	2
(b)	2	3	1	4
(c)	3	2	4	1
(d)	1	4	2	3

9. Fill in the blanks

List 1	List 2
A. Metal extraction process from ore	Smelting
B. Method of trapping solid waste fromwaste water	… … … .

(a) Flocculation   (b) Particulate matter   (c) Screening   (d) Sewage treatment

10. Identify the incorrect option.
    (a) Disguised unemployment - More people working than actually needed
    (b) Unemployment - Not getting jobs at a particular time of the year
    (c) Underemployed - Not employed according to skill or education
    (d) Labour effort- the hard work done by a labour to earn income

11. Study the following table and answer the question that follows.

Region/Country	Reserves 2017 (Thousand Millions Barrels)	Number of Years Reserves will last
Middle East	808	70
United States of America	50	10.5
World	1697	50.2

For how many years will the reserves of crude oil last in Middle East, if they continue extracting it at the present rate?
    (a) 50 years   (b) 70 years   (b) 100 years   (d) 60 years

12 In the question given below, there are two statements marked as **Assertion (A)** and **Reason (R)**.
Read the statements and choose the correct option.
Assertion (A) An equitable distribution of resources has sustained quality of life and global peace.
Reason (R) They promote equality among classes.
    (a) Both A and R are true and R is the correct explanation of A
    (b) Both A and R are true but R is not the correct explanation of
    (c) A is true, but R is false.
    (d) A is false, but R is true.

13. The following table gives the GDP in Rupees (crores) by the three sectors.

Year	Primary	Secondary	Tertiary
2000	52000	48500	133500
2013	800500	1074000	3668000

What is the share of the secondary sector in the total GDP of 2013.
    (a) 45.78%   (b) 18.70%   (c) 32.67%   (d) 14.55%

14. Which of the following statements is correct about developmental goals?
    (a) They are the same for all the citizens of a country.
    (b) These goals do not matter to the citizens
    (c) They are different and sometimes even contradictory for different groups and people
    (d) There are no developmental goals

15. Which of the following services rise rapidly?
    - (a) Banking and Trade
    - (b) Software companies
    - (c) Information and Communication Technology
    - (d) Education
16. How would you calculate Body Mass Index?
    - (a) Dividing the weight by the square of the height.
    - (b) Dividing the height by weight.
    - (c) Dividing the weight by height.
    - (d) Adding height to the weight of the person.
17. Who elects the members of the Gram Panchayat?
    - (a) The Presiding officer　(b) The Gram Panchayat　(c) The Gram Sabha　(d) The Nyaya Panchayat
18. Which of the following was the main reason responsible for the killing of thousands of people in Sri Lanka? Identify from the given options.
    - (a) Cold War between Sinhala and Tamil speaking population,
    - (b) Civil War between Sinhala and Tamil speaking population.
    - (c) Cultural riots between Sinhala and Tamil Speaking population
    - (d) None of the above
19. In the question given below, there are two statements marked as **Assertion (A)** and **Reason (R)**.
    Read the statements and choose the correct option.
    Assertion (A) : India is a holding together Federation.
    Reason (R) : All the states have equal powers and are strong as Union Government Codes
    - (a) Both A and R are true and R is the correct explanation of A.
    - (b) Both A and R are true but R is not the correct explanation of A.
    - (c) A is true, but R is false.
    - (d) A is false, but R is true.
20. Mark the correct features of 'Holding Together Federation' from the given options
    - (a) States exercise equal powers with the Union.
    - (b) The Central government is more powerful than the states.
    - (c) The jurisdictions of the respective levels of the government are not mentioned in the Constitution.
    - (d) States tend to be more powerful than the central government.

SECTION B (Very Short Answer Questions)　　　　　　**(2 × 4 =8)**

21. What is the difference between personal communication and mass communication?
22. Explain any two facts about the new economic situation created in India by the First World War.
23. What do you understand by GDP of a country?
24. What is an alternative political formation?

OR

Evaluate the meaning of defection.

SECTION C (Short Answer Based Questions)　　　　　　**(5 × 3 =15)**

25. Describe any three features of secularism which is an integral part of our Indian Constitution.

OR

Caste can take various forms in Indian politics. Examine this statement by giving a suitable example.
26. What were the consequences of the expansion of print culture for the poor people in the 19th century in the Indian Subcontinent?
27. Why are the demand deposits considered as money?
28. Write the meaning and features of demand deposit.
29. What is the need for water conservation and management?

SECTION D (Long Answer Based Questions)　　　　　　**(5 × 4 =20)**

30. What was the role of technology in transforming the world in the 19th Century?

OR

Explain the impact of the Great Depression on the Indian Economy.
31. How Banks play an integral role in the economic development of the economy.

OR

RBI plays a crucial role in controlling formal sector loans." Explain.

32. Write a brief note on waterways mentioning the national waterways of India.

OR

Enlist and describe the five major ports situated on the Western coast of India alongside the Arabian Sea.

33. Explain the major differences between democracy of Sri Lanka and Belgium.

OR

Describe the ways by which Belgium has accommodated the existing regional differences and cultural.diversities

SECTION E (Case Based Questions) (4 × 3 =12)

34. Read the given extract and answer the following questions.

The Bretton Woods conference established the International Monetary Fund (IMF) to deal with external surpluses and deficits of its member nations. The International Bank for Reconstruction and Development (popularly known as the World Bank) was set up to finance post-war reconstruction: The IMF and the World. Bank are referred to as the Bretton Woods institutions or sometimes the Bretton Woods twins. The post-war international economic system is also often described as the Bretton Woods system. The IMF and the World Bank commenced financial operations in 1947.0

Decision-making in these institutions is controlled by the Western industrial powers. The US has an effective right of veto over key IMF and World Bank decisions.

The international monetary system is the system linking national currencies and monetary system. The Bretton Woods system was based on fixed exchange rates. In this system, national currencies for example, the Indian rupee, were pegged to the dollar at a fixed exchange rate. The dollar itself was anchored to gold at a fixed price of $35 per ounce of gold.

34.(1) Why was the International Monetary Fund (IMF) set up?

34.(2) What was the Bretton Woods system?

34.(3) What decision was taken at Bretton Woods in New Hampshire, USA?

35. Read the given extract and answer the following questions.

The recent efforts and suggestions in our country to reform political parties and its leaders:

The Constitution was amended to prevent elected MLAs and MPs from changing parties. This was done because many elected representatives were indulging in Defection in order to

become ministers or for cash rewards. Now the law says that if any MLA or MP changes parties, he or she will lose the seat in the Legislature.

This new law has helped bring defection down. At the same time this has made any dissent even more difficult. MPs and MLAS have to accept whatever the party leaders decide. The Supreme Court passed an order to reduce the influence of money and criminals. Now, it is mandatory for every candidate who contests elections to file an Affidavit giving details of his property and criminal cases pending against him.

It should be made mandatory for political parties to give a minimum number of tickets, about one-third, to women candidates. Similarly, there should be a quota for women in the decision making bodies of the party.

There should be state funding of elections. The government should give parties money to support their election expenses. This support could be given in kind: petrol, paper, telephone etc. Or it could be given in cash on the basis of the votes secured by the party in the last election.

35.(1) What is defection?

35.(2) Analyse the merits of an Affidavit given by the candidate during the contesting election.

35.(3) How does the position of women changed due to the reforms made for political parties?

36. Read the given extract and answer the following questions.

Planning is the widely accepted strategy for judicious use of resources. It has importance in a country like India, which has enormous diversity in the availability of resources. There are regions which are rich in certain types of resources, but are deficient in some other resources. There are some regions which can be considered self sufficient in terms of the availability of resources and there are some regions which have acute shortage of some vital resources. For example, the states of Jharkhand, Chhattisgarh and Madhya Pradesh are rich in minerals and coal deposits. Arunachal Pradesh has abundance of water resources, but lacks in infrastructural development.

36.(1) How judicious use of resources can be done. by planning?

36.(2) Give two examples of resource availability in India.

36.(3) Why is planning necessary in India?

SECTION F (Map Skill Based Questions) (2 + 3 =5)

37.(a) On the outline map of India, Identify them and write their correct names on the lines drawn near them.

    A. The place where an incident occurred due to which Mahatma Gandhi called off the Non-cooperation Movement.

    B. The place associated with the cotton Mill's worker's satyagraha

(b) On the same outline map of India, locate and label any three of the following with suitable symbols.

    (i) A dam in Rajasthan

    (ii) A airport in Delhi

    (iii) A software technology park

    (iv) A sea port

5 Sample Paper

BLUE PRINT

SR NO	CHAPTER NAME	PER UNIT MARKS	MCQ	VSATQ	SATQ	LATQ	CBQ	MBQ	TOTAL MARKS
	UNIT-1 : HISTORY								
1	The rise of nationalism in Europe	20							
2	Nationalism in India		Q (2,3,4)					Q (1a)	5
3	The making of a global world		Q (1)	Q (1)	Q (4)				6
4	The age of industrialization								
5	Print Culture and the modern world		Q (5)			Q (4)	Q (1)		10
	Unit-2 : GEOGRAPHY								
1	Resources and development	20	Q (7)			Q (3)			6
2	Forest and Wildlife resources								
3	Water resources		Q (9)					Q (1b-II)	2
4	Agriculture		Q (6,8,10)						3
5	Minerals and energy resources			Q (4)			Q (2)		6
6	Manufacturing Industries				Q (1)				3
7	Lifelines of national economy							Q (1b-I, III, IV)	3
	UNIT – 3 : POLITICAL SCIENCE								
1	Power sharing	20	Q (12, 13, 14)			Q (6)			8
2	Federalism		Q (11, 15)		Q (2)				5
3	Gender, religion and caste								
4	Political parties			Q (3)	Q (5)				5
5	Outcomes of Democracy								
	UNIT-4 : ECONOMICS								
1	Development	20	Q (16,19)						2
2	Sectors of Indian Economy		Q (17,18,20)			Q (2)	Q (3)		3
3	Money and Credit				Q (3)				3
4	Globalization of the Indian economy			Q (2)					2
	TOTAL MARKS		20(20)	4(8)	5(15)	4(20)	3(12)	5	80

Time Allowed : 3 Hours   **Max. Marks : 80**

General Instructions

1. Question paper comprises Six Sections – A, B, C, D, E and F. There are 37 questions in the question paper. All questions are compulsory.
2. **Section A** – From question 1 to 20 are MCQs of 1 mark each.
3. **Section B** – Question no. 21 to 24 are Very Short Answer Type Questions, carrying 2 marks each. Answer to each question should not exceed 40 words.
4. **Section C** – contains Q.25 to Q.29 are Short Answer Type Questions, carrying 3 marks each. Answer to each question should not exceed 60 words
5. **Section D** – Question no. 30 to 33 are long answer type questions, carrying 5 marks each. Answer to each question should not exceed 120 words.
6. **Section-E** – Questions no from 34 to 36 are case based questions with three sub questions and are of 4 marks each
7. **Section F** – Question no. 37 is map based, carrying 5 marks with two parts, 37a from History (2 marks) and 37b from Geography (3 marks).
8. There is no overall choice in the question paper. However, an internal choice has been provided in few questions. Only one of the choices in such questions have to be attempted.
9. In addition to this, separate instructions are given with each section and question, wherever necessary.

SECTION A (MCQS)   (1 × 20 = 20)

1. Find the incorrect option
   (a) Mahatma Gandhi returned to India from South Africa in 1918.
   (b) In 1918, Gandhiji went to Ahmedabad to organise a Satyagraha Movement.
   (c) Khilafat Movement was started in 1921.
   (d) Jallianwala Bagh massacre took place on 13th April, 1919.
2. Which of the following statements is true about the process of unification of Britain?
   (a) The unification was based on an attack and conquer plan by the King of England
   (b) The process was a political struggle.
   (c) The unification was achieved through political and social subjugation of various ethnicities by the English.
   (d) The process was a result of thirty year long war between people of different ethnicities in which only the English remained unscathed.
3. Choose the incorrect pair
   (a) Greek Struggle for Independence begins: 1707
   (b) William I, the Prussian King: 1861
   (c) The Act of Union: 1707
   (d) Ireland was incorporated into United Kingdom: 1801
4. What happened to Poland at the end of the 18th century? Which of the following statement is this correct?
   (a) Poland achieved independence at the end of the 18th century.
   (b) Poland came totally under the control of Russia and became part of Russia.
   (c) Poland became part of East Germany.
   (d) Poland was partitioned at the end of the 18th century by three Great Powers: Russia, Prussia and Austria.
5. Find the incorrect option
   (a) Richard Ark wright is credited to create the cotton mill.
   (b) The most dynamic industries in Britain were cotton and metals.
   (c) Seth Hukumchand set up the first Indian Jute Mill in Calcutta in 1917.
   (d) In 1903, London underground railway starts operation.
6. Identify the following crop with the help of given clues.
   (i) The Arabica variety initially brought from Yemen is produced in the country.
   (ii) Its cultivation was introduced on the Baba Budan Hills.
   (iii) It is cultivated in Nilgiri in Karnataka, Kerala and Tamil Nadu.
   (a) Tea   (b) Coffee   (c) Rubber   (d) Millets

7. Match the following

List 1	List 2
A. Community Resource	1. Solar Energy
B. Renewable Resource	2. Public Parks
C. Non-Renewable Resource	3. Ocean
D. International Resource	4. Coal

    (a) 1, 4, 3, 2   (b) 2, 1, 4, 3   (c) 3, 2, 1, 4   (d) 4, 3, 2, 1

8. In the question given below, there are two statements marked as **Assertion (A)** and **Reason (R)**. Read the statements and choose the correct option.

   Assertion (A) : Pulses are grown in rotation with other crops.

   Reason (R) : It helps in restoring soil fertility by fixing nitrogen from the air.

   (a) Both A and are true and R is the correct explanation of A.

   (b) Both A and R are true, but R is not the correct explanation of A.

   (c) A is true, but R is false.

   (d) A is false, but R is true.

9. Ground water over use is particularly found in which of the following states?

   (a) Gujarat and Rajasthan   (b) Punjab and Western UP

   (c) Nagaland and Assam   (d) Himachal and Uttarakhand

10. Following is the image of crop cultivation which is used both as food and fodder. It is a Kharif crop which requires temperature between 21°C to 27°C and grows well in old alluvial soil, Identify the crop from the given options.

   (a) Wheat   (b) Maize   (c) Bajra   (d) Rice

11. Which among the following is known as a system of checks and balances?

   (a) The Supreme Court Judges can check the powers of the High Court Judges.

   (b) The President of India appoints the Prime Minister and further the Prime Minister checks the Powers of the President.

   (c) The judges are appointed by the executive and further judges can check the functioning of executive or laws made by the legislature.

   (d) All of the above

12. In the question given below, there are two statements marked as **Assertion (A)** and **Reason (R)**. Read the statements and choose the correct option.

   Assertion (A) : Power is shared among different social groups in Belgium.

   Reason (R) : Community Government in Belgium has the power regarding cultural, educational and language related issue.

   (a) Both A and R are true and R is the correct explanation of A

   (b) Both A and R are true and R is not the correct explanation of A

   (c) A is true, but R is false

   (d) A is false, but R is true

13. Annette studies in a Dutch medium school in the Northern region of Belgium. Many French speaking students in her school want the medium of instruction to be French. Her parents approach the respective government to realise the desire of the child. What could be the measure the Belgian government will adopt in such a situation?

   (a) Majoritarian measures   (b) Policy of accommodation

   (c) Despotic measures   (d) All of these

14. Identify the community with the help of following information. They form a majority in Belgium. They do not speak French. They are concentrated in the Flemish region.

   (a) Dutch speaking community   (b) German speaking community

   (c) Spanish speaking community   (d) Portuguese speaking community

15. Which of the following is incorrect regarding a unitary government?
    (a) There is either only one level of government or the sub-units are subordinate to the central government.
    (b) The central government can pass on orders to the provincial government.
    (c) A state government is conservable to the central government.
    (d) The powers of state governments are guaranteed by the Constitution.
16. Read the following data carefully and select the appropriate answer from the given options.

State	Infant Mortality Rate per 1,000 live births (2017)	Literacy Rate % 2017-18	Net Attendance Ratio (Per 100 persons) secondary stage (age 14 and 15 years) 2017-18
Haryana	30	82	61
Kerala	10	94	83
Bihar	35	62	43

Why does Bihar has High Infant Mortality Rate as compared to other states? Identify the reason from the given options:
(a) Due to lack of health facilities
(b) Due to lack of education facilities
(c) Low guidance
(d) Both A and B
17. Which among the following sectors is the most important sector in terms of share of the total production in the initial stages of development of developed countries?
    (a) Primary sector   (b) Secondary sector   (c) Tertiary sector   (d) Private sector
18. Identify the sector
    Sector is categorised based on ownership of activities. Private individuals and companies own most of the assets.
    Main driving force of this sector is profit.
    (a) Public sector   (b) Private sector   (c) Social Service sector   (d) None of these
19. How GDP is calculated?
    (a) The value of final goods and services produced in each sector during the last three years provides the total production of the sector for that year.
    (b) The value of final goods and services produced in each sector during a particular year provides the total production of that sector for that year and the sum of production in the three sectors.
    (c) The value of intermediate goods and services produced in each sector during a particular year and the sum of production in the three sectors.
    (d) The value of intermediate goods and services produced in each sector during a particular year provides the approximate production of the sector for that year.
20. Tertiary sector has replaced the primary sector as the largest producing sector. There are hindrances in the development of the tertiary or service sector.
    Identify the hindrances from the given options.
    (i) Inadequate Infrastructure
    (ii) Unfair competition in the Telecom sector
    (iii) Lack of Financial services
    (a) Only (i)   (b) Both (i) and (ii)   (c) Both (ii) and (iii) (d) All of these

SECTION B (VERY SHORT ANSWER QUESTIONS)   (2 × 4 =8)

21. Why did Gandhiji call off the Non-Cooperation Movement?
22. State any two reasons/ ways which states that the world has been converted into a global village?
23. Evaluate any two guidelines for devising ways and means for political reforms in India.

OR

How do parties form and run governments?
24. Evaluate the term Rat-hole mining.

SECTION C (SHORT ANSWER BASED QUESTIONS)   (5 × 3 =15)

25. Transport, communication and trade are complementary to each other. Do you agree with this statement? If yes, why?
26. How are the 'Coming together federations' formed?

OR

Define the Union and State Lists with respect to the Indian Constitution.

27. Highlight the meaning of the terms of credit? Why does the lender ask for collateral against the loan?
28. What was the impact of the First World War on the economic and political situation in India?
29. Write a detailed note on political party founded by Kanshi Ram

SECTION D (LONG ANSWER BASED QUESTIONS) (5 × 4 =20)

30. Explain the demands of the Sri Lankan Tamils. How did they struggle for their demands?

OR

What was the reason behind the civil war of Sri Lanka? State the impact of that war on Sri Lanka.

31. What do you understand about the private sector and public sector industries? Explain the significance of public sector industries in the economy.

OR

Write a detailed note on the following-
A-Organised Sector
B-Unorganized Sector

32. Explain the alluvial soil on the basis of following criterias-
    A- Formation
    B- Distribution
    C- Classification
    D- Nutrients

OR

What do you understand about Alluvial Soils? State the features of alluvial soils.

33. Explain the labour recruitment and retaining process of Europeans?

OR

What were the factors responsible for indentured labour migration from India.

SECTION E (CASE BASED QUESTIONS) (4 × 3 =12)

34. **Read the given text and answer the following questions given below.**

In the countryside poor peasants and artisans began working for merchants. This was a time when open fields were disappearing and commons were being enclosed. Cottagers and poor peasants who had earlier depended on common lands for their survival, gathering their firewood, berries, vegetables, hay and straw, had to now look for alternative sources of income. Many had tiny plots of land which could not provide work for all members of the household. So when merchants came around and offered advances to produce goods for them, peasant households eagerly agreed, By working for the merchants, they could remain in the countryside and continue to cultivate their small plots. Income from proto-industrial production supplemented their shrinking Income from cultivation. It also allowed them a fuller use of their family labour resources. This proto-industrial system was thus part of a network of commercial exchanges. It was controlled by merchants and the goods were produced by a vast number of producers working within their family farms, not in factories. At each stage of production 20 to 25 workers were employed by each merchant. This meant that each clothier was controlling hundreds of workers.

34.(1) What is a proto -industrial system?

34.(2) Which phase of industrialisation is called proto industrialization and why?

34.(3) Explain the main features of proto industrialization.

35. **Read the given text and answer the following questions given below.**

Decaying plants in swamps produce peat which has a low carbon and high moisture content and low heating capacity. Lighite is low grade brown coal, which is soft with high moisture content. The principal lignite reserves are in Neyveli in Tamil Nadu and are used for generation of electricity. Coal that has been buried deep and subjected to increased temperatures is bituminous coal. It is the most popular coal in commercial use. Metallurgical coal is high grade bituminous coal which has a special value for smelting iron in blast furnaces. Anthracite is the highest quality hard coal. In India coal occurs in rock series of two main geological ages, namely Gondwana, a little over 200 million years in age and in tertiary deposits which are only about 55 million years old. The major resources of Gondwana coal, which are metallurgical coal, are located in Damodar valley (West Bengal, Jharkhand).

Jharia, Raniganj, Bokaro are important coalfields. The Godavari, Mahanadi, Son and Wardha valleys also contain coal deposits. Tertiary coals occur in the North-Eastern states of Meghalaya, Assam, Arunachal Pradesh and Nagaland.

35.(1) Which reserves are important for lignite in India?

35.(2) To what extent do you agree that bituminous coal is metallurgical coal? State its one property. (1)

35.(3) Why is coal associated with geological ages? State where it is found? (2)

36. **Read the given text and answer the following questions given below.**

Another way of classifying economic activities into sectors could be on the basis of who owns assets and is responsible for the delivery of services. In the public sector, the government owns most of the assets and provides all the services. In the private sector, ownership of assets and delivery of services is in the hands of private individuals or companies.

Railways or post office is an example of the public sector whereas companies like Tata Iron and Steel Company Limited (TISCO) or Reliance Industries Limited (RIL) are privately owned. Activities in the private sector are guided by the motive to earn profits. To get such services we have to pay money to these individuals and companies.

The purpose of the public sector is not just to earn profits. Governments raise money through taxes and other ways to meet expenses on the services rendered by it.

Modern day governments spend on a whole range of activities. There are several things needed by the society as a whole but which the private sector will not provide at a reasonable cost.

36.(1) The bifurcation into public and private sector is on what basis?

36.(2) State one reason each as to why railways and post offices are counted in the public sector.

36.(3) State two reasons why the public sector is needed in our country.

SECTION F (MAP SKILL BASED QUESTIONS) (2 + 3 =5)

37.(a) On the outline map of India, Identify them and write their correct names. on the line drawn near them

    A. The place associated with the Congress session of September 1920.

    B. The place where a violent incident Caused Mahatma Gandhi to call off the Non Cooperation movement.

(b) On the same outline map label any THREE the following with suitable symbols

    I. Software technology park

    II. Dam located in Mahanadi river

    III. Rajiv Gandhi International Airport

    IV. Nuclear power plant in Maharashtra.

6 Sample Paper

LATEST PATTERN

BLUE PRINT

SR NO	CHAPTER NAME	PER UNIT MARKS	MCQ	VSATQ	SATQ	LATQ	CBQ	MBQ	TOTAL MARKS
	UNIT-1 : HISTORY								
1	The rise of nationalism in Europe	20	Q ((1, 3, 4)					Q (1a)	5
2	Nationalism in India		Q (2, 5)						2
3	The making of a global world						Q (1)		4
4	The age of industrialization			Q (2)		Q (1)			7
5	Print Culture and the modern world				Q (2)				3
	Unit-2 : GEOGRAPHY								
1	Resources and development	20					Q (3)		4
2	Forest and Wildlife resources								
3	Water resources		Q (9)		Q (5)	Q (3)		Q (1b-I, IV)	10
4	Agriculture		Q (6, 7)						2
5	Minerals and energy resources		Q (8)						1
6	Manufacturing Industries								
7	Lifelines of national economy			Q (1)				Q (1b-II, III)	4
	UNIT – 3 : POLITICAL SCIENCE								
1	Power sharing	20	Q (18, 19)			Q (4)			7
2	Federalism		Q (17, 20)						2
3	Gender, religion and caste				Q (1)				3
4	Political parties			Q (4)			Q (2)		6
5	Outcomes of Democracy								
	UNIT-4 : ECONOMICS								
1	Development	20	Q (11, 12, 14, 16)	Q (3)					6
2	Sectors of Indian Economy		Q (10, 13, 15)						3
3	Money and Credit				Q (3, 4)	Q (2)			11
4	Globalization of the Indian economy								
	TOTAL MARKS		20(20)	8(4)	15(5)	20(4)	12(3)	5	80

Time Allowed : 3 Hours   **Max. Marks : 80**

General Instructions

1. Question paper comprises Six Sections – A, B, C, D, E and F. There are 37 questions in the question paper. All questions are compulsory.
2. **Section A** – From question 1 to 20 are MCQs of 1 mark each.
3. **Section B** – Question no. 21 to 24 are Very Short Answer Type Questions, carrying 2 marks each. Answer to each question should not exceed 40 words.
4. **Section C** – contains Q.25 to Q.29 are Short Answer Type Questions, carrying 3 marks each. Answer to each question should not exceed 60 words
5. **Section D** – Question no. 30 to 33 are long answer type questions, carrying 5 marks each. Answer to each question should not exceed 120 words.
6. **Section-E** – Questions no from 34 to 36 are case based questions with three sub questions and are of 4 marks each
7. **Section F** – Question no. 37 is map based, carrying 5 marks with two parts, 37a from History (2 marks) and 37b from Geography (3 marks).
8. There is no overall choice in the question paper. However, an internal choice has been provided in few questions. Only one of the choices in such questions have to be attempted.
9. In addition to this, separate instructions are given with each section and question, wherever necessary.

SECTION A (MCQS)   (1 × 20 = 20)

1. Who ruled France in 1830's and was forced to flee after unemployment caused workers to revolt on roads?
   (a) King Emmanuel II   (c) King Louis Philippe   (b) King William I   (d) King Wilhelm
2. Which province did not boycott the council election?
   (a) Madras   (b) Ahmedabad   (c) Hyderabad   (d) Lucknow
3. Find the incorrect option.
   (a) The system of indentured labour was abolished in 1921.
   (b) The Bretton Woods conference was established in 1950.
   (c) By the 1890, a global agricultural economy had developed.
   (d) World War I was the first Modern Industrial War.
4. Following image is a caricature of which personality in the German Reichstag (Parliament) from Figaro, Vienna. Identify.
   (a) King Victor Emmanuel II   (b) Otto von Bismarck
   (c) Giuseppe Mazzini   (d) Giuseppe Garibaldi
5. Arrange the following events in a chronological order-
   I.   Unification of Germany
   II. Vienna Peace Settlement
   III. Greece gained independence
   IV. Unification of Italy
   (a) IV, II, III, I   (b) II, III, IV, I   (c) II, III, I, IV   (d) I, III, IV, II
6. Identify the soil with the help of given clues
   It is acidic in nature.
   It is rich in Iron.
   It is found in Hills summits of Eastern, Western Ghats and Assam Hills.
   (a) Red soil   (b) Laterite soil   (c) Black soil.   (d) Alluvial soil
7. Which are the following resources renewable but excessively used?
   (a) Air   (b) Solar Energy   (c) Wind Energy   (d) Trees
8. Find the incorrect match.
   (a) Sugarcane - Tropical as well as subtropical crop
   (b) Cotton- Grows in Jammu and Kashmir and Himachal Pradesh
   (c) Pulses- India is largest producer
   (d) Maize - Both food and fodder crop
9. In the question given below, there are two statements marked as **Assertion (A)** and **Reason (R)**.
   Read the statements and choose the correct option.
   Assertion (A) Floodgate dams are built across rivers so that water flows into inlets and gets trapped during high tides.
   Reason (R) Trapped water flows back via a pipe.that carries it through a power generating turbine.

(a) Both A and R are true and R is the correct explanation of A
(b) Both A and R are true, but R is not the correct explanation of A
(c) A is true, but R is false
(d) A is false, but R is true

10. Match the following-

List 1	List 2
A. Copper smelting	1. Consumer Industry
B. Sewing machines	2. Private Sector
C. Bajaj Auto Ltd	3. Basic Industry
D. Sugar Industry	4. Cooperative

(a) 3,4,2,1   (b) 1,4,3,2   (c) 2,1,3,4   (d) 3,4,1,2

11. Consider the following statements on parties.
    A. Political parties do not enjoy much trust among the people.
    B. Parties are often rocked by scandals involving top party leaders.
    C. Parties are not necessary to run governments.
    Which of the statements given above are correct?
    (a) A, B and C   (b) B and C   (c) A and B   (d) A and C

12. In which year the amendment in the Indian Constitution was made that led the third tier of democracy more effective and powerful?
    (a) 1990   (b) 1994   (c) 1992   (d) 1995

13. In the question given below, there are two statements marked as **Assertion (A)** and **Reason (R)**.
    Read the statements and choose the correct option.
    Assertion (A) Community Government in Belgium is elected by one language community.
    Reason (R) Community Government helped in resolving conflict between different linguistic groups..
    (a) Both A and R are true and R is the correct explanation of A.
    (b) Both A and R are true, but R is not the correct explanation of A.
    (c) A is true, but R is false
    (d) A is false, but R is true.

14. Pokhran, the place.where India conducted its nuclear tests, lies in Rajasthan. Suppose the Government of Rajasthan was opposed to the Central Government's nuclear policy, could it prevent the Government of India from conducting the nuclear tests? Identify the reason from the given options.
    (a) Yes, the state government could prevent it as Defence is a subject of State List.
    (b) No, the state government could not prevent the Central government from conducting the nuclear tests because 'Defence' is the subject of Union List and nuclear tests are the part of the Defence.
    (c) Yes, the state government could prevent it as conducting nuclear tests is a subject of Concurrent List.
    (d) No, the state government could not prevent

15. Which of the following is a regional party?
    (a) Bharatiya Janata Party (BJP)
    (b) Bahujan Samaj Party (BSP)
    (c) Dravida Munnetra Kazhagam (DMK)
    (d) Communist Party of India (Marxist) CPI (M)

16. Fill in the blanks-

Party	Year
A- Indian National Congress	1885
B- Communist Party of India	… . . …

(a) 1946   (b) 1925   (c) 1976   (d) 1932

17. In the question given below, there are two statements marked as Assertion (A) and Reason (R).
    Read the statements and choose the correct code.
    Assertion (A) GDP (Gross Domestic Product) shows how big the economy is.
    Reason (R) GDP of a country is the value of all intermediate goods.and services produced within a country during a particular year.

(a) Both A and R are true and R is the correct explanation of A.
(b) Both A and R are true, but R is not the correct explanation of A.
(c) A is true, but R is false.
(d) A is false, but R is true.

18. Analyse the table given below and answer the question that follows. The source shows a database of workers employed in different sectors (in millions)

Sector	Unorganised	Organised	Total
Primary	200	2	202
Secondary	50	5	55
Tertiary	80	20	100
Total	330	27	357
Total percentage			**100%**

Calculate the percentage of people in an organised sector.
(a) 10%　　　(b) 7.6%　　　(c) 9.6%　　　(d) 8.4%

19. Ram weighs 98 kgs and his height is 165 cm. Find out his Body Mass Index (BMI) from the following options:
(a) 18.5　　　(b) 36.0　　　(c) 15.2.　　　(d) 25.0

20. Which of the following would be an ideal goal for a multinational company?
(i) More Money.
(ii) To get rid of its waste without having to pay for its disposal.
(iii) More Profit.
(iv) More Employees.
(a) Only (i)　　　(b) (i), (ii) and (iii)　　　(c) Only (ii).　　　(d) (i), (ii) and (iv)

SECTION B (VERY SHORT ANSWER QUESTIONS) (2 × 4 =8)

21. What is the cheque in banking and commerce?
22. Explain the Anti Defection Law in your own words.
23. State the challenges faced by the Sugar Industry in India.
OR
What is the difference between the joint sector and labour intensive industries?
24. How has literacy rate improved in India due to the spread of print culture in India?

SECTION C (SHORT ANSWER BASED QUESTIONS) (5 × 3 =15)

25. State the merits and demerits of a multi-party system.
OR
Give any two merits and demerits of a one-party system.
26. Write a short essay on Establishment of the IMF and World Bank in the wake of globalisation.
27. State the highest tier of the Panchayati Raj? Explain its significance in detail.
28. What efforts are made to protect forest and wildlife in India?
29. What is the literal meaning of sustainability of development? How to achieve sustainable development?

SECTION D (LONG ANSWER BASED QUESTIONS) (5 × 4 =20)

30. The pace of change in the communication sector has been rapid in modern times," Support the statement with examples.
OR
Explain the importance of railways as a means of transport.
31. Evaluate the meaning of the Human Development Index. Also explain its various indicators.
OR
Explain with the example that there are many other important development goals rather than income goals.
32. Can democracy be judged by its outcome? Explain.
OR
Enumerate the various loopholes of democracy.
33. Describe the causes of conflict between weavers and gomasthas in weaving villages.
OR
Analyse the numerous problems faced by weavers of the Indian cotton industry in the 19th century.

SECTION E (CASE BASED QUESTIONS)   (4 × 3 =12)

34. Read the given text and answer the following questions given below.

New forms of popular literature appeared in print, targeting new audiences. Booksellers employed pedlars who roamed around villages, carrying little books for sale. There were almanacs or ritual calendars, along with ballads and folktales. But other forms of reading matters, largely for entertainment, began to reach ordinary readers as well. In England, penny chapbooks were carried by petty pedlars known as chapmen, and sold for a penny, so that even the poor could buy them. In France, were the 'Biliotheque Bleue', which were low-priced small books printed on poor quality paper, and bound in cheap blue covers. Then there were the romances, printed on four to six pages, and the more substantial 'histories' printed on four to six pages and the more substantial 'histories' which were stories about the past. Books were of various sizes, serving many different purposes and interests.

34.(1) What do you understand from Chapbooks?

34.(2) How Bibliotheque Bleue was different from chapbooks?

34.(iii) What were the new forms of literature introduced in Europe to attract the new readers?

35. Read the given text and answer the following questions given below.

Tea cultivation is an example of plantation agriculture. It is also an important beverage crop introduced in India initially by the British. Today, most of the tea plantations are owned by Indians. The tea plant grows well in tropical and sub-tropical climates endowed with deep and fertile well-drained soil, rich in humus and organic matter Tea bushes require warm and moist frost free climate all through the year. Frequent showers evenly distributed over the year ensure continuous growth of tender leaves. Tea is a labour intensive industry. It requires abundant cheap and skilled labour. Tea is processed within the tea garden to restore its freshness. Major tea producing states are Assam. hills of Darjeeling and Jalpaiguri districts, West Bengal, Tamil Nadu and Kerala. Apart from these, Himachal Pradesh, Uttarakhand, Meghalaya. Andhra Pradesh and Tripura are also tea-producing states in the country. In 2015, India was the second largest producer of tea after China.

35.(1) Who is responsible for introducing tea cultivation In India?

35.(2) What are the required climatic conditions for tea plantations ?

35.(3) State two advantages of "Tea industry in Indian Economy.

36. Read the given text and answer the following questions given below.

The various types of loans can be conveniently grouped as formal sector loans and informal sector loans Among the former are loans from banks and cooperatives. The dommal lenders include moneylenders, traders The Reserve Bank of India supervises the functioning of formal sources of loans. For instance, we employers, relatives and friends, esc have seen that the banks maintain a minimum cash balance out of the deposits they receive The RBI monitors the banks in actually maintaining cash balance, Similarly, the RBI sees that the banks give loans not just to profit-making businesses and traders but also to small cultivators.

There is no organisation which supervises the credit activities of lenders in the informal sector. They can lend at whatever interest rate they choose; there is no offe to stop them from using unfair means to get their money back. Compared to the formal lenders, most of the informal lenders charge a much higher interest on los Thus the cost to the borrower of informal loans is much higher

36.(1) Describe the formal sources of credit.

36.(2) Highlight the role of RBI in regulating the credit market of India.

36.(3) Evaluate any one difference between formal and informal sources of credit

SECTION F (MAP SKILL BASED QUESTIONS)   (2 + 3 =5)

37.(a) On the outline map of India, Identify them and write their correct names. On the line drawn near them

    A. Aplace of Bihar where Gandhiji inspired the peasants to struggle against the oppressive plantation system.

    B. A place where gandhiji violated salt law

(b) On the same outline map label any THREE the following with suitable symbols

    I. Tungabhadra dam

    II. Ramagundam thermal power plant

    III. Paradip sea port

    IV. Meenam bakkam airport

7 Sample Paper

BLUE PRINT

SR NO	CHAPTER NAME	PER UNIT MARKS	MCQ	VSATQ	SATQ	LATQ	CBQ	MBQ	TOTAL MARKS
	UNIT-1 HISTORY								
1	The rise of nationalism in Europe	20	Q (1, 4, 5)						3
2	Nationalism in India			Q (1)		Q (2)		Q (1a)	9
3	The making of a global world		Q (3)		Q (3)		Q (3)		8
4	The age of industrialization		Q (2)						1
5	Print Culture and the modern world								
	Unit-2 GEOGRAPHY								
1	Resources and development	20	Q (10)		Q (4)		Q (2)		8
2	Forest and Wildlife resources								
3	Water resources					Q (3)		Q (1b - III)	4
4	Agriculture		Q (6, 7, 9)						3
5	Minerals and energy resources								
6	Manufacturing Industries			Q (4)					3
7	Lifelines of national economy		Q (8)					Q (1b-I, II, IV)	4
	UNIT-3 POLITICAL SCIENCE								
1	Power sharing	20	Q (11, 13)		Q (1)				5
2	Federalism		Q (12, 14)	Q (2)					4
3	Gender, religion and caste								
4	Political parties		Q (15)			Q (4)			6
5	Outcomes of Democracy						Q (1)		4
	UNIT-4 ECONOMICS								
1	Development	20	Q (17, 18)						2
2	Sectors of Indian Economy		Q (16, 19)	Q (3)	Q (5)				7
3	Money and Credit				Q (2)				3
4	Globalization of the Indian economy		Q (20)			Q (1)			6
	TOTAL MARKS		20(20)	4(8)	5(15)	4(20)	3(12)	5	80

Time Allowed : 3 Hours   **Max. Marks : 80**

General Instructions

1. Question paper comprises Six Sections – A, B, C, D, E and F. There are 37 questions in the question paper. All questions are compulsory.
2. **Section A** – From question 1 to 20 are MCQs of 1 mark each.
3. **Section B** – Question no. 21 to 24 are Very Short Answer Type Questions, carrying 2 marks each. Answer to each question should not exceed 40 words.
4. **Section C** – contains Q.25to Q.29 are Short Answer Type Questions, carrying 3 marks each. Answer to each question should not exceed 60 words
5. **Section D** – Question no. 30 to 33 are long answer type questions, carrying 5 marks each. Answer to each question should not exceed 120 words.
6. **Section-E** – Questions no from 34 to 36 are case based questions with three sub questions and are of 4 marks each
7. **Section F** – Question no. 37 is map based, carrying 5 marks with two parts, 37a from History (2 marks) and 37b from Geography (3 marks).
8. There is no overall choice in the question paper. However, an internal choice has been provided in few questions. Only one of the choices in such questions have to be attempted.
9. In addition to this, separate instructions are given with each section and question, wherever necessary.

SECTION A

1. Why did the Frankfurt Parliament fail to achieve its goals? Identify from the given options-
   (a) Women were excluded from the membership.
   (b) Did not have the support of Peasants.
   (c) Kaiser William refused to accept the crown and opposed the assembly.
   (d) None of the above
2. Which of the following companies gradually gained power in the 1750s after the decline of Indian merchant's trade capacity?
   (a) Chinese companies   (b) Russian companies   (c) English companies   (d)   European companies
3. Which country introduced 'Corn Laws' to restrict the import of corn?
   (a) France   (b) Germany   (c) Britain   (d) Spain
4. Choose the correct option from the following.

List 1	List 2
(a) Liberalism	Customs Union.
(b) French Revolution	Individual Freedom and Equality before law.
(c) Zollverein	Transfer of sovereignty from monarch to the French citizens.
(d) Act of Union	Formation of the United Kingdom.

5. Following image depicts the fear of repression which drove many liberal-nationalists underground. Which of the following events is marked as per the given image? Identify.

   (a) Signing of Treaty of Vienna
   (b) Founding of Young Europe in Berne,
   (c) Giuseppe Mazzini unifying Italy
   (d) William I unifying Germany

6. Choose the correctly matched pair about the crops and the areas they are grown in
   (a) Ragi-Punjab
   (b) Maize-Uttar Pradesh
   (c) Coffee- Jammu and Kashmir
   (d) Jowar-Kerala
7. How will diversification of Indian cropping patterns help?
   (i) It will attract investment from people.
   (ii) It will replenish the fertility of the soil.
   (iii) It will save the environment.
   (iv) It will supply nitrogen to the soil.
   (v) It will increase incomes.
   (a) (i) (ii) (iii) and (v)   (b) (ii) and (iii)   (c) (iii), (iv) and (v) (d) (i), (iv) and (v)
8. Gas pipelines from Hazira in Gujarat connect Jagdishpur in which of the following states?
   (a) Madhya Pradesh   (b) Uttar Pradesh   (c) Bihar   (d) Himachal Pradesh
9. Match the following states with a type of slash and burn agriculture.

List 1 (Types of Slash and Burn Agriculture)	List 2 (States)
A. Khil	1. Odisha
B. Kuruwa	2. Himalaya Belt
C. Koman	3. Madhya Pradesh
D. Bewar	4. Jharkhand

   (a) 1,2,4,3   (b) 2,4,1,3   (c) 3,1,2,4   (d) 4,3,2,1
10. Which of the following is essential for the sustainable existence of all forms of life?
    (a) Resource planning
    (b) Resource management
    (c) Resource extraction
    (d) Resource generation
11. What features of democracy could be realised with linguistic reorganisation of the states?
    Choose the correct option.
    (i) Recognition and accommodation of diversities.
    (ii) Inception of isolationist tendencies.
    (iii) Fear of linguistic division of the country.
    (iv) Equal respect to all social groups.
    (a) Only (i)   (b) Both (i) and (ii)   (c) Both (iii) and (iv) (d) Both (i) and (iv)
12. Fill in the blanks-

Subject	Authority
Defense	Union Government
Computer Software	… .. … …. .

    (a) Union Government   (b) State government   (c) Both a and b   (d) Neither a nor c
13. In democracy, power is not shared with which of the following?
    (a) People who live in the democracy
    (b) Leaders of the government
    (c) Social Groups
    (d) Neighbouring countries
14. In the question given below, there are two statements marked as **Assertion (A)** and **Reason (R)**.
    Read the statements and choose the correct option.
    Assertion (A): Although judges are appointed by the Executive, they can check the functioning of the executive or laws made by the Legislatures.
    Reason (R): Judges are superior and more experienced than the Executive.
    (a) Both A and R are true and R is the correct explanation of A
    (b) Both A and R are true, but R is not the correct explanation of A.
    (c) A is true, but R is false.
    (d) A is false, but R is true.

15. Under which system, only one-party is allowed to function?
    (a) Single-party system (b) Bi-party system (c) Multi-party system (d) None of these
16. Identify the sector from the given information
    (i) Activities which are included in this sector are undertaken by directly using natural resources.
    (ii) This sector employs the most number of people.
    (a) Tertiary Sector (b) Primary Sector (c) Secondary Sector (d) Public Sector
17. Read the given table and answer the following question. Some comparative data on Haryana, Kerala and Bihar

State	Infant Mortality Rate per 1000 live births (2017)	Literacy Rate % 2011	Net Attendance Ratio (per 100 persons) secondary stage (age 14 and 15 years) 2013-2014
Haryana	30	82	61
Kerala	10	94	83
Bihar	35	62	43

As per the data, the literacy rate is highest in Kerala while the infant mortality highest in Bihar. What does it show?
    (a) Most of the people living in Kerala and Bihar have good living conditions.
    (b) Both Bihar and Kerala lack basic necessities of life.
    (c) The standard of living is better in Kerala as compared to Bihar.
    (d) The standard of living is better in Bihar as compared to Kerala.
18. In the question given below, there are two statements marked as **Assertion (A)** and **Reason (R)**.
    Read the statements and choose the correct option.
    Assertion (A) : Suppose the literacy rate in a state is 78% and the net attendance ratio secondary stage is 47%.
    Reason (R) : More than half of the students are going to other states for elementary education.
    (a) Both A and R are true and R is the correct explanation of A.
    (b) Both A and R are true, but R is not the correct explanation of A.
    (c) A is true, but R is false
    (d) A is false, but R is true.
19. What kinds of workers are employed in the tertiary sector?
    (a) Unskilled (b) Only skilled (c) Semi-skilled (d) Both skilled and semi-skilled
20. A situation in which all the countries reap equally the benefits of foreign trades equally is known as?
    (a) Internationalisation (b) Fair globalisation (c) Liberalisation (d) Equal globalisation

SECTION B (VERY SHORT ANSWER QUESTIONS) (2 × 4 =8)

21. Highlight the role of Alluri Sitaram Raju in Indian Independence
OR
Give a brief note about the Simon Commission. Why was it boycotted by Indians?
22. Evaluate the nature of local government in India before and after the constitutional amendment act of 1992.
23. What are secondary activities? Explain with suitable examples.
24. What are mineral based industries? Give four examples.

SECTION C (SHORT ANSWER BASED QUESTIONS) (5 × 3 =15)

25. Briefly define the language policy of our country. 1- Language Policy of India-
26. "Credit can play a negative role." Justify the statement with arguments.
OR
Explain any three reasons for the banks and cooperative societies to increase their lending facilities in rural areas.
27. "The global transfer of diseases became instrumental in colonisation of Africa and South America'. Explain the statement.
28. Distinguish between laterite soil and red soil in brief.
29. Distinguish between public sector and private sector in brief.

SECTION D (LONG ANSWER BASED QUESTIONS) (5 × 4 =20)

30. "MNCs often opt for foreign collaborations to expand and diversify. But their foreign collaborations have given rise to growth of monopolies and concentration of power in few hands". Comment.
OR
Evaluate the impact of globalisation on our daily life. Explain with examples.

31. What circumstances led to the Calling off of the Civil Disobedience Movement and Relaunching of Civil Disobedience Movement.

OR

Illustrate the meaning of Swaraj from the perspective of different social groups.

32. Multi purpose projects and large dams have also been the cause of many environmental movements. Justify the statement with the help of examples.

OR

Define the adverse effects and limitations of multi purpose projects.

33. State the recent efforts and suggestions in our country which are implemented for reforming the political parties

OR

Evaluate the reasons behind adoption of the Multi party system in India.

SECTION E (CASE BASED QUESTIONS) (4 × 3 =12)

34. **Read the given text and answer the following questions given below.**

Democracies are based on political equality. All individuals have equal weight in electing representatives. Parallel to the process of bringing individuals into the political arena on an equal footing, we find growing economic inequalities. A small number of ultra-rich enjoy a highly disproportionate share of wealth and incomes. Not only that, their share in the total income of the country has been increasing.

Those at the bottom of the society have very little to depend upon. Their incomes have been declining. Sometimes they find it difficult to meet their basic needs of life, such as food, clothing, house, education and health.

In actual life, democracies do not appear to be very successful in reducing economic inequalities. The poor constitute a large proportion of our voters and no party will like to lose their votes. Yet democratically elected governments do not appear to be as keen to address the question of poverty as.you would expect them to. The situation is much worse in some other countries. In Bangladesh, more than half of its population lives in poverty. People in several poor countries are now dependent on the rich countries even for food supplies.

34.(1) Why is it expected that democracy will reduce the economic disparities?

34.(2) Infer the reason of inability of democracy to achieve higher economic development.

34.(3) Why do some poor countries depend on the rich countries?

35. **Read the given text and answer the following questions given below.**

Irrigation has also changed the cropping pattern of many regions with farmers shifting to water intensive and commercial crops. This has great ecological consequences like salinisation of 191 or the soil. At the same time, it has transformed the asy social landscape i.e., increasing the social gap between the richer landowners and the landless 701 poor. As we can see, the dams did create conflicts between people wanting different uses and benefits from the same water resources.

In Gujarat, the Sabarmati-basin farmers were agitated and almost caused a riot over the higher priority given to water supply in urban areas, particularly during droughts. Interstate water disputes are also becoming common with regard to sharing the costs and benefits of the multi-purpose project.

Do you know that the Krishna-Godavari dispute is due to the objections raised by Karnataka, and Andhra Pradesh governments? It is regarding the diversion of more water at Koyna by the Maharashtra government for a multi-purpose project. This would reduce downstream flow in their states with adverse consequences for agriculture and industry.

Most of the objections to the projects arose due to their failure to achieve the purposes for which they were built. Ironically. the dams that were constructed to control floods have triggered floods due to sedimentation in the reservoir. Moreover, the big dams have mostly been unsuccessful in controlling floods at the time of excessive rainfall.

You may have seen or read how the release of water from dams during heavy rains aggravated the flood situation in Maharashtra and Gujarat in 2006. The floods have not only devastated life and property but also caused extensive soil erosion. Sedimentation also meant that the flood plains were deprived of silt, a natural fertiliser, further adding on to the problem of land degradation.

It was also observed that the multi-purpose projects induced earthquakes, caused water-borne diseases and pests and pollution resulting from excessive use of water.

35.(1) To what extent do you agree that farmers are also responsible for salinisation of soil?

35.(2) How can you say that multi-purpose projects fail to achieve their aim for which they were built? State with examples.

35.(3) How can you say that dams create conflicts between people? State any one example.

36. Read the given text and answer the following questions given below.

The Bretton Woods conference established the International Monetary Fund (IMF) to deal with external surpluses and deficits of its member nations. The International Bank for Reconstruction and Development (popularly known as the World Bank) was set up to finance post-war reconstruction: The IMF and the World. Bank are referred to as the Bretton Woods institutions or sometimes the Bretton Woods twins. The post-war international economic system is also often described as the Bretton Woods system. The IMF and the World Bank commenced financial operations in 1947.

Decision-making in these institutions is controlled by the Western industrial powers. The US has an effective right of veto over key IMF and World Bank decisions.

The international monetary system is the system linking national currencies and the monetary system. The Bretton Woods system was based on fixed 01 exchange rates. In this system, national currencies for example, the Indian rupee, were pegged to the dollar at a fixed exchange rate. The dollar itself was anchored to gold at a fixed price of \$35 per ounce of gold.

36.(1) Why was the International Monetary Fund (IMF) set up?

36.(2) What was the Bretton Woods system?

36.(3) What decision was taken at Bretton Woods in New Hampshire, USA?

SECTION F (MAP SKILL BASED QUESTIONS)   (2 + 3 =5)

37.(a) On the given political map of India, Two places are marked. are them as A and B. Identify help of given information.

    A. The place where peasant Satyagraha took place

    B. The place associated with Jallianwala Bagh incident

  (b) On the same outline map label any THREE the following with suitable symbols

    (I) Airport in Punjab

    (II) Software technological park in Maharashtra

    (III) Marmagao sea port

    IV) Kakrapar Nuclear Power Plant

8 Sample Paper

LATEST PATTERN

BLUE PRINT

SR NO	CHAPTER NAME	PER UNIT MARKS	MCQ	VSATQ	SATQ	LATQ	CBQ	MBQ	TOTAL MARKS
	UNIT-1 : HISTORY								
1	The rise of nationalism in Europe	20							
2	Nationalism in India		Q (3, 4, 5)						3
3	The making of a global world		Q (2)			Q (1)	Q (3)	Q (1a)	12
4	The age of industrialization		Q (1)	Q (1)					3
5	Print Culture and the modern world				Q (1)				3
	Unit-2 : GEOGRAPHY								
1	Resources and development	20							
2	Forest and Wildlife resources				Q (4)				3
3	Water resources		Q (7, 10)						2
4	Agriculture					Q (2)		Q (1b-I)	6
5	Minerals and energy resources		Q (6, 8, 9)				Q (2)		4
6	Manufacturing Industries								
7	Lifelines of national economy							Q (1b-iv)	1
	UNIT – 3 : POLITICAL SCIENCE			Q (2)				Q (1b-ii, iii)	4
1	Power sharing	20							
2	Federalism		Q (14)						1
3	Gender, religion and caste		Q (11, 12, 15)		Q (2)				6
4	Political parties			Q (3)		Q (4)	Q (1)		12
5	Outcomes of Democracy		Q (13)						1
	UNIT-4 : ECONOMICS								
1	Development	20							
2	Sectors of Indian Economy		Q (16, 18, 19)		Q (3)	Q (3)			11
3	Money and Credit		Q (17, 20)	Q (4)	Q (5)				7
4	Globalization of the Indian economy								
	TOTAL MARKS								

Time Allowed : 3 Hours   **Max. Marks : 80**

General Instructions

1. Question paper comprises Six Sections – A, B, C, D, E and F. There are 37 questions in the question paper. All questions are compulsory.
2. **Section A** – From question 1 to 20 are MCQs of 1 mark each.
3. **Section B** – Question no. 21 to 24 are Very Short Answer Type Questions, carrying 2 marks each. Answer to each question should not exceed 40 words.
4. **Section C** – contains Q.25to Q.29 are Short Answer Type Questions, carrying 3 marks each. Answer to each question should not exceed 60 words
5. **Section D** – Question no. 30 to 33 are long answer type questions, carrying 5 marks each. Answer to each question should not exceed 120 words.
6. **Section-E** – Questions no from 34 to 36 are case based questions with three sub questions and are of 4 marks each
7. **Section F** – Question no. 37 is map based, carrying 5 marks with two parts, 37a from History (2 marks) and 37b from Geography (3 marks).
8. There is no overall choice in the question paper. However, an internal choice has been provided in few questions. Only one of the choices in such questions have to be attempted.
9. In addition to this, separate instructions are given with each section and question, wherever necessary.

SECTION A (MCQS)   (1 × 20 = 20)

1. Which of the following is a correct definition of custom barrier?
   (a) It is a measure of limiting trade across borders of different cities and principalities.
   (b) It is a physical barrier between two cities.
   (c) It is a tax collected at railway stations to boost exports.
   (d) Custom duties decreased the price of products.
2. Arrange the following in the correct sequence
   1. Depressed Class Association
   2. Rowlatt Act
   3. Poona Pact Signed
   4. Gandhiji travelled to Champaran Codes
   (a) 1, 2, 3, 4   (b) 1, 3, 2, 4   (c) 4, 2, 1, 3   (d) 2, 1, 3, 4
3. Following image represents the Republic of France and became popular in 1850. Identify the given image by choosing the correct option. 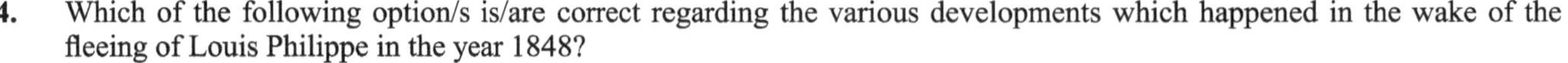
   (a) Caricature of Ottovon Bismarck
   (b) Picture of Germania
   (c) Postage Stamp with a picture of Marianne.
   (d) Aposter of Cavour
4. Which of the following option/s is/are correct regarding the various developments which happened in the wake of the fleeing of Louis Philippe in the year 1848?
   (i) The National Assembly was proclaimed a republic.
   (ii) National Workshops were set-up to provide employment.
   (iii) Suffrage to all women
   (iv) Right to work was guaranteed
   (a) (i), (ii) and (iv)   (b) (ii) and (iii)   (c) Only (iii)   (d) (iii) and (iv)
5. Who founded the revolutionary militia 'Red Shirt'?
   (a) Wilson   (b) Tsar Alexander II   (c) Giuseppe Garibaldi   (d) Duke Metternich
6. Choose the correctly matched pair about the crops and the areas they are grown in
   (a) Rubber- Assam   (b) Pulses- Uttar Pradesh   (c) Jowar-Punjab   (d) Rice- West Bengal
7. Consider the following statements about unclassed forests
   I. Unclassed forests are mostly managed by both private communities and the government.
   II. All human activities are allowed in these forests.
   III. Northern-Eastern states and parts of Gujarat have mostly unclassed forests.
   Which of the following is correct?
   (a) I and II   (b) II and III   (c) I and III   (d) All of these

8. Which is the most important plantation crop grown in Karnataka?
    (a) Tea   (b) Coffee   (c) Rice   (d) Banana

9. Match the following items given in Column (A) with those in Column (B).

Column A (Crops)	Column B (Areas)
A. Sugarcane	1. Karnataka and Tamil Nadu
B. Rice	2. Uttar Pradesh and Andhra Pradesh
C. Millets	3. Bihar and Punjab
D. Maize	4. Uttar Pradesh and Bihar

    (a) 3, 4, 2, 1   (b) 2, 1, 3, 4   (c) 4, 3, 2, 1   (d) 2, 4, 1, 3

10. Consider the following statements about reserved forests?
    I. Reserved forests are owned by the government and all human activities are not allowed in these forests.
    II. These forests are regarded as the most valuable forests in terms of conservation of forests and wildlife.
    III. These forests constitute about more than half of the total forest land in India.
    Which of the following is correct?
    (a) I and II   (b) II and III   (c) I and III   (d) All of these

11-. In what sense Federations are contrasted with unitary forms of government? Identify the correct option.
    (a) Powers in the federations are not concentrated in single hands but distributed among units.
    (b) In a federation, the central government can pass orders to the provincial or local government in an effective manner as compared to the Unitary government.
    (c) In a federation, state governments are answerable to the central government for every decision.
    (d) In a federation, state government powers are in the hands of the central government.

12. Which of the following statements are correct regarding the Panchayat Samiti in India?
    (a) Panchayat Samiti at the block level is an advisory body.
    (b) Panchayat Samiti at the block level is an administrative body.
    (c) Panchayat Samiti at the block level is a consultant committee.
    (d) Panchayat Samiti at the block level is a coordinating and supervisory authority.

13. Political parties can be reformed by?
    (a) reducing the role of muscle power
    (b) reducing the role of money
    (c) state funding of election
    (d) All of the above

14. Which of the following reasons of Power sharing stress that power sharing will bring out better outcomes? Identify the correct option:
    (a) Moral   (b) Prudential   (c) Legitimate   (d) Political

15. Fill in the blanks-.

List 1	List 2
Union of States	Prime Minister
Municipal Corporation	… .. …

    (a) Governor   (b) Gram Panchayat   (c) MLA   (d) Mayor

16. The task of measuring GDP is undertaken by which of the following levels of government?
    (a) Central Government   (b) State Government   (c) Local Government   (d) Both (a) and (b)

17. In the question given below, there are two statements marked as **Assertion (A)** and **Reason (R)**.
    Read the statement and choose the correct option.
    Assertion (A): Rakesh is an educated and skilled worker who earns a high salary as he is employed in a private bank in a city.
    Reason (R): All service sectors in India are growing extremely well and each individual engaged in any kind of tertiary activity earns a high income. monthly
    (a) Both A and R are true and R is the correct explanation of A.
    (b) Both A and R are true, but R is not the correct explanation of A.
    (c) A is true, but R is false.
    (d) A is false, but R is true.

18. Read the data given in the following table and answer the given question. Monthly income of citizens

Country	Group I	Group II	Group III	Group IV	Group V	Average income
Country A	9000	1000	8000	11000	12500	?
Country B	5000	4000	6800	5050	29650	?
Country C	2000	1600	3500	3000	10000	?

Which country has a more equitable distribution of income?

(a) Country A   (b) Country B   (c) Country C   (d) Both Country A and Country B

19. Raman's weight is 79kgs and his height is 1.54 meters. In which category can we place him from the following options?

(a) Underweight   (b) Normal weight   (c) Overweight   (d) Obesity

20. A man is employed on a corn farm where he does not have much manual work. He solely works on the farm every day. Of which type of employment is this an example?

(a) Disguised Employment

(b) Seasonal Employment

(c) Over Employment

(d) Cyclical Employment

SECTION B (VERY SHORT ANSWER QUESTIONS) (2 × 4 =8)

21. What are the consequences of abolition of corn laws?
22. Differentiate between international and local trade in a brief manner.
23. What do you understand about communal politics?
24. Write the major objectives of implementing the NREGA 2005.

OR

Do you think workers are exploited in the unorganized sector? If yes, give reason to support your answer.

SECTION C (SHORT ANSWER BASED QUESTIONS) (5 × 3 =15)

25. How historians agreed to the fact that print culture created the conditions within which the French Revolution occurred.
26. Briefly analyse the major difference between a federal form of government and a unitary one.
27. Is it right that development of a nation depends on the availability of public facilities. If yes, explain.
28. "India is rich in certain types of resources, but deficient in some other resources." Do you agree with the statement? Support your answer with examples.

OR

What are the main advantages of India's land under a variety of relief features?

29. Is it correct to agree with the fact that several services which cannot be provided by the private sector can be provided by the public sector? Explain.

SECTION D (LONG ANSWER BASED QUESTIONS) (5 × 4 =20)

30. Why did Mahatma Gandhi start the Civil Disobedience Movement? How did this movement unite the country? Explan.

OR

What was the reason behind non participation of Dalits in Non Cooperation Movement. Explain in an elaborate manner.

31. List out some suggestions for minimising industrial pollution of freshwater sources.

OR

Enlist some measures to curb the environmental pollution in general.

32. State the meaning of the term. HDI. Also explain its key indicators.

OR

Highlight the emphasis of sustainable development in the 21st century.

33. Is it justified to state that it is not politics that gets caste ridden, but it is the caste that gets politicised? Explain.

OR

Experts state that women still lag behind men in India despite some improvements since independence' Analyse the statement."

SECTION E (CASE BASED QUESTIONS) (4 × 3 =12)

34. Read the given text and answer the following questions given below.

Communalism becomes more acute when religion is expressed in politics in exclusive and partisan terms, when one religion and its followers are pitted against another. This happens when beliefs of one religion are presented as superior to those of other religions, when the demands of one religious group are formed in opposition to another and when state power is used to establish domination of one religious group over the rest. This manner of using religion in politics is communal politics. Communal politics is based on the idea that religion is the principal basis of social community. Communalism involves thinking along the following lines. The followers of a particular religion must belong to one community. Their fundamental interests are the same. Any difference that they may have is irrelevant or trivial for community life. It also follows that people who follow different religions cannot belong to the same social community. If the followers of different religions have some commonalities, these are superficial and immaterial. Their interests are bound to be different and involve conflict. In its extreme form communalism leads to the belief that people

34.(1) When does communalism happen in our society?

34.(2) Infer what will happen if the followers of different religions have some commonalities?

34.(3) How does communal politics suppress many voices within the same community?

35. Read the following passage and answer the questions that follow.

Through the 'right of inheritance' leading to the division of land among successive generations has rendered land-holding size uneconomical, the farmers continue to take maximum output from the limited land in the absence of alternative source of livelihood. Thus, there is enormous pressure on agricultural land.

The main characteristic of Commercial farming is the use of higher doses of modern inputs. e.g. High Yielding Variety (HYV) seeds, chemical fertilisers, insecticides and pesticides in order to obtain higher productivity.

The degree of commercialisation of agriculture varies from one region to another. For example, rice is a commercial crop in Haryana and Punjab, but in Odisha, it is a subsistence crop.

35.(1) Which two states of India produce rice commercially?

35.(2) Why is rice considered a subsistence crop in Odisha?

35.(3) How do farmers continue to take maximum output from limited land?

36. Read the following passage and answer the questions that follow.

Workers too had their own understanding of Mahatma Gandhi and the notion of swaraj. For plantation workers in Assam, freedom meant the right to move freely in and out of the confined space in which they were enclosed, and it meant retaining a link with the village from which they had come. Under the Inland Emigration Act of 1859, plantation workers were not permitted to leave the tea gardens without permission, and in fact they were rarely given such permission. When they heard of the Non Cooperation Movement, thousands of workers defied the authorities, left the plantations and headed home. They believed that Gandhi Raj was coming and everyone would be given land in their own villages They however, never reached their destination. Stranded on the way by a railway and steamer strike, they were caught by the police and brutally beaten up. The visions of these movements were not defined by the Congress programme. They interpreted the term swaraj in their own ways, imagining it to be a time when all suffering and all troubles would be over. Yet, when the tribals chanted Gandhi's name and raised slogans demanding Swatantra Bharat, they were also emotionally relating to an all-India agitation.

When they acted in the name of Mahatma Gandhi, or linked their movement to that of the Congress, they were identifying with a movement which went beyond the limits of their immediate locality.

36.(1) What was the motive of the Non Cooperation Movement?

36.(2) What positive impact was laid by the non cooperation movement?

36.(3) What did freedom mean for the plantation workers in Assam?

SECTION F (MAP SKILL BASED QUESTIONS) (2 + 3 =5)

37.(a) On the given political map of India, Two places Identify areas marked as A and B with the help of given information.

    (A) A region in Bihar which is concerned with movement of Indigo planters.

    (B) A place where Congress session held in 1927

(b) On the same outline map of India, locate and label any three following with suitable symbols

    I. A sea port in Gujarat

    II. An international airport in West Bengal

    III. Software Technology Park in Maharashtra

    IV. Narora Atomic Power Station

9 Sample Paper

BLUE PRINT

SR NO	CHAPTER NAME	PER UNIT MARKS	MCQ	VSATQ	SATQ	LATQ	CBQ	MBQ	TOTAL MARKS
	UNIT-1 HISTORY								
1	The rise of nationalism in Europe	20	Q (1, 2, 3,4, 5, 6)						6
2	Nationalism in India			Q (1)			Q (1)	Q (1a)	8
3	The making of a global world								
4	The age of industrialization				Q (3)	Q (1)			8
5	Print Culture and the modern world								
	Unit-2 GEOGRAPHY								
1	Resources and development	20	Q (7, 8, 9)						3
2	Forest and Wildlife resources								
3	Water resources							Q (1b-I)	1
4	Agriculture		Q (10)				Q (3)		6
5	Minerals and energy resources					Q (2)			5
6	Manufacturing Industries			Q (3)				Q (1b-IV)	3
7	Lifelines of national economy				Q (4)			Q (1b-II, III)	5
	UNIT – 3 POLITICAL SCIENCE								
1	Power sharing	20	Q (11, 12, 13, 14)						4
2	Federalism		Q (15, 16)		Q (2)				5
3	Gender, religion and caste			Q (2)		Q (4)			7
4	Political parties								
5	Outcomes of Democracy								
	UNIT-4 ECONOMICS								
1	Development	20	Q (17, 18, 20)		Q (5)	Q (3)			11
2	Sectors of Indian Economy		Q (19)						1
3	Money and Credit			Q (4)			Q (2)		6
4	Globalization of the Indian economy				Q (1)				3
	TOTAL MARKS		20(20)	4(8)	5(15)	4(20)	3(12)	5	80

Time Allowed : 3 HoursMax. Marks : 80

1. Question paper comprises Six Sections – A, B, C, D, E and F. There are 37 questions in the question paper. All questions are compulsory.
2. **Section A** – From question 1 to 20 are MCQs of 1 mark each.
3. **Section B** – Question no. 21 to 24 are Very Short Answer Type Questions, carrying 2 marks each. Answer to each question should not exceed 40 words.
4. **Section C** – contains Q.25to Q.29 are Short Answer Type Questions, carrying 3 marks each. Answer to each question should not exceed 60 words
5. **Section D** – Question no. 30 to 33 are long answer type questions, carrying 5 marks each. Answer to each question should not exceed 120 words.
6. **Section-E** – Questions no from 34 to 36 are case based questions with three sub questions and are of 4 marks each
7. **Section F** – Question no. 37 is map based, carrying 5 marks with two parts, 37a from History (2 marks) and 37b from Geography (3 marks).
8. There is no overall choice in the question paper. However, an internal choice has been provided in few questions. Only one of the choices in such questions have to be attempted.
9. In addition to this, separate instructions are given with each section and question, wherever necessary.

SECTION A (MCQS) (1 × 20 = 20)

1. Identify the correct statement with regard to the Zollverein' from the following options.
   (a) It was a coalition of Prussian states formed to manage political alliances (b) Its aim was to bind Prussia politically into an association.
   (c) It was a Custom Union at the initiative of Prussia.
   (d) It helped to awaken and raise national sentiment in Europe.
2. Which of the following countries were involved in the Three Wars with Prussia and ended with victory and unification of Germany?
   (a) Austria, Poland and France
   (b) Austria, Denmark and France
   (c) Austria, Turkey and France
   (d) Austria, England and France
3. Which of the following option(s) is/are correct about Balkan nationalism?
   (i) The Balkan region became part of the conflict because of the Ottoman Empire
   (ii) The region comprised of ethnic groups included Greeks, Serbs, Montenegro, etc
   (iii) British and ethnic nationalities struggled to establish their identity.
   (a) (i) and (ii)   (b) (ii) and (iii)   (c) Only (ii)   (d) Only (i)
4. Identify the major aspect that helped in the formation of a nation-state in Britain.

    (a) In 1688, the monarch of Britain fought war with the English Parliament.

    (b) The Parliament through a bloodless revolution seized power from the monarchy. (c) The British nation was formed as a result of a war with Ireland and Wales.

    (d) The formation of a nation-state in Britain was the result of many revolts.

5. Arrange the following events in a chronological order-

    (i)   Integration of Italy

    (ii) Greek struggle for independence initiated

    (iii) Unification of Germany

    (iv) Agreement on Vienna peace settlement

    (a) i, iv, ii, iii   (b) iv, ii, iii, i   (c) iv, ii, i, iii   (d) i, ii, iii, iv

6. Following image is the personification of Germany commonly associated with the Romantic Era and the Revolutions of 1848. Identify its name from among the following options.

    (a) Marianna   (b) Philip Viet   (c) Germania   (d) La Italia

7. The piece of land left uncultivated for the past 1 to 5 agricultural years is called?

    (a) Barren land   (b) Forest land   (c) Grazing land   (d) Fallow land

8. Identify the soil with the help of clues given below.

    (i)   Develops in areas with high temperature and heavy rainfall.

    (ii) Is low in humus content.

    (iii) Found in the hilly areas of Karnataka, Kerala and Tamil Nadu.

    (a) Forest soil   (b) Yellow soil   (c) Black soil   (d) Laterite soil

9 Which one of the following conferences was convened to discuss environmental protection and socio-economic development at the global level in 1992?

    (a) Kyoto Protocol

    (b) Montreal Protocol

    (c) Rio de Janeiro Earth Summit

    (d) World Summit on Sustainable Development

10. Choose the correctly matched pair about the crops and the areas they are grown in

    (a) Groundnut- Assam   (b) Tea-Gujarat   (c) Coffee-Karnataka (d) Sugarcane-Chhattisgarh

11. Identify the significant reason for power sharing from the following options.

    (a) Reduces socio-economic conflicts

    (b) Provides ethnic-cultural development

    (c) Allows people to enjoy specific rights

    (d) Restricts supremacy of one party

12. Consider the following statements on power sharing and select the answer using the codes given below

    (i)   It is good for democracy.

    (ii) It creates harmony in different groups.

    (iii) It brings transparency in the governance.

    (iv) It brings socio-political competition among parties.

    (a) (i), (ii) and (iii)   (b) (ii), (iii) and (iv)   (c) (i), (iii) and (iv)   (d) (i), (ii) and (iv)

13. Two statements are given in the question below as **Assertion (A)** and **Reason (R)**.

    Read the statements and choose the appropriate option.

    Assertion (A) : Sri Lanka adopted Sinhala as the only official language of the state in 1956

    Reason (R) : The Government of Sri Lanka wanted to foster their culture, language and religion.

    (a) Both A and R are true and R is the correct explanation of A.

    (b) Both A and R are true, but R is not the correct explanation of A.

    (c) A is true, but R is false.

    (d) A is false, but R is true

14. Anita is appearing in an examination conducted for recruitment to Central Government positions. In how many languages as mentioned in the 8th Schedule can she opt to take the exam? Select the appropriate option.

    (a) 18   (b) 21   (c) 22   (d) 25

15. Identify the correct statement/s about the theory of Federalism in the Indian Constitution.

    (i)   The Constitution declared India as a Union of States.

    (ii) Sharing of power between the Union Government and the State governments isbasic to the structure of the Constitution

    (iii) It is easy to make changes to this power sharing arrangement.

    (iv) The Parliament can on its own change this arrangement.

    (a) (i) and (ii)   (b) (ii) and (iii)   (c) (i) and (iii)   (d) (ii) and (iv)

16. Match the following-

List 1	List 2
A. Information Technology	1. Concurrent List
B. Police	2. Union List
C. Education	3. State List
D. Defence	4.Residuary Subject

  (a) 4,3,1,2   (b) 3,4,1,2   (c) 4,1,3,2   (d) 4,2,1,3

17. Vijay is undernourished as his weight is 45 kgs and his height is 1.78 meters. Find out his Body Mass Index (BMI) from the following options.

  (a) 12.6   (b) 13.5   (c) 14.7   (d) 15.2

18. Read the following data and information carefully and select the most appropriate answer from the given options.

Table for Comparison of Three Countries

	I	III	III	IV	V
Country A	9500	10500	9800	10000	10200
Country B	500	500	500	500	48000
Country C	5000	1000	15000	5000	5000

Rita is an employee of a multinational company who gets transferred to different countries after every three years of service. She has been given an opportunity to choose any one out of the three countries mentioned in the table above as her next job location. She calculates average income of all these countries as per the given data and chooses to be transferred to Country A. Identify the reason for which Rita has chosen country A.

  (a) Most of its citizens are rich and stable.

  (b) Has the most equitable distribution of income

  (c) National income of its citizens is higher

  (d) Average income of its citizens is lower.

19. According to 2017-2018 data, the share of different sectors in employment (percentage) in India was

  (i) Primary Sector-44%

  (ii) Secondary Sector-25%

  (iii) Tertiary Sector-31%

Out of the three sectors, why did the ratio of employment in the Primary Sector high?

Select the most suitable option from the following:

  (a) Workers in the Primary Sector are underemployed

  (b) Low job opportunities in the Secondary Sector.

  (c) Efforts of labour are not equivalent in all the sectors.

  (d) Outsourcing of job opportunities in the Secondary Sector.

20. Two statements are given in the question below as **Assertion (A)** and **Reason (R)**.

Read the statements and choose the appropriate option.

Assertion (A): Human Development mentions how much socio-economic development has happened in a country.

Reason (R) : Comparison of national income of two countries explains Human.Development Index.

  (a) Both A and R are true and R is the correct explanation of A:

  (b) Both A and K are true, but R is not the correct explanation of A.

  (c) A is true, but R is false.(d) A is false, but R is true.

SECTION B (VERY SHORT ANSWER QUESTIONS)   (2 × 4 =8)

21. Why were canal colonies built by Britishers?

22. If casteism and communalism are bad, what makes feminism a good thing? Why don't we oppose all those who divided the society on any lines-caste, religion or gender?

23. State any one difference between agro and mineral based industries.

OR

State any one negative impact of waste from the nuclear plant.

24. Why payments made in rupees cannot be refused in India?

SECTION C (SHORT ANSWER BASED QUESTIONS) (5 × 3 =15)

25. How does the Government attract foreign investment? Explain different ways.
26. Which is the highest tier of the Panchyati Raj? Explain its composition.
27. Highlight the position of weavers who produced coarse cloth in the 20th century.

OR

Describe the conditions of workers in Europe after the industrial revolution?

28. Mention any four features of the telecom network of India.
29. What do you mean by Per Capita Income of a country? How can it be used to compare two countries?

SECTION D (LONG ANSWER BASED QUESTIONS) (5 × 4 =20)

30. What series of changes affected the pattern of industrialization in India.

OR

Advertisements played a vital role in expanding the markets for products.' Explain the statement in the context of the pre-independence period of our country.

31. Minerals are integral parts of our lives. Justify this statement with suitable examples.

OR

How can biogas solve the energy problems in rural India. State some suggestions for the same.

32. With the support of examples, Illustrate how two groups may have different notions of development.

OR

Write a brief note on-
(i) Body mass index
(ii) Human development report

33. Explain the term Secularism. Explain any four features of secularism in India.

OR

How caste inequalities are still prevalent in India?

SECTION E (CASE BASED QUESTIONS) (4 × 3 =12)

34. **Read the given text and answer the following questions given below.**

For plantation workers in Assam, freedom meant the right to move freely in and out of the confined space in which they were enclosed, and it meant retaining a link with the village from which they had come. Under the Inland Emigration Act of 1859, plantation workers were not permitted to leave the tea gardens without permission, and in fact they were rarely given such permission. When they heard of the Non-Cooperation Movement, thousands of workers defied the authorities, left the plantations and headed home. They believed that Gandhi Raj was coming and everyone would be given land in their own villages. They, however, never reached their destination. Stranded on the way by a railway and steamer strike, they were caught by the police and brutally beaten up.

The visions of these movements were not defined by the Congress programme. They interpreted the term swaraj in their own ways, imagining it to be a time when all suffering and all troubles would be over. Yet, when the tribals chanted Gandhiji's name and raised slogans demanding Swatantra Bharar, they were also emotionally relating to an all-India agitation. When they acted in the name of Mahatma Gandhi, or linked their movement to that of the Congress, they were identifying with a movement which went beyond the limits of their immediate locality,

34.(1) What was the main motive behind the non cooperation movement?

34.(2) State Gandhi's idea of Swaraj.

34.(3) Define the role of plantation workers in the non cooperation movement.

35. **Read the given text and answer the following questions given below.**

We have seen that people obtain loans from various sources. The various types of loans can be grouped as formal sector loans and informal sector loans. Among the former some are from banks and cooperatives. The informal lenders include moneylenders, traders, employers, relatives and friends, etc). The Reserve Bank of India supervises the functioning of formal sources of loans. For instance, we have seen that the banks maintain a minimum cash balance out of the deposits they receive. The RBI monitors the banks in actually maintaining cash balance, Similarly, the RBI sees that the banks give loans not just to profit-making businesses and traders but also to small cultivators, small scale industries, to small borrowers etc. Periodically, banks have to submit information to the RBI on how much they are lending, to whom at what interest rate, etc. There is no organisation which supervises the credit activities of lenders in the informal sector. They can lend at whatever interest rate they choose. There is no one to stop them from using unfair means to get their money back. Compared to the formal lenders, most of the informal lenders charge a much higher interest on loans. Thus, the cost to the borrower of informal loans is much higher.

35.(1) Explain the formal sources of credit.

35.(2) Evaluate any one difference between formal and informal sources of credit.

35.(3) State any three functions of RBI in the credit market of India.

36. **Read the given text and answer the following questions given below.**

The main characteristic of commercial type of farming is the use of higher doses of modern inputs e.g. High Yielding Variety (HYV) seeds, chemical fertilisers, insecticides and pesticides in order to obtain higher productivity. The degree of commercialisation of agriculture varies from one region to another. For example, rice is a commercial crop in Haryana and Punjab, but in Odisha, it is a subsistence crop. Plantation is also a type of commercial farming. In this type of farming a single crop is grown on a large area. The plantation has an interface of agriculture and industry. Plantations cover large tracts of land, using capital intensive inputs, with the help of migrant labourers. All the produce is used as raw material in respective industries.

In India, tea, coffee, rubber, sugarcane, banana, etc., are important plantation crops. Tea in Assam and North Bengal and coffee in Karnataka are some of the important plantation crops grown in these states. Since the production is mainly for market, a well-developed network of transport and communication connecting the plantation areas, processing industries and markets plays an important role in the development of plantations.

36.(1) What do you understand about commercial farming?

36.(2) What are the required climatic conditions of rubber plant

36.(3) Evaluate the merits of commercial farming

SECTION F (MAP SKILL BASED QUESTIONS)　　　　　　(2 + 3 = 5)

37. (a)　On the given political map of India, Two places Identify areas marked as A and B with the help of given information.

　　A.　A place where movement of Indigo workers took place.

　　B.　A place where the civil disobedience movement took place.

(b)　On the same outline map of India, locate and label any three following with suitable symbols

　　I.　New Mangalore Sea Port

　　II.　Software technology park in Tamil Nadu

　　III.　Chhatrapati Shivaji International Airport

　　IV.　Singrauli Thermal Power plant

10 Sample Paper

BLUE PRINT

SR NO	CHAPTER NAME	PER UNIT MARKS	MCQ	VSATQ	SATQ	LATQ	CBQ	MBQ	TOTAL MARKS
	UNIT-1 HISTORY								
1	The rise of nationalism in Europe	20	Q1,2,5				Q2		7
2	Nationalism in India		Q4	Q2	Q2			Q1a	8
3	The making of a global world								
4	The age of industrialization		Q3						1
5	Print Culture and the modern world					Q4			6
	Unit-2 GEOGRAPHY								
1	Resources and development	20	Q6				Q3		7
2	Forest and Wildlife resources								
3	Water resources		Q9,		Q3				4
4	Agriculture					Q3			5
5	Minerals and energy resources		Q7,8						2
6	Manufacturing Industries							Q1b-I	1
7	Lifelines of national economy		Q10	Q1				Q1b-II,III,IV	6
	UNIT-3 POLITICAL SCIENCE								
1	Power sharing	20	Q15						1
2	Federalism		Q13		Q5				4
3	Gender, religion and caste		Q12						1
4	Political parties		Q14			Q2			6
5	Outcomes of Democracy		Q11	Q3	Q4				6
	UNIT-4 ECONOMICS								
1	Development	20	Q16,17,18		Q1	Q1			11
2	Sectors of Indian Economy		Q19	Q4			Q1		7
3	Money and Credit		Q20						1
4	Globalization of the Indian economy								
	TOTAL MARKS		20(20)	4(8)	5(15)	4(20)	3(12)	5	80

General Instructions

1. Question paper comprises Six Sections – A, B, C, D, E and F. There are 37 questions in the question paper. All questions are compulsory.
2. **Section A** – From question 1 to 20 are MCQs of 1 mark each.
3. **Section B** – Question no. 21 to 24 are Very Short Answer Type Questions, carrying 2 marks each. Answer to each question should not exceed 40 words.
4. **Section C** – contains Q.25to Q.29 are Short Answer Type Questions, carrying 3 marks each. Answer to each question should not exceed 60 words
5. **Section D** – Question no. 30 to 33 are long answer type questions, carrying 5 marks each. Answer to each question should not exceed 120 words.
6. **Section-E** – Questions no from 34 to 36 are case based questions with three sub questions and are of 4 marks each
7. **Section F** – Question no. 37 is map based, carrying 5 marks with two parts, 37a from History (2 marks) and 37b from Geography (3 marks).
8. There is no overall choice in the question paper. However, an internal choice has been provided in few questions. Only one of the choices in such questions have to be attempted.
9. In addition to this, separate instructions are given with each section and question, wherever necessary.

SECTION A (MCQS)   (1 × 20 = 20)

1. Following image is the Frankfurt Parliament in the Church of St Paul. When this Parliament convened in the church of St. Paul, who were admitted only as observers to stand in the visitors gallery?
   (a) Women   (b) Peasant class   (c) Non-propertied men   (d)   All of these
2. Match the following items

Column A (Year)	Column B (Important Events)
(a) 1814-15	1 Period of Economic Crises in Europe
(b) 1797	2 Victor Emmanuel II declared King of United Italy
(c) 1830	3 Fall of Napoleon
(d) 1861	4 The beginning of Napoleonic War

   (a) 4,3,2,1   (b) 2,1,3,4   (c) 3,4,1,2   (d) 1,2,4,3
3. Which image of a God was most commonly used to popularise baby products?
   (a) Ram   (b) Shiva   (c) Krishna   (d) Hanuman
4. Two statements are given in the question below as **Assertion (A)** and **Reason (R).**
   Read the statements and choose the appropriate option.
   Assertion(A) : The Chauri-Chaura incident occurred at Chauri-Chaura in Gorakhpur district of United province on 4th February, 1922.
   Reason (R) : Large number of people participated in the Non-Cooperation movement.
   (a) Both A and R are true and R is the correct explanation of A
   (b) Both A and R are true, but R is not the correct explanation of A
   (c) A is true, but R is false
   (d) A is false, but R is true
5. Arrange the following in the correct sequence
   1. Unification of Italy
   2. French Revolution
   3. Unification of Germany
   4. Napoleon invaded Italy
   (a) 2, 4, 1, 3   (c) 4, 3, 2, 1   (b) 3, 4, 2, 1   (d) 1, 2, 3, 4

6. Fill in the blanks

List A	List B
Arid soil	Source of salt
....	Problem of leaching

    (a) Black soil   (b) Laterite soil   (c) Regur soil   (d) Alluvial soil

7. Which type of sand in Kerala is rich in thorium?
    (a) Monazite sands   (b) Gypsum sands   (c) Silica sands   (d) Black sands

8. Arrange the following manganese producing In states from highest to lowest production.
    1. Odisha
    2. Madhya Pradesh
    3. Karnataka
    4. Andhra Pradesh
    (a) 2, 1, 3, 4   (b) 1, 2, 3,4   (c) 3, 2, 1, 4   (d) 2, 3, 4, 1

9. Which of the following was the first port developed soon after Independence to use the volume of trade on the Mumbai port?
    (a) Kandla   (b) Karachi   (c) Kochi   (d) Vizag

10. Find the Incorrect option
    (a) National Highways link extreme parts of India
    (b) National Highways are the Primary road system.
    (c) National Highways are laid and mentioned by the State Public Works Department.
    (d) National Highways No. 1 connects Delhi and Amritsar.

11. Why is the democratic government regarded as a better choice?
    (a) It promotes equality among citizen
    (b) It ensures economic development
    (c) It provides a method to resolve conflict
    (d) Both (a) and c

12. Two statements are given in the question below as **Assertion (A)** and **Reason (R)**.
Read the statements and choose the appropriate option.
Assertion (A) : There is no official religion for the Indian state for maintaining its democratic status.
Reason (R) : Communalism is one of the major challenges to democracy in our country.
    (a) Both A and R are true and R is the correct explanation of A
    (b) Both A and R are true, but R is not the correct explanation of A
    (c) A is true, but R is false
    (d) A is false, but R is true

13. Major step towards decentralisation in India was taken up in
    (a) 1992   (b) 1993   (c) 1991   (d) 1990

14. Which of the following is a regional party?
    (a) Bharatiya Janata Party (BJP)
    (b) Bahujan Samaj Party (BSP)
    (c) Dravida Munnetra Kazhagam (DMK)
    (d) Communist Party of India (Marxist) CPI (M)

15. Choose the correctly matched pair from the given options.
    (a) Community Government- India
    (b) Unitary Government- Sri Lanka
    (c) Majoritarian Measures- Belgium
    (d) Federal Government- Sri Lanka

16. Choose the correctly matched pair from the given options
    (a) Net Attendance Ratio- National Income divided by total income.
    (b) World Bank-Classify the countries on per capita income.
    (c) Sustainable development- To calculate the nutrition level.
    (d) Body Mass Index- Caring for the needs of future generations.

17. Assume there are four families in a country. The average per capita income of these families is 5,000. If the income of three families is 4,000, 7,000 and 3,000 respectively, what is the income of the fourth family?
    (a) 7500   (b) 8000   (c) 6500   (d) 6000

18. Rahul is 150 cm tall and have weight of 40 kg. Find out his BMI and choose the answer from the options given below:
(a) 19   (b) 17.5   (c) 18.5   (d) 16.5

19. The following table gives the GDP in rupees (crores) by the three sectors

Year	Prmary	ary	ary
2000	52000	48500	133500
2013	800500	1074000	3868000

Calculate the share of the three sectors in GDP for 2000 and 2013.
(a) 60%   (b) 57%   (c) 48%   (d) 65%

20. What is the most important function of money?
(a) Used in banking transactions
(b) Payment of loans
(c) Medium of exchange
(d) Stock market exchange

SECTION B (VERY SHORT ANSWER QUESTIONS)   (2 × 4 =8)

21. State the vital difference between State highways and district roads.

OR

State any two important reasons due to which road transportation is growing faster as compared to railways.

22. Mention any one reason for which the rich peasants communities took active participation in the civil disobedience movement

23. How democracy helps in enhancing the quality of decision making?

24. How does the public sector contribute to economic development?

SECTION C (SHORT ANSWER BASED QUESTIONS)   (5 × 3 =15)

25. Define the term-
(i) Per Capita Ratio
(ii) Net attendance ratio

OR

Sunita a 25 year old woman lives in a village. Her height is 1.45m and weight is 36 kg, while Nisha of the same age and height weighs 48 kg. What can be said about their nutritional condition?

26. Describe the effects of non cooperation movement in the economy of British and India.

27. Describe the working of the rainwater harvesting technique.

28. Explain in brief the meaning of dictatorship.

29. Write a brief note on the Union and Concurrent list.

SECTION D (LONG ANSWER BASED QUESTIONS)   (5 × 4 =20)

30. What is Gross Domestic Product (GDP)? How do we count the various goods and services for calculating GDP? Explain with examples.

OR

"Primary sector was the most important sector of economic activity at initial stages of development." Evaluate the statement.

31. "Political parties are rightly called the government in disguise." Justify the statement with reference to democratic politics by four arguments.

OR

How the lack of internal democracy is a challenge to efficient functioning of Indian Political Scenario. Explain

32. Write a short note on horticulture in India. Mention the states that are famous for the production of oranges and apricots.

OR

Which crop is known as the 'golden fibre'? Explain two geographical conditions essential for the cultivation of this crop. Mention its any four uses.

33. Mention some great women contributors to print culture in the 19th century.

OR

Explain the different stages of development of printing technology in China.

SECTION E (CASE BASED QUESTIONS) (4 × 3 =12)

34. **Read the given text and answer the following questions given below.**

The secondary sector covers activities in which natural products are changed into other forms through ways of manufacturing that we associate with industrial activity. It is the next step after primary. The product is not produced by nature but has to be made and therefore some process of manufacturing is essential. This could be in a factory, a workshop or at home. For example, using cotton fibre from the plant, we spin yarn and weave cloth. Using sugarcane as a raw material, we make sugar or gur. We.convert earth into bricks and use bricks to make houses and buildings. Since this sector gradually became associated with the different kinds of industries that come up it is also called as industrial sector

34.(1) What are three sectors of an economy?

34.(2) Evaluate the meaning of secondary activities with examples.

34.(3) Differentiate between primary, secondary and tertiary activities in brief.

35. **Read the given text and answer the following questions given below.**

Following the defeat of Napoleon in 1815, European governments were driven by a spirit of conservatism. Conservatives believed that established, traditional institutions of state and society-like the monarchy, the Church, social hierarchies, property and the family-should be preserve. Most conservatives, however, did not propose a return to the society of pre-revolutionary days. Rather, they realised, from the changes initiated by Napoleon, that modernisation could in fact strengthen traditional institutions like the monarchy. It could make state power more effective and stronger. A modern army, an efficient bureaucracy, a dynamic economy, the abolition of feudalism and serfdom could strengthen the autocratic monarchies of Europe. In 1815, representatives of the European powers who had collectively defeated Napoleon, met at Vienna to draw up a settlement for Europe. The Congress was hosted by the Austrian Chancellor Duke Metternich. The delegates drew up the Treaty of Vienna of 1815 with the object of undoing most of the changes that had come about in Europe during the Napoleonic wars. The Bourbon dynasty, which had been deposed during the French Revolution, was restored to power, and France lost the territories it had annexed under Napoleon.

35.(1) How did the Congress of Vienna ensure peace in Europe?

35.(2) Who were conservatives?

35.(3) State the main features of Napoleonic Code.

36. **Read the given text and answer the following questions given below.**

Laterite has been derived from the Latin word 'later' - which means brick. The laterite soil develops under tropical and subtropical climate with alternate wet and dry season. This soil is the result of intense leaching due to heavy rain. Laterite soils are mostly deep to very deep acidic (pH 6.0) generally deficient in plant nutrients and occur mostly in Southern states, Western Ghats region of Maharashtra, Odisha, some parts of West Bengal and North-East regions, where these soils support deciduous and evergreen forests. It is human rich, but under sparse vegetation and in semi-arid environment, it is generally humus poor. They are prone to erosion and degradation due to their position on the landscape. After adopting appropriate soil conservation techniques particularly in the hilly areas of Karnataka, Kerala and Tamil Nadu, this soil is very useful for growing tea and coffee. Red Laterite soils in Tamil Nadu, Andhra Pradesh and Kerala are more suitable for crops like cashew nut.

36.(1) What is the required climate for laterite soil

36.(2) State any two features of laterite soil.

36.(3) How laterite soil is different from red soil. Explain

SECTION F (MAP SKILL BASED QUESTIONS) (2 + 3 =5)

37.(a) On the given political map of India, Two places Identify areas marked as A and B with the help of given information.

    A. A place where Congress Session of December 1920 held

    B. A place where the Jallianwala bagh incident happened.

(b) On the same outline map of India, locate and label any three following with suitable symbols

    I. Namrup Thermal Power Plant

    II. Gandhinagar Software Technology Park

    III. Kochi sea port

    IV. Indira Gandhi International Airport

SOLUTIONS

1. **(b)** The Buddhist missionaries from China introduced hand-printing technology into Japan around 768 . 770 AD. The Buddhist Diamond Sutra which was printed in 868 AD was the oldest Japanese book.

2. **(a)** To Curb the Threats and repressions, autocratic monarchies of Europe (Central and Eastern) began to introduce changes and concessions to lure these rebels. Thus both serfdom and bonded labour were abolished. Thus both assertion and reason are true and the reason is the correct explanation of the assertion.

3. **(a)** The appropriate reason for the formation of the Swaraj party was that it wanted members of Congress to return to Council Politics.

4. **(a)** The courier of Rhineland loses all that he has on his way home from Leipzig Napoleon here is represented as a postman on his way back to France after he lost the battle of Leipzig in 1813. Each letter dropping out of his bag bears the names of the territories he lost.

5. **(b)** The earliest kind of print technology was developed in China around AD 594. Buddhist missionaries from China introduced hand printing technology into Japan around 768-770 AD. IN 1295, Marco Polo brought wood block printing technology to Italy. Gutenberg developed the first known printing press in the 1430s.

6. **(a)** Kerala accounts for more than 90 percent of the total rubber production in the country. The total area under rubber cultivation in the state is 5.45 lakh hectares.

7. **(b)** About 43 percent of the land area is plain, which provides facilities for agriculture and industry. Mountains account for 30 percent of the total surface area of the country. About 27 percent of the area of the country is the plateau region.

8. **(d)** Plantation agriculture is a form of commercial agriculture. The plantations have a large area and they are usually found in areas of low density of population.
They employ a large number of people, most of them unskilled low paid labourers.
Plantation farming is capital intensive.
It has been an agricultural practice primarily in tropical and subtropical regions.

9. **(b)** Sugarcane-Uttar Pradesh is the country's biggest sugarcane growing and producing state.
Coffee- Among all coffee producing states in India, Karnataka is the indisputable leader and produces more than 70% of the total coffee produced in the country
Assam is the largest producer of Tea in India. West Bengal is the second largest tea producer state. Assam alone produces more than half of India's tea production.
Kerala accounts for more than 90 percent of the total rubber production in the country. The total area under rubber cultivation in the state is 5.45 lakh hectares

10. **(b)** There are some units of the Indian Union which enjoy very little power. These are areas which are too small to become an independent State but which could not be merged with any of the existing States. These areas are called Union Territories. These territories do not have powers of a State. The Central Government has special powers in running these areas.

11. **(c)** Statement c is incorrect as it is not an advantage of power sharing. This is because Power sharing helps to reduce the possibility of conflict between social groups and It doesn't create problems for the majority class of the population.
Power sharing is a good way to ensure the stability of political order as social conflict often leads to violence and political instability

12. **(c)** Statement i, ii and iv are correct. Holding together federation' is a federation in which the powers of the country are divided between the central government and constituent states.
The central government has greater authority when compared to states. It has the right to ensure the sovereignty of the country.

13. **(b)** Hospitals and dispensaries are listed in the State list of the Seventh Schedule of the Constitution of India. Seventh Schedule of the Indian Constitution provides for various items divided between Union, State and Concurrent list.

14. **(b)** Gram Sabha is the primary body of the Panchayati Raj system and by far the largest. It is a permanent body. Gram Sabha is the Sabha of the electorate.
Functions of Gram Sabha:
(i) It elects the members of the Gram Panchayat.
(ii) The Gram Sabha supervises the work of the village panchayat.
(iii) It approves the annual budget of the panchayat.
(iv) It reviews the performance of the Gram Panchayat.

15. **(d)** Sri Lanka has better Human Development ranking then India because of the following reasons-
(1) Per capita income: The per capita income of Sri Lanka is higher than that of India. The per capita income of India is about 3285, whereas it is around 5170 for Sri Lanka.
(2) Literacy rate: Literacy rate in Sri Lanka is also higher than India. It is 90.6 in Sri Lanka whereas it is 62.8 in India.
Population is not considered while calculating Human Development Index Report

16. **(c)** Average income of the family.
$7000 + 8000 + 10000 + 15000 = 40,000$
Sum of income = 40,000
Average = 40000 / 4 = 10,000

17. **(b)** Life expectancy at birth means the average number of years a person is expected to live for.

18. **(b)** If the BMI is less than 18.5 then the person would be considered undernourished. However, if this BMI is more than 25, then a person is considered overweight.

19. **(b)** Under Primary sector the production of a community through the natural process comes. The primary sector includes all those activities the end purpose of which consists in exploiting natural resources: agriculture, fishing, forestry, mining, deposits.

20. **(b)** The UNDP's HDR focuses on humans development approach that entails people and their opportunities and choices. The objectives behind publishing the report are: Advancement of human development. Expansion of opportunities, choices and freedom of people across the globe.

21. Absolutist is a government or system of rule that has no restraints on the power exercised. In history, the term refers to a form of monarchical government that was centralised, militarised and repressive.

22. Airways is the fastest, most comfortable and prestigious mode of transport. It can cover very difficult terrains like high mountains, vast deserts, dense forests and long oceanic stretches with great ease. Air Transport was nationalized in 1953. Air India provides domestic and international air services. Pawanhans Helicopters Limited provides helicopter services to inaccessible areas of India like North-Eastern region, Jammu and Kashmir, Himachal Pradesh and Uttarakhand

23. The national political party which espouses secularism and welfare of weaker sections and minorities is the Indian National Congress. The features of this party are listed below
- It was founded in 1885.
- It dominated Indian politics, both at the national and state levels, for several decades after India's independence.

24. Following are the negative effects of globalisation
(i) Thousands of uneducated and unskilled labourers have become jobless due to closure of domestic units.
(ii) Most of the small industries like toys, plastics, dairy products are affected due to foreign competition. This results in their closure thereby reducing production.

OR

The positive impacts of globalisation.
(i) This process is based on the basic premise of the free market. It is presumed that the free market begets competition and increase efficiency which is lacking in controlled markets.
(ii) Foreign investment flows into the domestic economy and domestic economy becomes strong and boisterous.

25. SEZs are industrial zones set up by the government to promote the establishment of MNCs. The facilities available in SEZ are:
- SEZ are provided with world class facilities i.e. electricity, water, roads, transport, storage, recreational and educational facilities.
- Companies operating in SEZ do not have to pay taxes for five years.
- Government has allowed flexibility in the labour laws to attract MNCs.

OR

The stability in jobs for the workers affected due to globalisation in the following ways:
- There is no permanent employment, but workers are employed only when needed, i.e. they are 'flexible workers'. In the slack season, they are out of work with no compensation.
- Due to globalisation, the MNC's main objective is to lower costs. To do this, they provide temporary employment only and are given lower wages or they may have to work on a per day basis.
- Workers may have to work for longer hours and be laid off from work without any compensation during the slack season.

26. The main contents of Indian National Congress in December 1929 held under the leadership of Jawaharlal Nehru were:
- The Lahore Session of the Congress in 1929 is called the historical session as at this session, the Congress President Jawaharlal Nehru passed a resolution declaring 'Purna Swaraj' in December 1929.
- In 1929, Viceroy Lord Irwin announced an uncertain offer of 'Dominion status' to India and a Round Table Conference to discuss a future Constitution. The expectations of the Congress were not met by this announcement.
- At that time liberals and moderates in Congress lost their influence and Radicals like Jawaharlal Nehru and Subhash Chandra Bose became more assertive in Congress. After declaring 'Purna Swaraj' or complete independence, the Congress declared 26th January, 1930 was Independence Day.

27. Caste has not disappeared from contemporary India. This can be clear by looking at the following facts:
According to the National Sample Survey Office (NSSO), the average economic status of caste groups in India still remains the same as was in the past. Most of the rich section belongs to higher castes, while people of lower castes are generally poor.
Despite the constitutional prohibition, many people are still considered as untouchables in the country.
Even now most people marry within their own caste or tribe.
Political parties often field their candidates in constituencies according to the caste prevailing in that constituency. People also tend to vote on the caste lines.

28. The dimensions of deforestation in India are staggering. The forest and tree cover in the country is estimated at 79.42 million hectare, which is 24.16% of the total geographical area (dense forest 12.2%; open forest 9.14%; and mangrove 0.14%). According to the State of Forest Report (2015), the dense forest cover has increased by 3,775 sq km since 2013.
However, this apparent increase in the forest cover is due to conservation measures, management interventions and plantation, etc., by different agencies.

29. Bharatiya Janata Party (BJP) founded in 1980 draws inspiration from India's ancient culture and values.

Features of Bharatiya Janata Party (BJP) are-

Cultural Nationalism (Hindutva) is an important element in its conception of Indian nationhood and politics.

Wants full territorial and political integration of Jammu and Kashmir with India.

A uniform civil code for all people living in the country irrespective of religion and ban on religious conversions. Earlier limited to north and west and to urban areas, the party expanded support in the south, east, the north-east and rural areas.

30. (i) In Awadh, the Peasant Movement developed under the leadership of Baba Ramchandra (a Sanyasi who had earlier been a Fiji as an indentured labourer). This Peasant Movement demanded reduction of revenue, abolition of begar and social boycott of oppressive landlords. In many places, nai-dhobi bandhs were organised by panchayats to deny services to all landlords. In October, 1920 the Oudh Kisan Sabha was set-up. It was headed by Jawaharlal Nehru, Baba Ramchandra and a few others. Within a month, over 300 branches of this sabha had been set up in the villages around the region. As the peasant movement spread, the houses of taluqdars (Indian land-holders) and merchants were attacked, bazaars were looted and grain hoards were taken over.

(ii) In the Gudem Hills of Andhra Pradesh, for instance, militant guerrilla movements spread in the early 1920's. It was not a form of struggle that the Congress could approve. During that time, in the forest regions, the colonial government had closed large forest areas, preventing people from entering the forests to graze their cattle, or to collect fuel wood and fruits. This enraged the hill people. This affected their livelihoods as well as they felt that their traditional rights were being denied to them. When the government began forcing them to contribute beggar for road building, the hill people revolted. The person who came to lead them was Alluri Sitaram Raju. He was inspired by the Non-Cooperation Movement and persuaded people to wear khadi and give up drinking. On the other hand, he asserted that India could be liberated only by the use of force, not non-violence. The Gudem rebels attacked police stations, attempted to kill British officials and carried on Guerrilla warfare for achieving Swaraj.

OR

(i) The role of poor peasantry in the Civil Disobedience Movement was:

• As the economic depression continued the poor peasants found it difficult to pay the rent. They wanted the unpaid rent to the landlord to be remitted. Thus, they joined a variety of radical movements, often led by socialists and communists.

• They came in huge numbers to support Gandhiji and his followers. It was because of them that the Civil Disobedience movement could become a mass movement.

• They launched a 'no rent' campaign but it was not supported by the Congress. So, the relationship between the poor peasant and Congress remained uncertain.

(ii) The role of merchants and the industrialists in the Civil Disobedience Movement was

• They became powerful in society and wanted to expand their business. So, they started opposing colonial policies that restricted their business. They wanted protection against imports of foreign goods and a rupee sterling foreign exchange ratio that would discourage imports.

• The industrialists criticised colonial control over the Indian economy and supported the Civil Disobedience Movement at its first stage. Most industrialists thought of 'Swaraj' as a time when colonial restriction did not exist in the business world. As a result, trade and business would flourish without constraints.

• They gave financial assistance and refused to buy or sell imported goods.

31. The measures to make formal sector loans beneficial for poor farmers and workers are:

(i) The formal sector like banks and cooperatives should lend more to poor people and workers, particularly in rural areas.

(ii) The formal sector should provide cheap and affordable credit to the poor people so that repayment is easy.

(iii) Formal sector should work out other ways of arranging collateral from the poor people.

(iv) By providing linkage between Self Help Groups and banks, the formal sector of credit can be increased.

(v) There should be more cooperatives and banks in rural areas and people should be made aware of their presence.

OR

(i) The lenders ask for collateral while lending due to the following reasons:

• Collateral is an asset that the borrower owns and uses as a guarantee to a lender until the loan is repaid. Lenders ask for collateral as a security against loans.

• If the borrower fails to repay the loan, the lender has the right to sell the asset or collateral to obtain the amount.

• For a bank in case of taking collateral, the repayment of the loan becomes easy because banks has no risk of non-performing assets. The items that can be kept as collateral against the loan are (a) Land Titles (b) Deposits with banks (c) Vehicle (d) Building.

(ii) The terms of credit becomes difficult for the small and marginal farmers because

- They are not capable of providing the collateral such as land titles, deposits with Banks, livestock's, etc.
- The terms of credit includes interest rate, collateral, documentation and the mode of repayment.
  They vary substantially from one credit arrangement to another depending on the nature of the lender and the borrower.
- They lack in the mode of payment as in case of crop failure, it becomes difficult for small farmers to repay the loan on time.

32. Democracy is undoubtedly better than other forms of government. We can give the following arguments in its favour:

(i) Democracy improves the quality of decision making. Democracy is based on consultation and discussion. A democratic decision always involves many persons, discussions and meetings. When a number of people put their head together, they are able to point out possible mistakes in any decision. This takes time but there is a big advantage in taking time over important decisions. This reduces the chances of rash or irresponsible decisions.

(ii) Democracy provides a method to deal with differences and conflicts. In any society people are bound to have differences of opinions and interests. These differences are particularly sharp in a country like ours which has an amazing social diversity. People belong to different regions, speak different languages,practice different religions and have different castes. They look at the world differently and have different preferences. The preference of one group can clash with those of other groups. This conflict can be solved peacefully in a democratic set-up. In democracy no one is a permanent winner, no one is a permanent loser. Different groups can live with one another peacefully.

OR

Democracy is often referred to as being an accountable, responsive and legitimate form of government. According to professor Jason Barabas, democratic responsiveness measures the degree to which governmental policies match public preferences. For example, during the rule of UPA, the Ministry of Environment, under pressure from the United Nations, some NGOs and several environmental protection groups, passed several legislations to regulate the process of industrialisation while at the same time protecting the environment

33. Roadways still have an edge over railways in India:
Construction cost of roadways is much lower than that of railways.
Roads can traverse comparatively more dissecting and undulating plains.
Roads can negotiate higher gradients of slopes and can traverse mountains like Himalayas.

Road transport is economical in transportation of few persons and small amount of goods over short distances. It also provides door to door services.
Cost of loading and unloading is much lower.
Road transport is also used as a feeder to other modes of transport such as they provide link between railway station, airports and sea ports.

OR

Indian Railways is a government body under the Ministry of Railways which operates the national railway system of India. It is run by the government in the public interest and manages the fourth largest railway network in the world, Improvement in Indian Railways- 64% of all broad-gauge routes have been electrified by 40,5 km or by August 2020 with 25 kV 50 Hz AC electric traction.
Railways have taken several initiatives to upgrade their aging infrastructure and improve the quality of their service. The Indian government plans to invest tr 9.05 trillion to upgrade IR by 2020.
All unmanned level crossings were abolished by January 2019, and manned level crossings are being gradually replaced by overbridge and underbridge.
Other security projects include the expansion of an automatic fire alarm system, which was first introduced in all air-conditioned coaches in Rajdhani Express trains in 2013; and 9095 GPS-enabled Fog Pilot Assistance Systems Railway signaling devices were installed in four zones in 2010: Northern, North Central, North Eastern and North Western and replacing ICF coaches with LHB coaches.
Electrification of railway lines to increase speed, and to burn less fuel.
Introduction of electronic ticketing or 'E-Ticketing' for convenience of passengers.
Construction of new railway lines to improve the connectivity of the country.
Introduction of new, superfast trains like Shatabdi.
Replacing steam engines, which cause heavy pollution, by diesel and electric engines.

34.(a) Indian Postal Network has helped the country to engage in communication and social-economic development.

34.(b) Mass Communication is the medium which provides entertainment as well as creates awareness among the masses. It includes radio, television, newspapers, magazines, books, films etc. whereas Personal Communication is between sharing of ideas and thoughts between person to person.

34.(c) Significance of communication for a nation-
Communication has a major role to play in that. It has brought all regions in a nation close and all nations in the world closer . Without a well developed communication infrastructure, no nation can assume an important position on the globe.
Essential roles of strategic communication in nation building and national development include: creating a clear image and strong positioning; agenda setting

and vision sharing; building support for government actions, policies and programmes; and creating and building credible profiles, images and personas for public.

35.(a) Hindustan Socialist Republican Army (HSRA) was established in 1928 at Feroz Shah Kotla in New Delhi by Chandrasekhar Azad, Bhagat Singh, Sukhdev Thapar and others.

35.(b) Bhagat Singh was put on trial because In April 1929, Bhagat Singh along with Batukeshwar Dutta threw a bomb in the Legislative Assembly in an attempt to blow up the train in which Lord Irwin was travelling.

35.(c) HSRA was founded when Mahatma Gandhi suspended the non violent movement after the spread of violence. The suspension of the Nonviolent movement irritated some nationalists who believed that the suspension was unjustified. This resulted in the emergence of revolutionary movements among the most radical of those who wanted to overthrow British rule and then HSRA then came into existence.

36.(a) Guls and Kuls are the terms used for channels built by the people living in hilly areas. They are built for irrigation. Guls and Kuls are diversion channels mostly used in the state of Himachal Pradesh. They require special care as their design and operation play a very important role.

36.(a) Rainwater harvesting (RWH) is the collection and storage of rain, rather than allowing it to run off. Rainwater is collected from a roof-like surface and redirected to a tank, cistern, deep pit (well, shaft, or borehole), aquifer, or a reservoir with percolation, so that it seeps down and restores the ground water.

36.(a) Benefit of Rainwater harvesting are-
Rainwater harvesting provides an independent water supply during regional water restrictions and in developed countries, it is often used to supplement the main supply.

It provides water when drought occurs, which can help reduce flooding in low-lying areas and reduce demand on wells that may be able to maintain groundwater levels.

It also helps in the availability of potable water, as rainwater is largely free from salinity and other salts.

37.(a) A. Amritsar
B. Kolkata

(b)

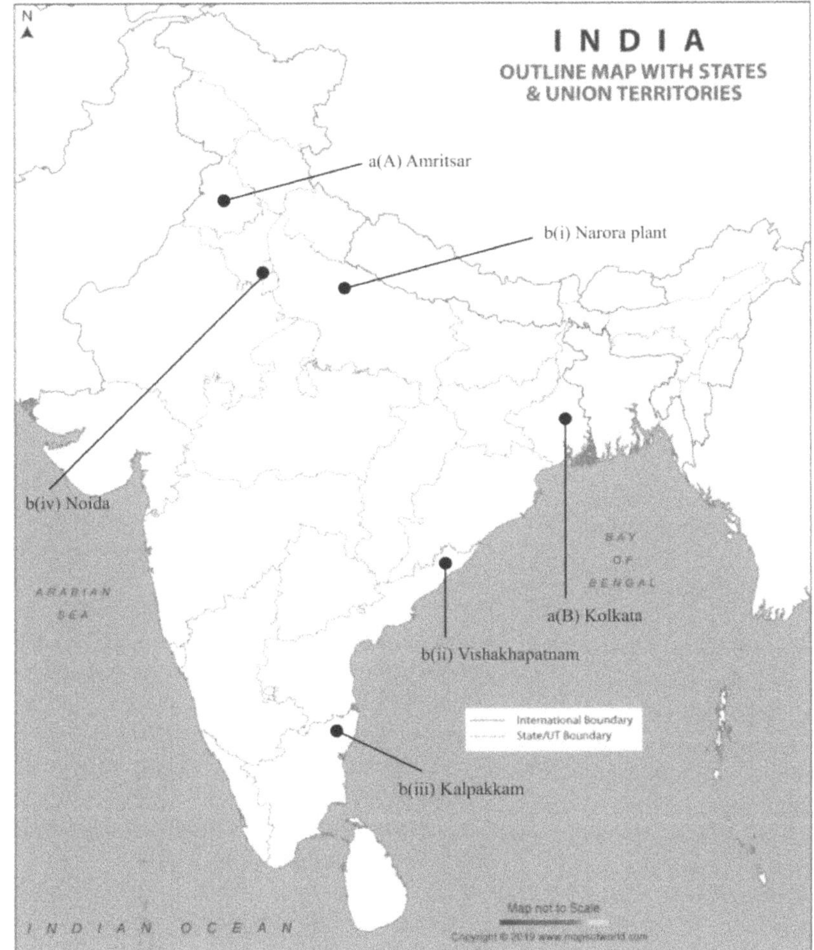

SAMPLE PAPER-2

1 **(c)** Only option c is correct. On 24 September 1932, the Poona Pact was sealed between Mahatma Gandhi and Dr B R Ambedkar in the Yerwada Central Jail, Pune.
Indian Industrial and Commerce Congress was formed in 1920
Federation of the Indian Chamber of Commerce and Industries formed in 1927 Mohammad Iqbal demanded Separate Electorates for Muslims in 1930.

2. **(c)** The female allegory of France was named Marianne, a popular Christian name, which underlined the idea of a people's nation. Her characteristics were drawn from those of Liberty and the Republic i.e. the red cap, the tricolour, the cockade. Statues of Marianne were erected in public squares to remind the public of the national symbol of unity.

3. **(c)** The events arranged in a chronological order are-
Earliest factories started in England in nearly 1730.
James Watt patented the steam engine in 1765.
First jute mill came up in Bengal in 1855.
First spinning and weaving mill of Madras began production in 1874

4. **(d)** The Planting of Tree of Liberty in Zweibrücken, Germany. The subject of this colour print by the German painter Karl Kaspar Fritz is the occupation of the town of Zweibrücken by the French armies.

5. **(a)** After the mid 19th century women's schools were set up in the cities and towns. This was because of many journals which were written by liberals to educate the citizens regarding the importance and scope of women's education.

6. **(c)** Jute grows well on well-drained fertile soils in the floodplains where soils are renewed every year. A high temperature is required during the time of growth.

7. **(c)** Among the following pairs only pair 2 is correctly matched. Yellow and red soils are also found in parts of Chhattisgarh.
Arid soil is found in the parts of Haryana, Western Rajasthan, and Punjab
Alluvial soil is found in the regions of Indo-Gangetic plains, Punjab, Haryana, Uttar Pradesh, Bihar, West Bengal and Assam

8. **(b)** The method followed in Madhya Pradesh was Watershed Management
Watershed management is a term used to describe the process of implementing land use practices and water management practices to protect and improve the quality of the water and other natural resources within a watershed by managing the use of those land and water resources in a comprehensive manner

9. **(c)** Jawaharlal Nehru port was planned with a view to decongest the Mumbai port and serve as a hub port to this region. Jawaharlal Nehru Port, also known as Nhava Sheva port is the largest container port in India. It is located in East of Mumbai, in the state of Maharashtra.

10. **(b)** Brussels has a separate government in which both the French and the Dutch have equal representation.
Belgian leaders between 1970 and 1993 amended their Constitution four times only to arrange so that the diverse communities can reside together peacefully within the same country without any conflicts.
French-speaking people Accepted equal representation in Brussels.
Citizens acquire a stake in the system through participation in a legitimate government. A legitimate government is one where citizen participate to acquire a stake in the system

11. **(d)** Forms of power sharing are-
Division of Powers between Central and State legislatures.
The division of power between the national and state governments is federalism. States have authority within their boundaries while the national authority extends across all the states.
Power sharing between the Union and the States through lists of subjects. The Union and the State government share the power between themselves via union list, state list and concurrent list.

12. **(a)** Mahatma Gandhi said the above words.
Gandhi said these words because India was a religious country with great traditions and customs which are mainly based on religion. So Gandhi foresaw that religion has been included in every part of Indian life and cannot be separated from politics. This was proved correct when Muhammad Ali Jinnah succeeded in the partitioning of India into Pakistan based not on colour, creed or anything but religion.

13. **(a)** Earlier education was a subject in the State List but the 42nd Amendment to the Constitution in 1976 shifted it to the Concurrent List. Now, education is available to both the Parliament and state assemblies to legislate upon.

14. **(b)** Events arranged in a chronological order is as follows- India's journey as a democracy begins - 1947
States on the basis of language created- 1953
Central government agrees to continue the use of English- 1965 Rise of regional political parties leading to coalitions- 1977

15. **(a)** Democracy has transformed people from subject to citizen because when there is a lack of democracy all the decision are taken by the ruler but when democracy established there is a important role of people in taking decision by the power of the right

16. **(c)** Percentage of tertiary sector workers employed in unorganised sector
No. of employees in unorganised sector/ Total no. of employees in tertiary sector $\times$ 100
$= 17 + 76 = 93$
% of employed in unorganised sector
$76/93 \times 100 = 81.70\%$

17. **(b)** The Bank is more likely to give credit to Sunil as he has regular employment and he will pay his debt in a more efficient and effective manner as compared to Anil

18. **(c)** Anubha works in the tertiary sector. Banking is included under the tertiary sector. The tertiary sector of the economy is the service sector. This sector provides services to the general population and to businesses.

19 **(c)** Under Barter system goods were exchanged without using money. Barter is an act of trading goods or services between two or more parties without the use of money

20. **(a)** To have a safe and secure work environment at the office will be the aspiration of a working woman.

21. The factors that promote the setting up of MNCs or the. reason for setting up MNCs at a certain place are
Availability of skilled and unskilled labour, e.g. India has highly skilled engineers who can understand the technical aspects of production.
Availability of raw materials at cheap prices e.g. China provides the advantage of being a cheap manufacturing location.

22. The Vernacular Press Act was passed in 1878 by the British Government in India. This Act provided the government with extensive rights to censor reports and editorials in the vernacular press. If a vernacular paper published any seditious material, the paper was banned and its printing machinery was seized. This was a complete violation of the freedom of expression.

23. The Chipko movement's main influence was that it encouraged the government of the Union to amend the Indian Forest Act, 1927, and adopted the 1980 Forest Protection Act, which specified that forest land should not be used for non-forest purposes.

24. The conditions laid down by the Election Commission to recognise a 'State Party' and 'National Party' are
Merits of two-party system are
- In this system, electorate has a very clear choice before him/her.
- This system promotes political stability in the country

25. (i) Automobile Industry This industry provides quick transportation vehicles for goods and passengers. In India, there are centers for manufacture of trucks, buses, cars, motor cycles, scooters, three-wheelers and multi-utility vehicles. The industry is located around Gurugram, Mumbai, Pune, Chennai, Kolkata, Lucknow, Indore, Hyderabad, Jamshedpur, Delhi and Bengaluru.
(ii) Information Technology (IT) and Electronics Industry It covers products from transistor sets to televisions, telephones, cellphones, telephone exchanges, radars, computers and other equipment required by the telecommunication and computer industry.
Bengaluru has emerged as the electronic capital of India. Other important centres for electronic goods are Noida, Mumbai, Chennai, Hyderabad, Pune, Delhi, Kolkata, Lucknow and Coimbatore.

OR

Industries create thermal and noise pollution in the following ways

- Thermal pollution of water bodies occurs when hot water from factories and thermal power plants is released into them before cooling. The consequence of thermal pollution are that aquatic life in the water bodies can be killed. This includes plants as well as fish.
- Noise pollution is generated by the unbearable noise from industrial and construction activities, machinery, generators, pneumatic and electric tools. The consequences of noise pollution create irritation, anger, stress, hearing impairment, increased heart rate and blood pressure among other physiological effects.

26. Giuseppe Mazzini was an Italian. He was born in Genoa in Italy. He became a member of the secret society of the Carbonari.
At the age of 24, he was sent into exile for attempting a revolution in Liguria. He subsequently established two more underground societies – Youthful Italy in Marseilles and Youthful Europe in Berne whose members were like-minded young men from Poland, France, Italy and the German States.
Mazzini accepted that God had intended nations to be the natural units of mankind.

27. Women in India have to face a lot of issues. They have to go through gender discrimination, harassment, sexual abuse, lack of education, dowry-related harassment, gender pay gap and much more.
Different aspects of life in which women are discriminated in India are:
Education: The literacy rate among women is only 54 per cent compared with 76 per cent among men. When it comes to higher education, a smaller proportion of girls, in comparison to the boys, are allowed to go for higher studies. This is because parents prefer to spend their resources on their sons' education.
Sex-ratio: In many parts of India, parents find ways to abort the girl child in a will to have a son. This has led to a decline in child sex ratio (number of girl children per thousand boys) in the country to merely 919.
High-Paid jobs: The proportion of women working in highly paid and valued jobs is still smaller than men.

28. The two reasons that say that caste alone cannot determine election results in India are:
(i) No parliamentary constituency in India has a clear majority of one single caste. So, parties need to win the confidence of more than one caste and community to win elections.
(ii) No party wins the votes of all the voters belonging to one particular caste or community. Voters have become wiser and they only vote for those candidates or parties which are expected to work towards the development of their constituency.

29. Credit is one of the major aspects that determine a country's development. There is a huge demand for loans for various economic activities. Cheap and affordable loans give people an opportunity to develop their business. Credit plays a very crucial role in agricultural activities. People can borrow money and use it to adopt modern farming methods to increase the crop production and grow crops which are more reliable than the traditional methods. By sanctioning loans to developing industries and trade, banks provide them with the necessary aid for improvement. This leads to increased production, employment and profits that ultimately help in the development of the country.

30. The statement is correct that some of the political organisations in India were lukewarm in their response to the 'Civil

Disobedience Movement'. This can be understood by the following examples-
   - Some of the Congress leaders were not willing to continue the non-cooperation because they were tired of the mass struggle, wanted to participate in the council elections and criticize the British policies within the council. The Swaraj party was formed within the Congress party by CR Das and Motilal Nehru. It was formed with the purpose to argue for return to council elections.
   - The Muslims and their political organisations were also not taking much interest in the Civil Disobedience Movement due to the decline of the Non Cooperation Khilafat Movement. They felt alienated from Congress. They felt that Congress is linked with the Hindu Mahasabha and their propagandas are Hindu oriented.

OR

The precise narrative of the genesis of Gandhi's idea of non-cooperation with the British and the circumstantial significance of launching the first mass movement in 1920 is given in 'Hind Swaraj' 1909. In this book, he declared that British rule was established in India with the cooperation of Indians. If Indians refused to cooperate, British rule in India would collapse within a year and Swaraj would come. Mahatma Gandhi proposed the following strategy for the implementation of the Non-Cooperation as a Movement
   - The movement would begin with a surrender of titles, honours and honorary posts by people.
   - The movement would boycott Civil Services, Army, Police, British Courts and Legislative Assemblies, School and Colleges and British goods.
   - The British goods would be replaced by domestic goods or Swadeshi to promote the native cottage industries.
   - In case of government suppression, the Civil Disobedience Movement would be launched. The Non-Cooperation Movement was adopted by the Congress during the Nagpur Conference in December 1920 and it began under the leadership of Mahatma Gandhi.

31. Dynastic succession is defined as a desire of few to concentrate political powers in their own hands. It is one of the most serious challenges before the political parties because
   - Most political parties do not practice open and transparent procedures for their functioning.
   - There are few ways for an ordinary worker to rise to the top in a party.
   - In many parties, the top positions are always controlled by members of one family. This practice is unfair to other members of that party and is also bad for a democracy.
   - People who do not have adequate experience or popular support come to occupy positions of power.

OR

Political parties are rightly called the government in disguise due to the following reasons
   - In most democracies, elections are fought mainly among the candidates put up by political parties.
   - Parties put forward different policies and programmes and the voters choose from them.
   - Parties play a decisive role in making laws for a country. They shape public opinions to raise and highlight issues.
   - Parties form and run governments.
   - Opposition role is important in democracy as it voices different views and criticises the government for its failures or wrong policies.
   - Parties provide people access to government machinery and welfare schemes implemented by governments.

32. India has enormous diversity in the availability of resources. Through planning, regions which have shortage of vital resources and those having adequate quantities, receive equal attention.
   - There are regions which are rich in certain types of resources but are deficient in some other resources. For example: Arunachal has an abundance of water but lacks infrastructural development.
   - There are some regions which can be considered self-sufficient in terms of availability of resources. For example: The states of Jharkhand, Chhattisgarh and Madhya Pradesh are rich in minerals and coal deposits.
   - There are some regions which have acute shortage of some vital resources. For example: The state of Rajasthan is well endowed with solar and wind energy but lacks in water resources.

OR

Four institutional efforts made at global level for 'resource conservation' are-
   - At the international level, the Club of Rome advocated resource conservation for the first time in a more systematic way in 1968.

- In 1974, the Gandhian Philosophy was presented once again by Schumacher in his book "Small is Beautiful".
- Brundtland Commission Report in 1987, introduced the concept of 'sustainable development' and advocated it as a means for resource conservation. This was subsequently published in a book entitled "Our Common Future".
- In June 1992, the first 'International Earth Summit' was held in Rio de Janeiro in Brazil, in which 100 heads of States met for addressing urgent problems of environmental protection and socio-economic development at the global level.

33. The banks might not be willing to lend certain borrowers due to the following reasons:
- A few people fail to provide the required set of documents to get a loan.
- There are some people who have not repaid previous loans. Such borrowers come in the defaulters list. Banks might not be willing to lend them further.
- The banks might not be willing to lend entrepreneurs who are going to invest in the business with high risks.
- The banks might not be willing to lend those people who earn irregular incomes or have no fixed salary because in such cases chances of repayment of the loan are very less.

OR

The terms of credit can be unfavorable for the small farmer which can be explained with the help of the following example:

If a farmer borrows money from the bank and during the harvest season his crops are ruined, then he shall not be able to repay the loan to the bank. He might have to sell a part of his land to repay the amount. In such condition he will further fall into the debt trap.

The small farmers can get cheap credit from the different sources like banks, agricultural cooperatives, and SHGs.

34.(1) Paper currency and coins made up of alloys, ATM cards and cheques can be counted as a modern form of money.

34.(2) Computerisation of banking systems primarily facilitates the expansion of newer currency emonetisation.

34.(3) The possible benefits from demonetisation include
(i) Reducing Counterfeit Currency - This allows the government to weed out counterfeit currency from the market.
(ii) Curbs Anti-social Activities -Through the medium of cash many anti-social activities are discouraged.

35.(1) Organic chemicals includes petrochemicals that are used for manufacturing of synthetic fibers, synthetic rubber, plastics, dyes stuffs, drugs and pharmaceuticals.

On the other hand, inorganic chemicals includes sulphuric acid, nitric acid, alkalis, soda ash and caustic soda. They are used to manufacture fertilizers, synthetic fibres, plastics, adhesives, paints, dyes, stuff, etc.

35.(2) Organic chemical plants are located near oil refineries or petrochemical plants..

35.(3) The features of chemical industries are
- It is a major source of employment to large number of people due to its diverse and fast growing nature.
- It comprises of both large and small scale manufacturing units.

36.(1) In 1916, Gandhiji initiated a movement in Champaran in Bihar against the oppressive indigo plantation system.

36.(2) Mahatma Gandhi ji launched the Civil Disobedience Movement because Lord Irwin ignored Gandhi's eleven demands including the abolition of the salt tax. Gandhiji started a civil disobedience movement with the famous Dandi March.

36.(3) Two impacts of the civil disobedience movement are
- Women and students participated in large numbers in the movement, which was a liberating experience for Indian women who were entering public space in such large numbers for the first time.
- The civil disobedience movement had a far-reaching impact. It instilled distrust in the British.government and laid the groundwork for the freedom struggle, as well as popularising new methods of propaganda such as the Prabhat, pheris, pamphlets, and so on.

37. (a)

A- Madras

B- Ahmedabad

(b)

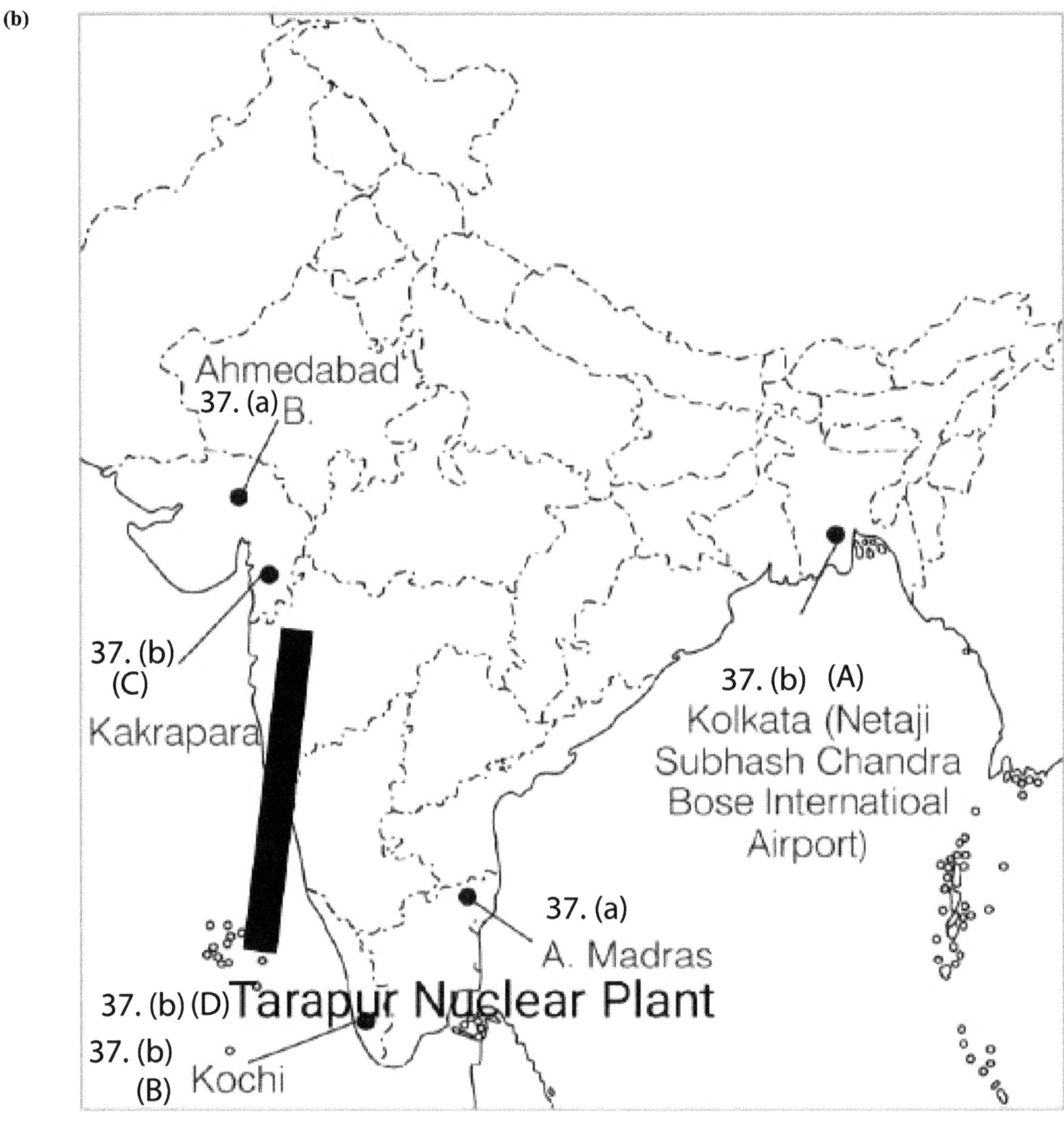

SAMPLE PAPER-3

1. **(b)** The Vienna Congress was convened in 1815 to restore conservative regime in Europe. The Congress of Vienna of 1814–1815 was an international diplomatic conference to reconstitute the European political order after the downfall of the French Emperor Napoleon Bonaparte.

2. **(d)** Among the following statement 4 is incorrect.
The Vernacular Act of 1878 was proposed by Lord Lytton, then Viceroy of India, and was passed on 14 March 1878. This act excluded English-language publications as it was meant to control seditious writing of Indians which were against the British policies in India.

3. **(c)** Bombay and Calcutta ports grew after the European companies gained power in trade. The European companies gained power in trade by securing a variety of concessions from the local courts.

4. **(c)** The features of the economic situation which existed in Europe were -migration of population from rural to urban regions, small producers had to face stiff competition from England and no. of Job seekers exceeded the employment opportunities. Developments in 19th-century Europe are bounded by two great events. The French Revolution broke out in 1789, and its effects reverberated throughout much of Europe for many decades.
Industrial revolution became more advanced in most countries of Europe, was not a feature of the economic situation which existed in Europe.

5. **(c)** Events arranged in chronological orders is as follows:
Martin Luther 'Ninety Five Theses' - 1517
The first Tamil Book Printed - 1812
The first Malayalam book was printed- 1887
Vernacular Press Act passed- 1878

6. **(d)** In the coalition government the leader decides every rule best signifies the given image. Coalition government is formed by the coming together of two or more political parties. Usually, partners in a coalition form of political alliance adopt a common programme for governance.

7. **(c)** Rubber is mainly an equatorial crop, but under special conditions it is also grown in tropical areas. It requires moist and humid climate with rainfall of more than 200 cm and temperature above 25° C. It is an important industrial raw material that supports many industries. Hence, statement 'A' is true and 'R' is false.

8. **(a)** Only statement 1 is correct. Other statements are incorrect because Odisha is the largest bauxite producing state in India.
Bellary-Chitradurga belt is famous for iron ore reserves in India.

9. **(c)** Inundation channel is largely practiced in Bengal. Inundation canals are long canals that are taken from large rivers having a huge capacity and receive water when the level of the river is high enough and especially when in flood.

10. **(c)** In a democracy, if the power to decide is dispersed, it is not possible to take quick decisions and enforce them. People are the source of all political power in a democracy because the Central Government, State Governments and Local body Governments are elected by the people through elections. If the Government does not perform to the expectations of the people, the Governments will be voted out in the elections which are conducted periodically in democracy.

11. **(c)** The origins of the Sri Lankan Civil War lie in the continuous political rancor between the majority Sinhalese and the minority Tamils, and the preference given to Sinhalese by the government in the policies enacted, especially the Sinhala Only Act

12. **(b)** Sri Lanka got independence in 1948.
Sinhala became the official language of Sri Lanka in 1956
The civil war of Sri Lanka was ended in 2009
Liberation Tigers of Tamil Eelam was established in 1976.

13. **(d)** Statements 1,3 and 4 are correct.
A federal state derives its existence from the constitution. The constitution is regarded as the supreme law of the land and no one is above the constitution.
In a Federal government, the constitution may be written or unwritten. The Indian Constitution is the world's second-longest written Constitution.
Legislature may be bicameral or unicameral in unitary government. Unicameral legislation is used to describe a government with only one legislative house or chamber. A bicameral parliament or legislature is one in which two assemblies share legislative power

14. **(d)** In a unitary government, all the powers of government are vested in the central governmentwhereas in a federal government, the powers of government are divided between the centre and the units.

15. **(a)** The sum of the total production of all goods and services in the three sectors are combinedly called as GDP (Gross Domestic Product). Gross domestic product (GDP) is the most commonly used measure for the size of an economy.

16. **(b)** A customs barrier is any implementation of fees, rules, or regulations designed with the intention to limit international trade. Restrictions can come in the form of tariffs, levies, duties, trade embargoes, and even currency manipulation.

17. **(d)** India ranks low in HDI despite of its huge size and population because of
- Less investment in social infrastructure in the country.
- In India gender inequality is still prevalent. Increasing income inequalities among different sections of the society.

18. **(a)** The workers of the unorganised sector are often exploited and not paid fair wages. Their earnings are low and not regular. These jobs are not secure and have no other benefits and they also face social discrimination. Thus, there is a need for measures to be adopted related to their protection and support. Hence, both statementare true and 'R' is the correct explanation of "A

19. **(a)** If the Body Mass Index (BMI) is less than 18.5 then the adult person would be consideredconsidered underweight.

20. **(a)** Statement 1 is incorrect regarding the features of informal source of credit. There is no organization that controls credit activities in informal sources

21. The Rowlatt Act affected the National Movement as the Indians disapproved this act in the following ways
   • Rallies were organized in various cities, workers went on strike in railway workshops and shops were closed down. The British administration suppressed the nationalists. As a result local leaders were picketed up from Amritsar and Mahatma Gandhi was barred from entering Delhi. The Rowlatt Act provided the foundation and channel for subsequent movements like Khilafat and Non Cooperation.

22. Border roads are those roads that are built in the border area for the defence of the country. They are built by the Border Roads Organisation or BRO. These roads have aided the economic development of these border areas and helped armed forces keep vigil in remote areas in north and north-eastern parts of the country.

23. The horizontal distribution of power ensures that power is shared among different organs of government—the legislature, executive and judiciary. It allows different organs of
   government placed at the same level to exercise different powers. The horizontal distribution of power is also called a system of checks and balances. This system ensures that none of these organs can exercise unlimited power. Each organ checks the other.

24. Special Economic Zones or SEZs are industrial zones set up by the government having word class facilities such as electricity, water, roads, transport, storage, recreational and educational facilities. Companies who set up production units in SEZs are exempted from taxes for an initial period of five years.

OR

FDI (Foreign Direct Investment') is the investment of foreign capital in the economic and productive activities of a country by foreign companies or MNCs with the aim of expanding capacity and production to earn profits

25. The effects of worldwide economic depression on India, towards late 1920's were-
   The depression immediately affected Indian trade. Indians exports and imports nearly came to half between 1928 and 1934.
   Between 1928 and 1934, wheat prices fell by 50%. The fall in prices had a deep impact on poor farmers. Though agricultural prices fell sharply, the colonial government refused to give any relief to the farmers in taxes.
   The unrest created the great depression, an opportunity for Mahatma Gandhi to launch the Civil Disobedience Movement in 1931.

OR

Gandhiji launched the Civil Disobedience Movement because Lord Irwin ignored Gandhi's eleven demands including the abolition of the Salt Tax. Gandhi's 'Salt March marked the beginning of the Civil Disobedience Movement all over India. The Civil Disobedience Movement came into force in various parts of the country and united different groups in the following ways . With the spread of the movement, foreign cloth was boycotted and liquor shops were picketed, Peasants refused to pay revenue and chaukidari taxes. Village officials resigned from their post. Forest people violated forest law.
In the countryside, rich peasant communities viz, Patidars of Gujarat and the Jats of Uttar Pradesh became the supporters of the Civil Disobedience Movement.
The poorer peasantry, often led by the socialist and the communist, joined a variety of radical movements for the remission of their unpaid rent to the landlords.

26. Humans are dependent on the ecological system because they are part of this system.
   This can be understood through the following points
   (i) Humans breathe air, drink water and grow crops in soil which are the non-living components of the ecological system.
   (ii) The living components like plants, animals and microorganisms recreate the quality of the air humans breathe, the water humans drink and the soil that produces human food. Without These elements human beings cannot survive.
   (ii) Human beings are dependent on both living and non-living components of the ecological existence

27. Money is a medium of exchange in transactions. A person holding money can easily exchange it for any commodity or service that he or she might want.
   Modern money currency is accepted as a medium of exchange because.it is certified for a particular denomination (For example, ₹10, ₹20, ₹100, ₹1,000). It is issued by the Central Bank of the country. It is authorized by the government of the country.

28. Status of women's representation in India's legislative bodies- Panchayati Raj in India has reserved one-third seats in Local Government bodies for women.
   In India, the proportion of women in the legislature has been very low.
   The percentage of elected women members in Lok Sabha is not even 10 per cent and in State Assemblies less than 5 per cent. India is behind several developing countries of Africa and Latin America. Women organisations have been demanding reservations of at least one-third seats in Lok Sabha and State Assemblies for women.

29. We can say that globalisation has been advantageous to both consumers as well as the producers due to the following reasons

Globalisation has led to an intense increase in industrial competition. As a result, producers are competing over each other to provide better and cheaper services to the consumers.

This has also resulted in reduction of the prices.

With the initiation of globalisation, producers now have actively free access to international markets. Also, they can avail more easily the credit facilities forwarded in terms of capital and technology. Like for instance in case of electronics goods and garments industry.

Consumers have more chances of goods and services as compared to earlier times especially in modern digital technological equipments like cell phones, cameras, etc.

30. The anthropogenic factors responsible for land degradation in India are

(i) Deforestation due to mining activities in Jharkhand, Chhattisgarh, Madhya Pradesh and Odisha have caused severe land degradation. Mining sites are abandoned after excavation work is completed, leaving deep scars.

(ii) Mineral processing like grinding of limestone for cement industry as well as calcite and soapstone for ceramic industry generate huge quantities of dust which falls down on land. This retards the process of infiltration of water into the soil.

(iii) Effluents as waste from industries have become a major source of land and water pollution in many parts of the country.

(iv) Over irrigation in Punjab, Haryana and Western Uttar Pradesh is responsible for land degradation due to waterlogging, leading to increase in salinity.

OR

Gandhiji said, "There is enough for everybody's need and not for anybody's greed." He blamed the greedy and selfish individuals and exploitative nature of modern technology as the root cause for resource depletion at the global level.

Irrational consumption and overutilisation of resources has led to the socio-economic and environmental problems of shortages and pollution.

As resources are vital for any developmental activity, resource conservation at various levels is important to overcome these problems. If resources are used up at the same rate as they are generated or formed, they will be maintained for use by future generations.

31. When power is taken from Central and State Governments and given to local governments, it is called decentralisation.

The advantages of decentralisation are

(i) The basic idea behind decentralisation is that there are a large number of problems and issues which are best settled at the local level. People have better knowledge of the problems of their own locality. They have better idea on where to spend money and how to manage things efficiently.

(ii) Decentralisation makes it possible for the people to directly participate in decision making. This helps the people to develop a habit to participate in democratic activities. Thus local government is the best way to realise the significance of local self-government in democracy.

(iii) Decentralisation reduces the burden of Central and State Governments. It helps to concentrate on matters of national of state importance in a better way.

(iv) Decentralisation leads to women empowerment as it provides that at least one-third of all positions are reserved for women in all the local bodies.

OR

The policies adopted by Indian Government have ensured the success of federalism in India.

Policies adopted by India to ensure this success are

(i) Centre-State Relations Federalism has been strengthened by restructuring of centre-state relations.

(i) Decentralisation In India, power has been decentralised to the local government. The local government includes panchayats and municipalities.

(ii) Linguistic States The policy of creating linguistic states has also strengthened federalism. Despite the division, this policy united the nation.

(iv) Language Policy Indian federation did not give status of national language to any language. This ultimately has strengthened federalism.

32. China was one of the countries where the earliest kind of print technology was developed.

The different stages of development of printing technology in China are

(i) (From AD 594 onwards, books in China were printed by rubbing paper against the inked surface of woodblocks. These papers were also invented in China. The imperial state of China was the major producer of printed material for a very long time. At that time, China possessed a huge bureaucratic system which recruited its personnel through civil service examination. From the 16th century, number of candidates for the examination the increased, so the number of books also increased.

(ii) By the 17th century, urban culture developed in China and merchants, rich women, wives of scholar-officials not only started reading different books like, fictions, poetry, autobiographies, anthologies of literary masterpieces, romantic plays, they also began to write.

(iii) In the late 19th century, Shanghai became the hub of the new print culture by importing Western printing techniques and mechanical presses. From hand printing, there was a gradual shift to mechanical printing in China.

OR

The Gutenberg Press It was the first printing press of Europe. It was invented by Johann Gutenberg of Strasbourg. He grew up in a large agricultural estate and had knowledge and experience in operating olive and wine presses. The olive press provided him the model for the printing press and he used moulds for casting metal types for letters of the alphabet. He invented the printing press around the year 1448.

Erasmus's Idea of the Printed Book Erasmus was a Latin scholar. He was not happy with the printing of books because he was afraid that this would lead to circulation of books with rebellious ideas. According to him only a few books were useful to read and may give useful information and the majority of books were just useless, controversial or may have irreligious ideas which may lead to provoking rebellion. According to him such books devalue the valuable books.

33. Rapid improvement in technology has been playing a key role in encouraging the globalisation process in the following ways

Improvements in transportation technology, e.g. container manufacturing and air transport has made faster delivery of goods across long distances at lower costs.

There have been rapid developments in information technology, c.g. computer, internet, etc. They have made easy access to information around the world thus stimulating globalisation.

Rapid development in means of communication are used to contact one another which have established trade links around the world.

Thus, it can be said that technology has stimulated the globalisation process.

OR

When local companies enter into a joint venture with MNCs:

First, the MNCs provide money for additional investments for faster production. Second, MNCs bring with them the latest technology for enhancing and improving the production.

Some Indian companies have gained from successful collaborations with foreign companies. Globalization has enabled some companies to emerge as multinationals.

Parakh Foods was a small company which was bought over by a large American Company – Cargill Foods. Parakh foods had built a large marketing network in various parts of India as a well- reputed brand. Parakh Foods had four oil refineries whose control has now shifted to Cargill. Cargill is now the largest manufacturer of edible oil in India making five million pouches daily.

34.(1) Decentralization is the transfer of authority, responsibility, and accountability from central to local. governments. Decentralization can take various forms, commonly described in public. administration terms as deconcentration, devolution, and delegation.

34.(2) In 1993, a constitutional amendment was passed in India that called for a random one third of village council leader, or sarpanch, positions in gram panchayat, to be reserved for women.

34.(3) Two advantages of having a Local Self-Government are:

• It gives an opportunity to provide foundations on which the entire democratic structure of our country can stand. It helps in making it possible for people to take interests in governing their own affairs and also to groom them well to take on larger responsibilities.

• Local Self- Governments provide training grounds for local leadership to manage national or state affairs. This training helps in gaining experience to deal with bigger challenges later on. Many of the peoples' political careers as member of local bodies have helped them to gain experience for the national level.

35.(1) NTPC refers to National Thermal Power Corporation. It is a major power providing corporation in India.

35.(2) NTPC has a proactive approach for preserving the natural environment and resources like water, oil and gas and fuels in places where it is setting up power plants.

35.(3) The ways adopted by the NTPC towards the preservation of natural environment include

• Optimum utilization of equipment by adopting latest techniques and upgrading existing equipment.

• Minimising waste generation by maximising ash utilisation.

36.(1) Italians were scattered over several dynastic states as well as the multi-national Habsburg Empire. During the middle of the nineteenth century, Italy was divided into seven states, of which only one, Sardinia-Piedmont, was ruled by an Italian princely house. The north was under Austrian Habsburgs, the centre was ruled by the Pope and the southern regions were under the domination of the Bourbon kings of Spain.

36.(2) Young Italy was an Italian Nationalist Movement for the youth of Italy (citizens under 40 years of age). It was founded by Giuseppe Mazzini in the year 1831

36.(3) Count Camillo de Cavour was Chief Minister of Sardinia-Piedmont state who led the movement to unify the regions of Italy. He was neither a revolutionary nor a democrat. Like many other wealthy and educated members of the Italian elite, he spoke French much better than he did Italian. He engineered a careful diplomatic alliance with France, which helped Sardinia-Piedmont defeat the Austrian forces in 1859, and thereby free the northern part of Italy from the Austrian Habsburgs.

37.(a)   A.   Madras
          B.   Dandi

(b)

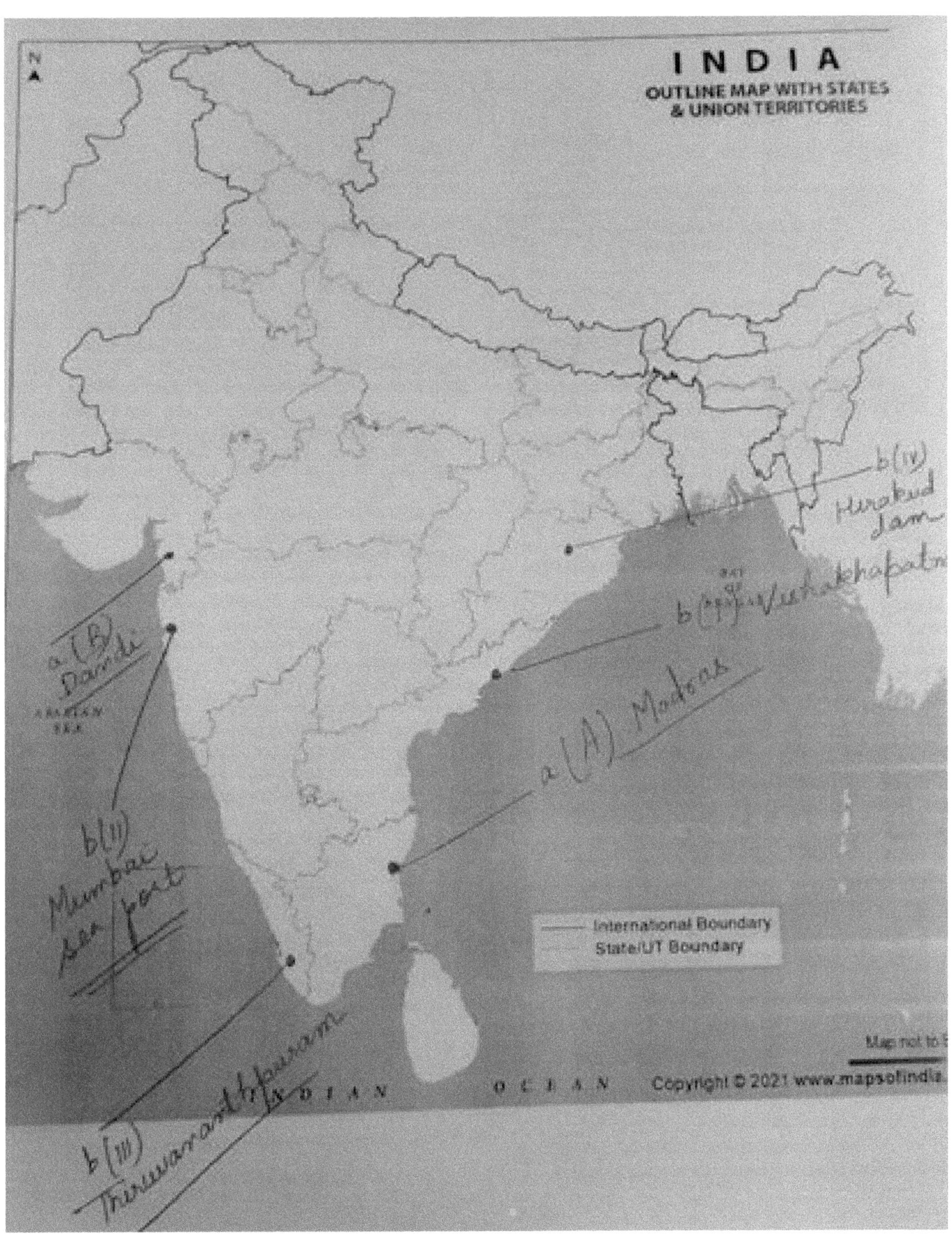

SAMPLE PAPER-4

1. (b) During early 18th and 19th century's women and non-propertied men organised opposition movements, demanding equal political rights. In France, the right to vote and to get elected was granted exclusively to persons who owned property. Men without properties and women were excluded from this right.

2. (b) The non-cooperation Khilafat movement began in January 1921. Various social groups participated in this movement, each with its own specific aspiration. All of them responded to the call of Swaraj, but the term meant different things to different people.

3. (c) Statements 1 and 3 are correct about the French Revolution.
Statements 2 and 4 are incorrect because The revolution proclaimed that it was the people who would henceforth constitute the nation and shape its destiny and monarchy should be abolished.
Internal customs duties and dues were abolished and a uniform system of weights and measures was adopted.

4. (a) Peasant Uprising is depicted in the image.Peasant Uprising first great popular rebellion in English history. Its immediate cause was the imposition of the unpopular poll tax of 1380, which brought to a head the economic discontent that had been growing since the middle of the century

5. (b) Events arranged in a chronological order-
Mahatma Gandhi returned to India from South Africa in 1915.
Distressed Uttar Pradesh peasants organised by Baba Ramchandra in 1918-19. Khilafat Committee was formed in Bombay in 1919.
The Chauri Chaura incident occurred at Chauri Chaura in the Gorakhpur district of the United Province, (modern Uttar Pradesh) in British India on 4 February 1922

6. (b) The crop described here is Sugarcane. It is a tropical as well as a subtropical crop. It grows well in hot and humid climate with a temperature of 21°C to 27°C and an annual rainfall between 75cm.

7. (b) Aus refers to the July- August season. Aman refers to the December- January seasons. Boro refers march-May seasons, these are the varieties of rice. Rice is a stable food for many countries around the world. Rice is the third highest worldwide production after maize and sugarcane.

8. (a) Ferrous minerals are those minerals that contain iron. Some examples of ferrous minerals include iron ore, manganese, nickel and chromite

Minerals that do not contain iron content are called non-ferrous minerals. These include copper, bauxite, lead, zinc and gold
Non-metallic minerals are those minerals that do not contain metal elements. Potash, Clay, Diamond, Dolomite, Gypsum, Mica, Amethyst, Quartz, etc. are some common examples.
Energy minerals are those minerals which are used for producing power, heat and energy It include coal, oil, natural gas and uranium.

9. (c) Method of trapping solid waste from waste water is known as screening. Screening is a wastewater pre-treatment, which aims to prevent coarse solids, such as plastics, rags and other trash, from entering a sewage system or treatment plant

10. (b) Option b is incorrect as The term unemployment refers to a situation where a person actively searches for employment but is unable to find work. Unemployment indicates the health of the economy. The unemployment rate is the most frequent measure of unemployment.

11. (b) For 70 many years will the reserves of crude oil last in Middle East, if they continue extracting it at the present rate.

12. (c) If there was no equitable distribution, resources will not be evenly spread among people and inequalities will increase leading to unrest and chaos. Hence, an equitable distribution of resources has become essential for a sustained quality of life and global peace. Hence, Assertion is true, but statement R is false.

13. (b) In 2013, primary sector = 13.94%, secondary sector = 18.70%, tertiary sector = 67.36%. So share of the secondary sector in the total GDP of 2013 is 18.7%

14. (c) Different persons can have different developmental goals and what may be development for one may not be development for the other person. It may even be destructive for the other.

15. (c) Information and Communication Technology Rise rapidly. Online retailing, cloud computing and e-commerce are all contributing to the speedy growth of the IT industry. The rate of growth in the IT sector for 2019-20 is approximately ten percent. The Indian IT industry has grown rapidly with an exponential growth rate after the economic reform of 1991-92.

17. (c) The Gram Sabha elects the members of the Gram Panchayat.The Pradhan and members of the Gram Panchayat shall be elected by direct election under secret ballot by the members of the Gram Sabha from amongst themselves in such manner as may be prescribed.

18. (b) The main reason responsible for the killing of thousands of people in Sri Lanka is the civil war between Sinhala and Tamil speaking population. It also caused great impact to the social, cultural and economic life of the country.

19. (c) Here the assertion is true but the reason is false. In India, there is a union government at the centre and the state governments at the state level. In this form of government, the central government has all the powers and there is no role of the state governments.

20. (b) Option b is correct regarding features of 'Holding Together Federation'. Holding together federation' is a federation in which the powers of the country are divided between the central government and constituent states. The central government has greater authority when compared to states.

21. Personal communication means a communication between two persons either through oral letter or through telephone etc while mass communication includes the use of radio television press films etc for wider public audience.

22. Two facts about the new economic situation created in India by the First World War are-

(i) It led to a huge increase in defence expenditure which was financed by war loans and increasing taxes.

(ii) Through the war years prices increased-doubling between 1913 and 1918 - leading to extreme hardship for the common people.

23. GDP is the calculation of total production in a country/state within a time period, normally a year. It is the calculation of values of all final goods and services within a year.

24. Alternative political formation is one of the concepts that helps in explaining the dissatisfaction of the people or the community in which the requirements and the demands of the people are not fulfilled by the political parties.

Due to the dissatisfaction act, the people are forming their own laws and rules so that they can govern their group and they also raised the public voice in front of the government.

OR

Defection in politics means moving of a person from one party to another party for some personal benefit. It means changing party allegiance from the party on which a person got elected to a different party.

25. Three features of secularism are-

(i) There is no official religion for the Indian state. Unlike the status of Buddhism in Sri Lanka, that of Islam in Pakistan and that of Christianity in England, our Constitution does not give a special status to any religion.

(ii) The Constitution provides to all individuals and communities freedom to prefer, practice and propagate any religion or not to follow any.

(iii) The Constitution allows the state to intervene in the matters of religion in order to ensure equality within religious communities. For example it bans untouchability.

OR

Caste can take various forms in Indian politics. For example-

(i) When parties choose candidates in elections, they keep in mind the caste composition of the electorate and nominate candidates from the same castes so as to get necessary support to win elections. A candidate from a particular minority community became a candidate from the constituency which is mostly inhibited by that particular minority.

(ii) During the campaigning, political parties and candidates make appeals to people to give their votes on the basis of caste. Some political parties are known to favour some castes and are seen as their representatives.

(iii) When governments are formed, political parties take care that representatives of different castes and tribes should get a place in the ministry.

26. Print culture came to India with the coming of Portuguese missionaries. Konkani was the first Indian language in which books were printed. The first Tamil book printed was printed in 1579 and Malayalam book in 1713. English printing in India commenced with the publication of Bengal Gazette in 1780.

The consequences of the expansion of print culture on poor people in 19th century in Indian Subcontinent were as follows

(i) The literacy rate improved in India. Printed material, especially for entertainment, began to reach even the poor in the 19th century. Publishers started producing small and cheap books for the poor. These books were sold at crossroads. Public libraries were setup by Christian missionaries and rich people.

(ii) Enlightening essays were written against caste discrimination and its inherent injustices. These were read by people across the country.

(iii) On the encouragement and support of social reformers, overworked factory workers set up libraries for self-education. Some of them even published their own works, like Kashibaba published Chhote Aur Bade Ka Sawal.

27. Due to following reasons the demand deposits are considered as money

(i) Demand deposits can be withdrawn from the bank whenever it is required.

(ii) Demand deposits widely accepted as a means of payment, along with the currency, thus they are considered as money.

(iii) Demand deposits are also accepted widely as means of payment by way of a cheque instead of cash.

28. Those deposits in the bank accounts that can be withdrawn on demand, are called demand deposits.

Some important features of demand deposits are

(i) Demand deposits are accepted widely as a means of payment by way of a cheque along with currency.

(ii) Demand deposits are closely linked to the working of the modern banking system. Such deposits earn Loan amount as interest.

29. It is the need of the hour to conserve and manage our water resources. This can be understood through the following points

- To meet the water demand effectively.
- To safeguard people from health hazards caused by drinking toxic water.
- To ensure food security.
- To ensure continuation of our livelihoods and productive activities.
- To prevent degradation of our natural ecosystems.
- To reduce over exploitation and mismanagement of water resources..
- Irrigated agriculture is the largest consumer of water.

So, there is a need to revolutionise agriculture through developing drought-resistant crops and dry farming techniques.

30. The role of technology in transforming the world in the 19th century is :

Transformation of World Economy Technology played an important role in transforming and developing railways, steam ships, telegraph, etc. Through these inventions, it was not possible to imagine the transformation of the 19th century world.

Inter-linking the Markets The new investments in transportation system in the form of faster railways and larger ships helped to move food more cheaply and quickly from far away farms to markets. This by 1890, a global agricultural economy had taken shape, accompanied by complex changes in labour movement patterns, capital flows, ecologies and technology.

Impact on Meat-trade Till the 1870s, animals were shipped live from America to Europe and then slaughtered when they arrived there. But live animals took up a lot of ship space, many also died in voyage, fell.ill, lost weight, or became unfit to eat. Meat was hence an expensive luxury beyond the reach of the European poor. High prices in turn kept demand and production down until the development of a new technology,.namely, refrigerated ships, which enabled the transport of perishable foods over long distances.

Social Peace and Imperialism The refrigerated ships reduced shipping costs and lowered meat prices in Europe. The poor people in Europe could now afford and consume a varied diet. Better living conditions promoted social peace and support for imperialism abroad.

OR

The Great Depression immediately affected Indian trade. India's exports and imports nearly halved between 1928 and 1934. As international prices crashed, prices in India also plunged. Between 1928 and 1934, wheat prices in India fell by 50 per cent. Peasants and farmers suffered more than urban dwellers. Though agricultural prices fell sharply, the colonial government refused to reduce revenue demands. Peasants producing for the world market were the worst hit. The depression proved less grim for urban India. Because of falling prices, those with fixed incomes such as urban landowners who received rents and middle-class salaried employees, now found themselves better off as everything cost less. Industrial investment also grew as the government extended tariff protection to industries.

31. Banks play an important role in the economy of India in the following ways

(i) Provide Deposits Bank accept the deposits and also pay an amount as interest on the deposits. In this way, people's money is safe with the banks and it earns an amount as interest. People also have the provision to withdraw the money as when they require it. Since the deposits in the bank account can be withdrawn on demand, So these deposits are called demand deposits.

(ii) Provide Loans Banks keep only a small portion of their deposits as cash with themselves. Banks use the major position of the deposits to give loans. There is a huge demand for loans for various economic activities. Banks make use of the deposits to meet the loan requirements of the people.

(iii) In this way, banks provide credit to set up od industries and in agriculture. This generates more O employment and raises income thereby bringing economic development.

OR

The Reserve Bank of India (RBI) supervises all formal sources of credit or loan approvals or disbursements in India. This is the Central Bank of India.

(i) Commercial Banks are also required to hold part of their cash with the Reserve Bank of India maintaining a minimum type of cash out deposits and banks also have to submit the lending information details to the Reserve Bank of India to ensure the bank gives loans to everyone in need.

(ii) Reserve Bank of India sees that the banks give loans not just to profit making business and traders but also to small cultivators, small-scale industries to small borrowers, etc. (iii) Banks have to submit the lending information details to the Reserve Bank of India to ensure that the bank give loans to all kinds of customer

32. Waterways are the cheapest means of transport. It is fuel-efficient, environment-friendly and suitable for carrying heavy and bulky goods. India has inland navigation waterways of about 14,500 km in length out of which 5,685 km are navigable by mechanised boats. The waterways declared as the National Waterways are .

NW-1 Allahabad to Haldia (1,620 km) on the Ganga river system. NW-2 Sadiya to Dhubri (891 km) on the Brahmaputra river.

NW-3 West-Coast canal in Kerala (205 km), (Kottapuram-Komman, Udyogamandal and Champakkara canals).

NW-4 Parts of Krishna and Godavari rivers along with Kakinada-Puducherry stretch of canals (1,078 km).

NW-5 Parts of Brahmani river along withMatai river, delta channels of Mahanadi and Brahmani rivers and East coast canal (588 km). There are some other inland waterways on which substantial transportation takes place. These are Mandavi, Zuari and Cumberjua, Sunderbans, Barak and backwaters of Kerala.

OR

The following are the major ports lying on the Western coast along the side of the Arabian Sea

(i) Kandla It is located in the Gulf of Kutch. It was the first port which was developed soon after independence when the Karachi port went to Pakistan due to partition. It was developed to facilitate the volume of trade on the Mumbai port. It is also known as the Deendayal port. It is a tidal port. It handles exports and imports of highly productive granary and industrial belt stretching across the states of Jammu and Kashmir, Himachal Pradesh, Punjab, Haryana, Rajasthan and Gujarat.

(ii) Mumbai It is the biggest port in India with a natural harbour. Jawahar Lal Nehru port developed nearby to ease off the decongestant in Mumbai port.

(iii) Marmagao (Goa) It is the premier iron ore exporting port in India. This port accounts for about 50% of India's iron ore export.

(iv) New Mangalore It is located in Karnataka. It caters to export of iron-ore from Kudremukh mines.

(v) Kochchi It is the extreme South-Western port located at the entrance of a lagoon with a natural harbour.

33. The major differences between the Belgium and Sri Lankar democracies were as follows

Policy Belgium adopted the policy of accommodation of social and ethnics divisions. On the other hand, Sri Lanka also adopted democratic system but followed majoritarian policies

Power Sharing Under the Belgium model of democracy, power was shared among two ethnic groups. Sri Lanka favoured the interests of the majority Sinhala community. Treatment of Communities In Belgium, both the communities had equal share in working of government but in Sri Lanka the minority community was isolated. To maintain political stability and unity, equal representation was provided to both the groups. Apart from that, community governments of both the ethnic groups also existed at the local level. Sri Lanka, however, had no such arrangement.

Constitutional Provision The Constitution of Belgium was amended four times before arriving at a final draft to prevent civil strife. In Sri Lanka, majoritarianism led to Civil War for long twenty years.

OR

The ways by which Belgium has accommodated the existing regional differences and cultural.diversities are as follows-

The Government of Belgium has equal number of Dutch-speaking and French-speaking ministers. This has been done to give equal power to the majority and the minority language speaking groups. Community Government

A third kind of government, named the Community government, was introduced in addition to the Central and the State Governments. This government has powers to decide cultural, educational and linguistic issues.

This government comprises members from all the three communities ie. Dutch-speaking, French-speaking and German-speaking.

Many powers of the Central Goverment in Belgium were given to the State governments of the two regions of the country. The State governments were not subordinate to the Central Government, but were made independent of it..Equal Representation In the State Government of Brussels, the capital city, both the French-speaking and Dutch-speaking communities have equal representation

34.1 The IMF was set up to promote International Monetary Cooperation.

34.2 The Bretton Woods System was based on fixed exchange rates. In this system, national currencies viz. the Indian rupees were pegged to the dollar at a fixed exchange rate. The dollar itself was anchored to gold at a fixed price of $35 per ounce of gold.

34.3 In Bretton Woods Conference New Hampshire USA, decisions were taken for establishing the World Bank and International Monetary Fund (IMF) to preserve Global economic stability and full employment in the industrial world.These institutions would also deal with surplus and deficit of member nations and finance post war reconstruction.

35.1 Defection is changing party allegiance (a person's continued support for a political party) from the party on which a person got elected to a legislative body to a different party.

35.2 Due to the Supreme's Court order candidate has to give the details of his property and criminal case report through an Affidavit. It helps the public to decide the suitable candidate to elect.

35.3 Many suggestions are made to reform political parties. Among these one of the most important reforms is to give at least one-third number of tickets to women candidate. This helps women to participate in direct politics and they can raise their voice for their own demands.

36.1 Planning involves identification and quantification of resources. By knowing their exact quantity, ways can be developed to use them properly.

36.2 The states of Jharkhand, Chhattisgarh and Madhya Pradesh are rich in minerals and coal deposits. Arunachal Pradesh has an abundance of water resources. This shows that India has resource availability.

36.3 Planning is necessary in India due to two reasons.

(a) There are regions which are rich in certain types of resources, but are deficient in some other resources.

(b) There are some regions that can be considered self-sufficient in terms of the availability of resources, and there are some regions which have acute shortage of some vital resources.

37.(a)

   A.   Chauri Chaura

   B.   Ahemdabad

(b)

SAMPLE PAPER-5

1. **(a)** Option A is incorrect as Mahatma Gandhi returned to India from South Africa in 1915.

2. **(c)** The Unification of Britain was achieved through political and social subjugation of various ethnicities by the English. English suppressed the Irish and Scottish ethnic iden tities through its political, social and territorial supremacy and forced them in a Union.

3. **(a)** Among the following pairs, Pair A is incorrectly matched. The Greek Struggle for Independence begins in February 1821 when Alexander Ypsilantis, leader of the Etairists, crossed the Prut River into Turkish-held Moldavia with a small force of troops

4. **(d)** At the end of the eighteenth century, Poland was partitioned between the great powers of Prussia, Russia and Austria. As a result of this partition, Poland did not remain an independent territory.

5. **(d)** Pair D is incorrect as The world's first underground railway opened in London in 1863. It was launched for reducing street congestion.

6. **(b)** The crop described here is coffee. Indian coffee is known in the world for its good quality. The Arabica variety initially brought from Yemen is produced in the country. This variety is in great demand all over the world. Initially its cultivation was introduced on the Baba Budan Hills and even today its cultivation is confined to the Nilgiri in Karnataka, Kerala and Tamil Nadu

7. **(b) Community Resources -** The resources which are accessible to all the members of the community are known as community resources. Village ponds, public parks, playgrounds, etc. are some examples of community resources.
Renewable resources are those resources that can be replenished or renewed naturally over time. Air, water, wind, solar energy etc are all renewable resources. Renewable resources can be easily renewed by nature
Non renewable resources are those which cannot be immediately replaced once they are depleted. Examples of Non-renewable resources include fossil fuels, such as coal, petroleum and natural gas and rare minerals typically found in meteorites
International Resources are resources that are governed by international organisations. For example, the open sea or ocean refers to the ocean and water beyond 200 miles of the Exclusive Economic Zone. Without the consent of international authorities, no country may use these resources.

8. **(a)** Pulses are the important source of protein and minerals that are also known as poor man's meat. Pulses need less soil moisture and can survive in dry conditions. All the pulses except arhar have the ability to fix nitrogen and restore the soil fertility. They are grown in crop rotation so that the soil gets its nutrient back. Hence, both 'A' and 'R' are correct and R is the correct explanation of A.

9. **(b)** Groundwater overuse is particularly found in the agriculturally prosperous regions of Punjab and Western U.P

10. **(c)** The crop described here is Bajra. Bajra grows very well in dry and warm climatic regions, and it is a drought – tolerant crop with quite low annual rainfall of 40 cm to 60 cm. The ideal temperature range for Bajra cultivation is 20°C to 30°C. During its vegetative growth, moist weather is beneficial.

11. **(c)** Power-sharing among organs of government (legislature, executive, judiciary) is called a system of checks and balances. According to the Constitution, there are three organs of the State. These are the legislature, the executive and the judiciary. The legislature refers to our elected representatives. The executive is a smaller group of people who are responsible for implementing laws and running the government. The judiciary refers to the system of courts in this country. In order to prevent the misuse of power by any one branch of the State, the Constitution says that each of these organs should exercise different powers. Through this, each organ acts as a check on the other organs of the State and this ensures the balance of power between all three.

12. **(b)** Here, the assertion and reason is correct, but the reason is not the correct explanation of the assertion. Power may be shared among different social groups such as the religious and linguistic groups. 'Community government' in Belgium is a good example of this arrangement. This power is shared among different social groups to give equal representation to each and every community of Belgium. It is made to protect every ethinc community of Belgium.

13. **(b)** Policy of accommodation could be the measure the Belgian government will adopt in such a situation. Belgium is a model for accommodative politics in Europe. The constitution allows for equal representation of Dutch and French-speaking ministers in the central government.
Brussels has a separate government where both the French and the Dutch have equal representation.

14. **(a)** Belgium's 59 % population lives in the Flemish Region and speaks Dutch language. They form a majority community in Belgium.

15. **(d)** Option d is incorrect regarding a unitary government. Under the unitary system, either there is only one level of government or the sub-units are subordinate to the central government. The central government can pass on orders to the provincial or the local government and state government is conservable to the central government

16. **(d)** Infant Mortality Rate can be substantially reduced only by improvements in the life and health of the majority. This is due to the fact that almost all the health and non-health components of a communit contribute to the morbidity and mortality of its children to a certain extent.

17. **(a)** Primary sector is the most important sector in terms of share of the total production in the initial stages of development of developed countries. The primary sector is a base for most of the other products that we subsequently make. Since most of the natural products we get are from agriculture and related sectors, the development of this sector leads to the development of services such as transport, trade, storage and the like. The greater the development of the primary sector, more would be the demand for such services

18. **(b)** The sector discussed here is private sector. The private sector is the part of the economy that is run by individuals and companies for profit and is not state controlled. Therefore, it encompasses all for-profit businesses that are not owned or operated by the government.

19. **(b)** The value of final goods and services produced in each sector during a particular year provides the total production of that sector for that year and the sum of production in the three sectors.
    The value of the final goods and services produced in each sector during a particular year provides the total production of the sector for that year. Thus, GDP is the sum value of the final goods and services of the three sectors (Primary, Secondary and Tertiary) produced within a country during a particular year.

20. **(d)** All of these statements are hindrances in the development of the tertiary or service sector. The tertiary sector covers a wide range of activities from commerce to administration, transport, financial and real estate activities, business and personal services, education, health and social work. The major hindrances of this sector are- (i) Inadequate infrastructure. (ii) Lack of Financial services. (iii) Lack of consular divisions. (iv) Unfair competition in the telecom sector.

21. Gandhiji called off the Non-Cooperation Movement in 1922 because
    The movement became violent at Chauri-Chaura (Gorakhpur) when a peaceful demonstration in a bazaar turned into a violent clash in which more than 20 policemen were killed. Gandhiji felt that the Satyagrahis needed to be properly trained before they would be ready for mass struggle.

22. The world has been converted into a global village with the help of efficient and fast moving transport and communication facilities in the following ways
    (i) Daily flights to different countries and improved technology to develop fast means of transportation has connected the countries.
    (ii) Computer and internet facilities supported by satellite services have made the world a small village wherein the information can be reached at almost instantly.

23. Two broad guidelines for devising ways and means for political reforms in India are

(i) A law should be made to regulate the internal affairs of political parties. Political parties should maintain a register of its members, to hold open elections, to follow its own Constitution, etc.
(ii) Political parties can be monitored by ordinary citizens, pressure groups, media, etc. Pressure on political parties can be done through petitions, publicity and agitation.

OR

Parties form and run governments by-
Different political parties take part in elections. A party winning the maximum number of seats in the election is invited to form the government.
The big policy decisions are taken by political executives that come from political parties. Parties recruit leaders, train them and then make them ministers to run the government in the way they want.

24. In the tribal areas of north-east India, minerals are owned by individuals or communities. Thus, coal mining in Jowai and Cherapunjee is done by family members in the form of a long narrow tunnel, known as 'Rat-hole' mining.

25. Yes, means of transport, communication and trade are complementary to each other as mentioned below :
    Transport and communication provide the infrastructural basis for conducting trade. The growth in trade also leads to creation of more infrastructure to match the volume of trade because increase in the volume of trade may need more means of transport.
    More trade creates an avenue for investment in infrastructure through the revenue generated by trade.
    The growth in trade means more transport like roads, railways, air, water and pipelines to be developed to keep the wheels of economy moving.
    Communication helps in commercial transactions to be completed across different places all over the world. It helps to cross the geographical barriers and keeps the traders informed about their business instantly. The modern means of communication such as e-mail, mobile etc. are of great help for the traders all over the world. The world has become a village

26. The exact balance of power between the central and the state government and within various state governments varies from one federation to another. This balance depends mainly on the historical context in which the federation was formed. There are two kinds of routes through which federations have been formed.
    The first route involves independent states coming together on their own to form a bigger unit, so that by pooling sovereignty and. retaining identity they can increase their security. This type of coming together' federations include USA, Switzerland and Australia. In this first category of federations, all the constituent stales usually have equal power and are strong vis-a-vis the federal government.

OR

(i) **Union List -** It includes subjects of national importance like defence, foreign affairs, banking, communications and currency as we need uniform policies on these matters throughout the country. The Union Government alone can make laws relating to the subjects mentioned in the Union list.

(ii) **State List -** It contains subjects of state and local importance like police, trade, commerce, agriculture and irrigation. The State Government alone can make laws relating to the subjects mentioned in the State list.

27. Interest rate, collateral and documentation requirements, and the mode of repayment together comprise the terms of credit. The terms of credit vary substantially from one another. Every loan agreement specifies an interest which the borrower must pay me lender along with the repayment of the principal.

    In addition, lenders may demand collateral (i.e. security against loan). Collateral is an asset that the borrower own, such as land, building, vehicle, livestock, deposits with the bank and uses this as guarantee to a lender until the loan is refunded. If the borrower fails to repay the loan, the lender has the right to sell the asset or collateral to obtain repayment payment such as land titles, deposits with banks and livestock are some common examples of collateral used for borrowing.

28. The implications of First World War on the economic and political situation of India were Economic Situation

    It led to a huge increase in defence expenditure which was financed by war loans. It resulted in raising custom duties and the introduction of income tax.

    - Increased prices of essential commodities le to extreme hardship for the common people Political Situation

    Forced recruitment of villagers into armies caused widespread anger among them.

    There was an acute food shortage due to failure of crops and influenza epidemic which resulted in the death of millions of people.

29. Bahujan Samaj Party (BSP) was founded by Kanshi Ram in 1984.

    It seeks to represent Bahujan Samaj, which includes Scheduled Castes (SCs), Scheduled Tribes (STs), OBCs and religious minorities. It gets inspiration from the ideas and teachings of

    Sahu Maharaj, Mahatma Phule, Periyar Ramaswami Naicker and BR Ambedkar. It stands for the cause of securing the interests and welfare of the dalits and oppressed people. It has its main base in Uttar Pradesh and substantial presence in neighbouring states like Madhya Pradesh,

    Chhattisgarh, Uttarakhand, Delhi and Punjab. After Kanshi Ram, Mayawati became the leader and formed the government in Uttar Pradesh.

30. The three demands of Sri Lankan Tamils were
    (i) Recognition of Tamil as an official language
    (ii) Provision of regional autonomy
    (iii) Equality of opportunity in securing education and jobs

    Sri Lankan Tamils struggle for their demands in the following ways
    (i) They formed several political organisations to demand an independent Tamil Eelam (state) in Northern and Eastern parts of Sri Lanka.
    (ii) Sri Lankan Tamils launched their own political party LTTE (Liberation Tigers of Tamil Eelam) to fight for their rights.
    (iii) When the demands of LTTE were denied repeatedly then they took to violent means that started the Civil War.

    OR

    The reasons for the civil war in Sri Lanka are-
    (i) The democratically elected government in Sri Lanka adopted a series of majoritarian measures to establish Sinhala supremacy in Sri Lanka.
    (ii) The government followed preferential policies that favoured Sinhalese in respect of job, religion and many more.
    (iii) All the measures taken by the government gradually increased the feeling of alienation among the Sri Lankan Tamils. They felt deprived.

    The impact of these measures on the country were
    (i) People got divided on the basis of ethnic and linguistic communities along with a widespread conflict of violent nature.
    (ii) Thousands of Sri Lankan Tamils were killed or were forced to leave their country.
    (iii) The civil war gave a terrible setback to the social,. cultural and economic life of Sri Lanka that influenced even the Sinhala community.
    (iv) People of both the communities suffered heavy losses.

31. **Public Sectors**
    In the public sector, government owns most of the assets and provides all the services, therefore it is also called state sector or government sector, e.g. Indian Railways. Bharat Heavy Electricals Limited, etc.
    Private Sector
    In the private sector, ownership of assets and delivery of services is in the hands of individuals or private companies, eg. Reliance Industries Limited (RIL), TISCO, etc. Motive of private sector is to earn profits.
    Role of Public/Government Sector in an economy
    Developing infrastructure which is done by developing. communication, heavy industries, building bridges, roads and railways, dams, generating electricity.
    Encouraging the private sector to open industries and generate employment. Support farmers by buying food grains at a fair price and supports poor people by supplying food grains at low price in ration shops.

Provides health care facilities and education in backward and rural areas especially elementary education.

Dealing with problems of malnutrition, high infant mortality rate, unsafe drinking water, lack of housing, food and nutrition, etc.

OR

Organised Sector

It covers those enterprises or places of work where workers are given regular employment.

The enterprises are registered by the government and follow the rules and regulations such as Factories Act, Minimum Wages Act, Payment of Gratuity Act, Shop and Establishment Act, etc.

Workers have job security, work for a fixed number of hours paid better wage and benefits like provident fund, medical leaves, paid holiday, etc.

The management ensures good working conditions like clean drinking water and a safe working environment.

Unorganized Sector

This sector is characterised by small and scattered units which are unregistered and donot follow governmental rules and regulations. Workers get lower wages and are not given facilities like paid holidays or paid leave due to sickness, etc. Working conditions are poor and there is no job security so employment is irregular.

32. Alluvial soil can be described as follows

    (a) Formation - Alluvial soil is made-up of silt, sand and clay. It is deposited by three important Himalayan river systems: the Indus, the Ganga and the Brahmaputra. It is bigger and coarser in the upper reaches of the river and becomes finer as the river flows down.

    (b) Distribution/Area- This soil is prevalent in the river valleys of the Northern plains (Indus, Ganga, Brahmaputra), strips in Gujarat and Rajasthan, as well as in the Eastern coastal plains in the deltas of rivers of the Peninsular plateau (Mahanadi, Krishna, Kaveri).

    (c) Classification- According to their age, alluvial soils can be classified as (Bangar) old alluvial and Khadar (new alluvial). Khadar has higher concentration of kankar and contains more fine particles than Bangar.

    (d) Nutrients/Minerals - This soil is rich in nutrients like potash, phosphoric acid and lime, which is suitable for growing paddy, wheat, sugarcane and other cereal and pulse crops.

OR

Alluvial soil is the most widespread soil in India, which has been deposited by three important Himalayan river systems i.e. the Indus, the Ganges and the Brahmaputra.

Due to its high fertility, areas having this soil are intensively cultivated and densely populated.

Some features of alluvial soil are given below

It is mostly found in river valleys of the Northern Plains (Indus, Ganga, Brahmaputra), parts of Gujarat and Rajasthan, in Eastern coastal plains, especially in the deltas of Peninsular rivers (Mahanadi, Godavari, Krishna, Kaveri).

It is made up of silt, sand and clay. It is rich in nutrients like potash, phosphoric acid and lime.

It is suitable for growing paddy, wheat, sugarcane and other cereal and pulse crops. It is more common in the piedmont plains that are at the foothills such as Duars, Chos and Terai.

On the basis of age, it can be categorised as Bangar (old alluvial) and Khadar (new alluvial). Bangar soil is coarse but Khadar soil has fine particles and is more fertile. Bangar contains Kankar noodles.

Alluvial soil in the drier areas is more alkaline and needs fertilisers and good irrigation.

The particles of this soil are bigger towards the river valleys and this soil is coarse in the upper reaches of the valley.

33. The European employers found it difficult to recruit labour in Africa because historically Africa had abundant land and a relatively small population. For centuries, land and livestock sustained African livelihoods and people had no need to work for a wage.

In late 19th century Africa, there were few consumer goods, so there was little reason to work for a wage. Europeans were attracted to Africa due to its vast resources of land and mineral. They came to Africa hoping to establish plantations and mines to produce crops and minerals for export to Europe. But there was an acute problem of shortage of labour.

The Europeans then used some methods to recruit and retain labour. These were

    (i) Heavy taxes were imposed which could be paid only by working for wages on plantations and mines.

    (ii) Inheritance laws were changed so that peasants were displaced from lands. Only one member of a family was allowed to inherit land, as a result of which the others were pushed into labour markets.

    (iii) Mine workers were confined to compounds and not allowed to move freely.

    (iv) Cattle disease rinderpest was introduced to destroy their dependence on livestock for sustenance.

OR

In the 19th century, a large number of Indian labourers went to work on plantations, in mines and in road and railway construction projects around the world. The following factors were responsible for indentured labour migration from India

    (i) In India, indentured labourers were hired under contracts. They promised with return travel to India. The agents provide them false information about the nature of work, living and working conditions. Hoping for a better future, the workers migrated in other countries.

(ii) Most Indian indentured workers came from the present-day regions of Uttar Pradesh, Bihar, Central India and the dry districts of Tamil Nadu. In these regions, cottage industries declined, land rents rose, lands were cleared for mines and plantations. All these factors forced the poor to migrate in search of work.

(iii) Many indentured labourers agreed to take up work hoping to escape poverty or oppression in their home villages. Labourers were largely required in other countries and the scope of employment forced the workers to migrate.

34.(1) The proto-industrial system was a network of early form of commercial exchange before industrialisation. It was controlled by the merchants.

34.(2) The early phase of industrialisation in which large-scale production was carried out for the international market not at factories but in decentralised units is called proto-industrialisation. It is called proto-industries because products are made by hand only. In this period, handmade products symbolises refinement and class. In proto-industrialisation, products were better finished, individually produced and carefully designed.

34.(3) Proto-industrialisation refers to the earliest phase of industrialisation.

The following were the main features of proto-industrialisation.

(i) The production was done by hand.

(ii) It was controlled by merchants or guilds who had monopoly rights to produce and trade goods.

(iii) Generally family members were involved in the production process. Production was carried out in the countryside.

35.(1) Neyveli reserves in Tamil Nadu are important lignite reserves in India.

35.(2) Bituminous coal is a high grade coal and thus, a metallurgical coal. This type of coal has a special value for smelting iron in blast furnaces Important Property of Bituminous Coal. Bituminous coal is buried deep under the earth surface and is subjected to increased temperature It makes it unique to use in smelting iron-ore in blast furnaces.

35.(3) Coal is associated with geological ages because coal is formed due to compression of plant material and takes million of years to come into existence. In India, coal occurs in rock series of two main geological ages, namely Gondwana rock series which is a little over 200 million year in age and in tertiary deposits rock series which are only about 55 million years old. Distribution of Coal Gondwana coal deposits are found in Damodar valley (West Bengal, Jharkhand), Jharia, Raniganj, Bokaro, coalfields. The Godavari, Mahanadi, Son and Wardha valleys also contain coal deposits. Tertiary coal deposits are found in the North-Eastern states of Meghalaya, Assam, Arunachal Pradesh and Nagaland.

36.(1) The bifurcation into public and private sector is based on who owns the assets and is responsible for delivery of services.

36.(2) Railways and post office are counted in public sector due to following reasons- Railways is owned by the government and not by any private individual, Government is responsible for the delivery of various services through Post Offices.

36.(3) Public Sector is needed in India due to

- Public Sector spends in different activities that are needed by the society which private sector cannot provide.

- Private sector will not provide services at reasonable prices, so the public sector is needed.

37.(a).   A.   Chauri Chaura
B.   Kolkata

(b)

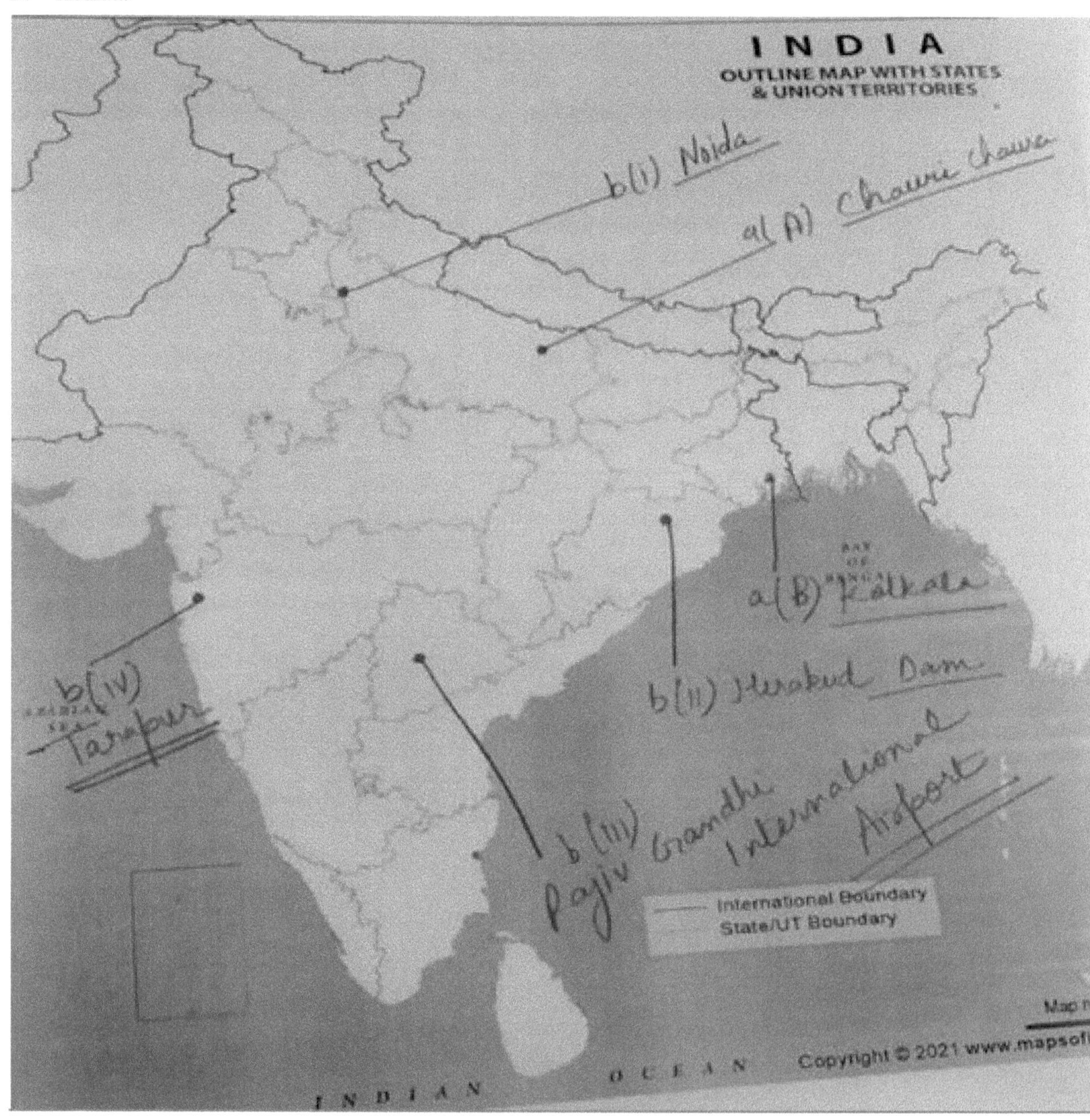

SAMPLE PAPER-6

1. **(c)** Louis Philippe was forced to flee in the year 1848. As economic conditions worsened in France, Philippe was forced to give up his crown after the outbreak of the French Revolution of 1848. Food shortages and widespread unemployment brought the population of Paris out on the roads. Barricades were erected and Louis Philippe was forced to flee.

2. **(a)** During the movement in town, the council elections were boycotted except at Madras, because Brahmans felt that entering the council will gain some power.

3. **(b)** Statement b is incorrect because The Bretton Woods conference was established in 1944.

4. **(b)** The following caricature is of Otto von Bismarck in the German reichstag (Parliament). from Figaro, Vienna, March 5, 1870. Otto von Bismarck was a Prussian politician who became Germany's first-ever chancellor, a position in which he served from 1871 to 1890. Through a series of wars, he unified 39 individual states into one German nation in 1871.

5. **(b)** The following events arranged in a chronological order is as follows-
Vienna Peace Settlement - 1815
Greece gained independence - 1821
Unification of Italy - 1859
Unification of Germany - 1871

6. **(b)** The soil described here is Laterite soil. Laterite soil develops in areas with high temperature and heavy rainfall. Humus content of the soil is low because most of the micro organisms, particularly the decomposer like bacteria, get destroyed due to high temperature. Laterite soils are suitable for cultivation with adequate doses of manures and fertilizers.

7. **(d)** Tree is a renewable resource but it is excessively used. Trees are also very important for us as a renewable resource. Trees are a natural resource that can be renewed by the planting of trees. The trees are excessively harvested. The loss of trees and other vegetation can cause climate change, desertification, soil erosion, fewer crops, flooding, increased greenhouse gases in the atmosphere, and a host of problems for indigenous people.

8. **(b)** Pair b is incorrectly matched. Cotton is not grown in Jammu and Kashmir and Himachal Pradesh of India. In India, cotton is grown in 9 major cotton growing States which is Punjab, Haryana and Rajasthan in the Northern zone, Gujarat, Maharashtra and MP in the Central zone and Andhra Pradesh, Karnataka and Tamil Nadu in the Southern zone.

9. **(d)** Floodgate dams are built across inlets. During high tide water flows into the inlet and gets trapped when the gate is closed. After the tide falls outside the flood gate, the water retained by the floodgate flows back to the sea via a pipe that carries it through a power-generating turbine.

10. **(a)** Consumer industries that produce goods for direct use by consumers – sugar, toothpaste, paper, sewing machines, fans etc.
Private sector industries owned and operated by individuals or a group of individuals
–TISCO, Bajaj Auto Ltd., Dabur Industries.
Basic industries are those that provide raw materials to other industries to manufacture goods. Further, these industries execute the discovery, development, and processing of raw materials. Examples of basic industries are copper smelting, iron and steel, metallurgical, wood, paper, milling, and chemicals.
Cooperative sector industries are owned and operated by the producers or suppliers of raw materials, workers or both. They pool the resources and share the profits or losses proportionately such as the sewing machine industry and the coir industry

11. **(c)** Option A is true as It is often said that political parties are facing a crisis because they are very unpopular and the citizens are indifferent to political parties. Political parties are one of the least trusted institutions all over the world.
Option B is also true because most political leaders are corrupt. They are involved in scams which tend to make the people feel that politics does not have good leaders.

12. **(c)** A major step towards decentralization was taken in 1992. The Constitution was amended to make the third-tier of democracy more powerful and effective. The provisions of Constitutional Amendment are as follows: To hold regular elections under the local government bodies has been made compulsory.

13. **(a)** The Community Government in Belgium is elected by one language community. In Belgium, the community government is elected by people belonging to a particular language-speaking community, no matter where they live. The community Government has the power related to educational, cultural and linguistic issues of the people of their people.

14. **(b)** Option b is the correct reason from the given options. Rajasthan Government could not prevent the Government of India from conducting the nuclear tests because "Defence" is the subject of Union List and nuclear tests are the part of the Defence.

15. **(c)** Dravida Munnetra Kazhagam (DMK) is a regional party. A "regional party" is any political party with its base in a single region, whatever its objectives and platform may be, whereas "regionalist" parties are a subset of regional parties that specifically campaign for greater autonomy or independence in their region.

16. **(b)** The Communist Party of India was formed on 26 December 1925 at the first Party Conference in Kanpur, which was then known as Cawnpore. S.V. Ghate was the first General Secretary of CPI.

17. **(c)** Here the assertion is true but the reason is incorrect. GDP measures the monetary value of final goods and services–that is, those that are bought by the final user—produced in a country in a given period of time (say a quarter or a year). It counts all of the output generated within the borders of a country.

18. **(b)** Percentage of x = x/Total × 100
27 / 357 × 00
7.6%

19. **(b)** 165 cm into meter = 1.65 m
1.65 × 1.65 = 2.725
98 / 2.725
= 36
Ram has BMI of 36.

20. **(b)** More Money, More Profit and More Employees. would be an ideal goal for a multinational company. An MNC is a company that owns or controls production in more than one nation. MNCs set up offices and factories for production in regions where they can get cheap labour and other resources.

21. A cheque is a document you can issue to your bank, directing it to pay the specified sum mentioned in digits as well as words to the person whose name is borne on the cheque.
Cheques are also called negotiable instruments.

22. According to Anti Defection law, MLAs or MPs cannot change the party after the election. If any MLA or MP changes parties, he or she will lose the seat in the Legislature. This was done because many elected representatives were involved in defection' in order to become ministers or for cash rewards.

23. Major challenges faced by the Sugar Industry in India include the seasonal nature of the industry, old and inefficient methods of production, transport delay in reaching cane to factories and the need to maximise the use of by-products like bagasse. The raw material is bulky making its transportation difficult and the sucrose content keeps on decreasing with time.

OR

An industry owned jointly by the state and individual or group of individuals is a joint sector venture. Labour intensive industry refers to those industries that employ a large number of workers directly or indirectly.

24. Literacy rate improved due to the spread of print culture in India because printed material began to reach even the poor section of the society in the 19th century. Publishers started producing small and cheap books for the poor. These books were sold at crossroads. Public libraries were also set up by Christian missionaries and rich people to encourage the underprivileged section of the society to read more.

25 **The merit of a multi-party system-**
- It enhances electoral transparency in a democratic form of government.
- Governments in Multi-party systems are responsive and accountable to the needs of the people.

- Multi-party system is best in diverse countries as it represents the voices and opinions of each section of the society.
- This system ensures a healthy competition among different parties and prevents the dictatorship of a single party. Thus, it provides chances for the growth of the nation.

Demerits of multi-party system are-
- In this system, the country may face political instability due to the presence of several political parties.
- The introduction and implementation of public policies may take much time due to discussions and deliberations of various parties.

OR

Merits of one-party system are-
(i) Strong and Stable Government Since there is no opposition party, the government is so strong and cannot be removed or voted out of power.
(ii) Less Expensive Since there is only one party and one candidate of the party, not much money is spent on the election.

Demerits of one-party system are
(i) Undemocratic Government can become dictatorial.
(ii) No Choice It gives no choice to the voters.

26. The Bretton Woods Conference established the International Monetary Fund (IMF) to deal with external surpluses and deficits of its member nations. The International Bank for Reconstruction and Development (known as World Bank) was set up to finance post-war reconstruction.
The IMF and World Bank are referred to as the Bretton Woods Institutions or Bretton Woods twins. They commanded financial operations in 1947 and the decision making in these Constitutions were mostly controlled by the Western Industrial powers.
The International Monetary System is the system linking national currencies and the monetary system. Under this system, the national currencies followed the fixed exchange rates" and were fixed to the US dollar.

27. The highest tier of the Panchayati Raj System in rural areas is the Zilla Parishad. The Zilla Parishad coordinates the activities of all the Block Samitis in the whole district. The composition of Zilla Parishad is
(i) All the Panchayat Samitis or Mandals in a district together constitute the Zilla Parishad.
(ii) Members of the Lok Sabha and MLAs of the district and some other officials of other district level bodies are also its members.
(iii) Zilla Parishad Chairperson is the political head of the Zilla Parishad.

28. Methods of forest conservation adopted by the Government of India are-
(i) The Government of India has implemented the Indian Wildlife (protection) Act in 1972 for conservation of wildlife and forests.

(ii) The government has classified forests into three categories such as reserved forests, protected forests and unclassed forests. Out of these forests two categories, the 'Reserved' and the 'Protected forests have been restricted for use.

(iii) The government has started Joint Forest Management (JFM) programmes involving local communities in management and restoration of degraded forests.

(iv) The Central and many State Governments established national parks, wildlife sanctuaries and biosphere reserves to protect forest and wildlife of India.

29. Sustainability of development means that development should take place without damaging the environment, and development in the present should not compromise with the needs of the future generations. Here, the natural resources should be used in such a way that environmental balance is also maintained.

Sustainable development can be achieved in the following ways

(i) By scientific and proper use of the resources.

(ii) By finding out ways to stop environmental pollution.

(iii) By developing renewable sources of energy like water, wind and solar energy.

30. (i) The Indian postal network is the largest in the world. It handles parcels as well as personal written communications. Cards and envelopes are considered first–class mail and are airlifted between stations covering both land and air. The second–class mail includes book packets, registered newspapers and periodicals. They are carried by surface mail, covering land and water transport. To facilitate quick delivery of mail in large towns and cities, six mail channels have been introduced recently. They are called Rajdhani Channel, Metro Channel, Green Channel, Business Channel, Bulk Mail Channel and Periodical Channel.

(ii) India has one of the largest telecom networks in Asia. Excluding urban places more than two-thirds of the villages in India have already been covered with Subscriber Trunk Dialling (STD) telephone facility. In order to strengthen the flow of information from the grass root to the higher level, the government has made special provision to extend the twenty-four hours STD facility to every village in the country.

(iii) All India Radio (Akashwani) broadcasts a variety of programmes in national, regional and local languages for various categories of people, spread over different parts of the country. Doordarshan, the national television channel of India, is one of the largest terrestrial networks in the world. It broadcasts a variety of programmes from entertainment, educational to sports, etc. for people of different age groups.

(iv) India publishes a large number of newspapers and periodicals annually. They are of different types depending upon their periodicity. Newspapers are published in about 100 languages and dialects. Largest numbers of newspapers published in the country are in Hindi, followed by English and Urdu.

OR

Importance of Railways railways as a means of transport.-

- Railways are the principal mode of transportation for freight and passengers in India. Railways also make it possible to conduct many activities like business, sightseeing, and pilgrimage along with transportation of goods over longer distances.

- Apart from an important means of transport the Indian Railways have been a great integrating force for more than 150 years. The Indian Railway have a network of more than 7133 stations spread over a route length of 64,460 km with a fleet of 9213 locomotives, 53,220 passenger service vehicles, 6,493 other coach vehicles and 2,29,381 wagons as on March 2011.

- The Northern plains with their vast level land, high population density and rich agricultural resources provided the most favourable condition for the growth of railways. The development of Konkan railway along the west coast has facilitated the movement of passengers and goods in this most important economic region of India.

- Thus, it has been rightly said that Railways in India bind the economic life of the country as well as accelerate the development of industry and agriculture.

31. Human Development is the process of enlarging people's choices as well as raising the level of well being so that they can lead a purposeful and a creative life. Though national income and per-capita income are the main indicators of human development, it also includes many other elements such as consumption, health, environment etc. The UNDP consider four criteria as central indicators of development.

These are as follows:

(i) Per Capita Income This is the total income of country divided by its total population.

(ii) Life expectancy at birth This is the number of years, a new born child is expected to live at the prevailing conditions.

(iii) Literacy rate This is the total percentage of the population of an area at a particular time aged 7 years or above, who can read and write with understanding at least one language.

(iv) Net Attendance Ratio The total number of children enrolled in or attending primary school, as a percentage of total number of children of primary school age.

OR

Besides income, the developmental goals of various of people are different from person to Some examples of developmental goals other than income are

(i) For rich farmer, development means higher support price for crops, cheap labour and subsidised inputs. person.

(ii) For landless rural labourer, development means more days of work, schools for their children and no social discrimination.

(iii) For adivasi, development means no social discrimination, year round employment, school education for children and PDS shop in his village.

(iv) For urban youth, development means opportunity for higher education, availability of an office job and own house.

(v) For urban girls from rich families, development means freedom to choose her profession or being able to pursue higher studies abroad.

32. Democracy should be judged by its outcome because it opens the path of expectations which is one of the criteria for judging any democratic country.

Following points justify the above statement

(i) The examination procedure of democracy is eternal, as it passes one test, it produces another test.

(ii) It automatically gives rise to expectations as well as complaints by the people when they want to know about the functioning of democracy.

(iii) The fact that people also complain about democracy indicates the awareness and the ability of people to expect and to look critically at power holders and the high and the mighty.

(iv) It transforms people from the status of a subject into that of a citizen.

(v) Most individuals today believe that their vote makes a difference to the way the government is run and to their own self-interest.

OR

Following are the various loophole of democracy -

(i) Unstable Government Lots of political parties are allowed to criticise the government and its policies. Sometimes, it leads to the downfall of the ruling party and re-elections in the country. This gives instability to the government.

(ii) Slow and Inefficient Government The most common demerit of democracy is that, it is slow in its functioning. The decision-making process involves long debates and deliberations in the Parliament. This takes a lot of time before the decisions are actually taken.

(iii) Incompetence Democracy gives every individual the right to voice his concern. As a result, everybody focusses on his personal interests and not the collective interests. This sometimes leads to incompetent and wrong selections of the candidates in the government.

(iv) Role of Money in a Democracy Money plays an important role at the time of the elections. A lot of money is needed to organise demonstrations, public meetings and speeches. Those candidates are chosen in the elections, who can raise a lot of money for the party.

33. The East India Company appointed paid servants called gomasthas to supervise weavers. They used to collect supplies and examine the quality of cloth. The causes of clashes between the weavers and the gomasthas were

(i) The gomasthas gave loans to the weavers to purchase the raw material for their production. Those who took loans had to hand over the product timely to the gomasthas. They had no option to sell their products to other traders.

(ii) Often the price given by the gomasthas (dictated by the company) was miserably low and the loans the weavers had accepted tied them to the company.

(iii) Weavers along with village traders revolted and opposed the company official and sometimes migrated to other villages.

(iv) The gomasthas had no feelings to the weavers. They marched into villages with sepoys and peons and punished the weavers. Thus, clashes between the weavers and gomasthas became very common.

OR

By the end of the 19th century, Indian textile industry started to decline due to the following reasons

(i) East India Company Gained Power Once the East India Company established political power, it asserted a monopoly right to trade. It proceeded to develop a system of management and control that would eliminate competition, control costs and to ensure regular supplies of cotton and silk goods.

(ii) Growth of Cotton Industries in England As cotton industries developed in England, industrial groups became worried about the imports from other countries. They pressured the government to impose import duties on cotton textile, so that Manchester goods could easily sell in Britain without facing any competition from outside. Further the industrialists persuaded the East India Company to sell British products forcefully in the Indian market.

(ii) The Result of Two Edge Policy To sell British products in India the East India Company followed a two edged policy, i.e. no taxes on imports but high taxes on exports. Due to this policy, the local Indian market shrank and flooded with cheap Manchester machine made products.

(iv) Shortage of Raw Material Due to the American Civil War, cotton supplies from the US were cut off and Britain turned to India for cotton supplies. As raw cotton exports from India increased, Indian weavers faced the problem due to the shortage of raw materials for the textile industry.

34. (1) Chapbooks were the pocket size books that were sold by travelling peddlers called chapmen.

34.(2) Bibliotheque Bleue' are low priced small books printed in France. They were printed on poor quality paper and bound in cheap blue covers. On the other hand chapbooks were pocket size book, published in England. These became popular from the time of the 16th century print revolution.

34.(3) The new forms of literature introduced in Europe to attract the new readers were

There were almanaces along with ballads and Folktales. In England chapbooks were carried by petty peddlers and sold for a penny.

Biliotheque Bleues were low priced books sold in France.

35. (1) British Government was responsible for introducing tea cultivation In India

35. (2) Tea requires well drained soil with high amount of organic matter and pH 4.5 to 5.5. The performance of tea is excellent at elevations ranging from 1000 - 2500 m. Optimum temperature: 20 - 270 C. The nursery soil should be well drained and deep loam in nature with a pH of 4.5 to 4.8.

35. (3) Two advantages of Tea Industry in Indian Economy-

• India is among the top 5 tea exporters in the world making about 10% of the total exports. In the year 2021, the total value of tea exports from India was around US$ 687.9 million. Indian Assam, Darjeeling, and Nilgiri tea are considered one of the finest in the world.

• Tea is one of the most important cash crops and plays a significant role in rural development, poverty reduction and food security in exporting and developing countries. It is a principal source of livelihood for millions of smallholder producers.

36.(1) Formal sector credits are those that are supervised by the government and the Reserve Bank of India (RBI). Banks come under the formal sector. Even cooperatives are registered with the government and fall under the formal sector. The RBI, directly or indirectly, supervises the functioning of the formal sources of loans.

36.(2) It supervises the functioning of formal sources of loans. It promotes financial inclusion by ensuring that banks give loans not just to profit-making businesses and traders but also to small cultivators, small scale industries, and small borrowers. It manages the foreign exchange .

36.(3) **Formal sources:**

(i) They follow those sources of credit, which are registered by the government and have to follow its rules and regulations.

Example: Banks and cooperatives.

Informal sources:

(i) These include those small and scattered units which are largely outside the control of the government.

Eg- Traders, Moneylender

37.(a)   (A) Champaran
          (B) Dandi

(b)

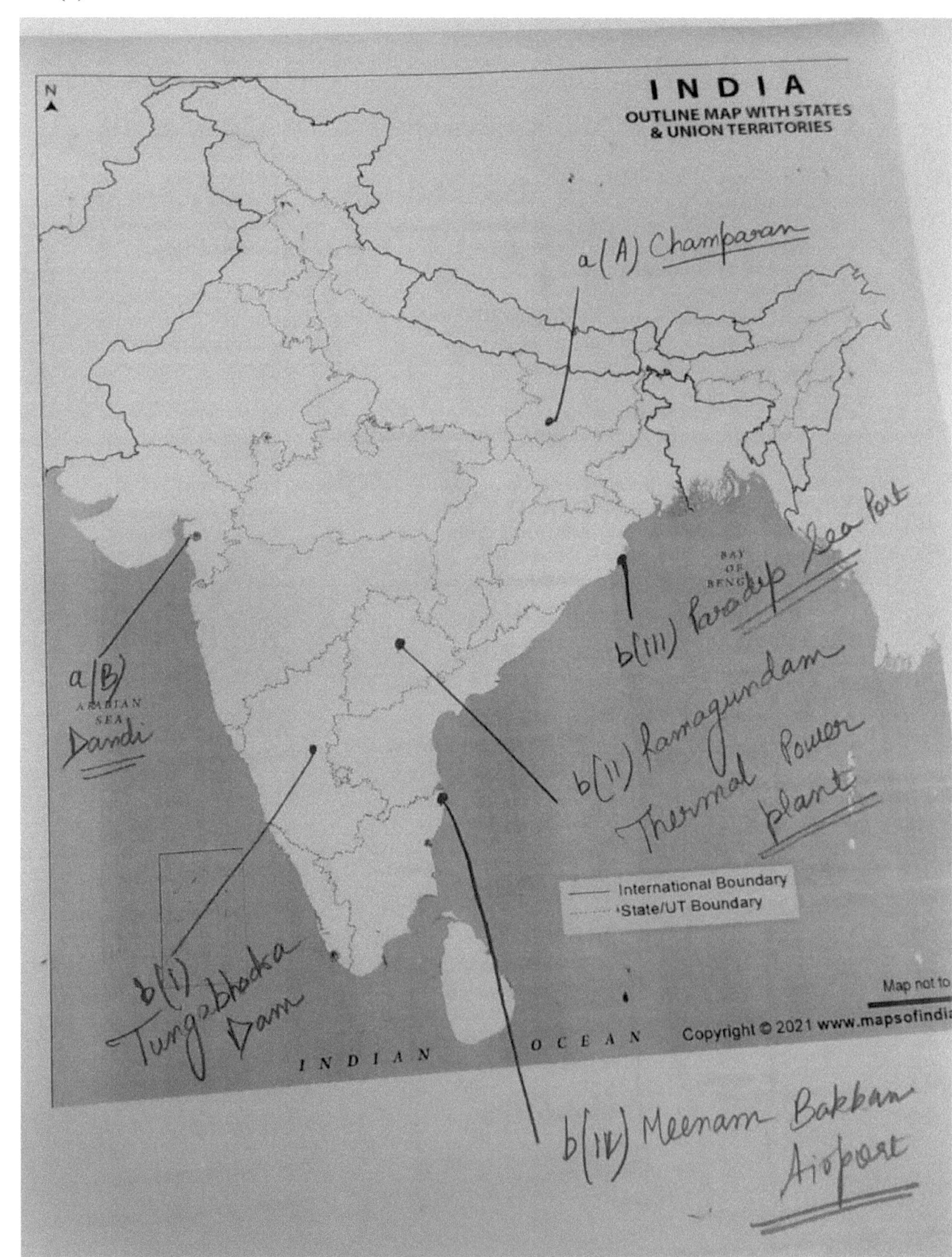

SAMPLE PAPER-7

1. **(c)** Frankfurt Parliament fail to achieve its goal because Kaiser William refused to accept the crown and opposed the assembly. This led the opposition of aristocracy and military to come stronger, the social basis of Parliament eroded.

2. **(d)** European companies gradually gained power in the 1750s after the decline of Indian merchant's trade capacity.

3. **(c)** The Corn Laws were tariffs and other trade restrictions on imported food and corn enforced in Britain in between 1815 and 1846. The word corn in British English denotes all cereal grains, including wheat, oats and barley.

4. **(d)** Pair D is correct. The Acts of Union, passed by the English and Scottish Parliaments in 1707, led to the creation of the United Kingdom of Great Britain on 1 May of that year. Liberalism is a political and economic doctrine that emphasizes individual autonomy, equality of opportunity, and the protection of individual rights (primarily to life, liberty, and property) French Revolution-Transfer of sovereignty from monarch to the French citizens.
The Zolloverein was a German customs union that was founded in 1834 during the Prussian rule. It formulated many rules for free trade and economic cooperation among the German states.

5. **(b)** The event described in the image is Founding of Young Europe in Berne. Guiseppe Mazzinni was a revolutioanry who fought for his liberal ideas. He joined Carbonari to overthrow the absolutist regime in Italy. He founded a secret society called 'Young Italy' in Marseille. Thereafter, he founded 'Young Europe', a secret society that consisted of like-minded young men from France, Poland, Italy, and some German states.

6. **(b)** Maize is grown in Uttarpradesh.
Ragi is grown in Karnataka, Maharashtra, Uttarakhand, Tamilnadu, Andhra Pradesh Coffee is grown in Karnataka, Kerala and Tamil Nadu.
Jowar is grown in Maharashtra, Karnataka and Tamil Nadu.

7. **(a)** Agriculture Diversification helps in reducing risk factors as it ensures that the farmers do not lose all of their resources.Since multiple crops can be harvested from a small field, the production increases ten-fold it makes provision for additional employment in rural areas. It effectively increases soil fertility and controls pest incidences. The boost in rural employment impacts the overall economy of the nation

8. **(b)** Gas pipelines from Hazira in Gujarat connect Jagdishpur in Uttarpradesh via Vijaypur in Madhya Pradesh. It has branches in Kota in Rajasthan, Shahjahanpur, Babrala and other places in Uttar Pradesh.

9. **(b)** Khil is generally practiced in the Himalaya Belt. Kuruwa is generally practiced in Jharkhand.
Koman is generally practiced in Odisha.
Bewar is generally practiced in the Madhya Pradesh

10. **(a)** Resource planning is essential for the sustainable existence of all forms of life.
Resource planning refers to the strategy for planned and judicious utilisation of resources. Resource planning is essential for the sustainable existence of all forms of life. This shows that resource planning is needed at the national, regional, state and local levels for the balanced development of a country.

11. **(d)** Statements 1 and 4 are the features of democracy that could be realised with linguistic reorganisation of the states. Linguistic states are those created on the basis of language. It was hoped that if the demands for separate states on linguistic basis were accepted, the threat of division and separation would be reduced. Accommodation of regional demands and the formation of Linguistic states were seen as more democratic.

12. **(a)** Subject of computer software comes in residuary subjects. Subjects which are not present in any of the lists mentioned in the constitution are known as Residuary Subjects. Union Government has the powers to make laws on Residuary Subjects. Such subjects include: Computer software, e-commerce etc. These subjects came into being after the constitution was created.

13. **(d)** In democracy power is not share between Neighbouring countries. In modern democracies, power sharing arrangements can take many forms. Power is shared among different organs of government, such as the legislature, executive and judiciary.
Power can be shared among governments at different levels – a general government for the entire country and governments at the provincial or regional level. Power may also be shared among different social groups, such as the religious and linguistic groups.

14. **(c)** Here the assertion is correct but the reason is incorrect. Judges of supreme court and high courts are appointed by the president of India who is here an executive. They can check the functioning of the executive or laws made by the Legislatures.
Judiciary is the guardian of the constitution of India. So judges have the responsibility to check over legislative,executive organs to avoid misuse of power.

15. **(a)** Under the Single-party system only one-party is allowed to function. It is a form of government where the country is ruled by a single political party, meaning only one political party exists and the forming of other political parties is forbidden.

16. **(b)** The sector described here is Primary Sector. The primary sector includes all those activities the end purpose of which consists in exploiting natural resources: agriculture, fishing, forestry, mining, deposits.

17. **(c)** The data shows the standard of living is better in Kerala as compared to Bihar.

18. **(c)** Net Attendance Ratio is the total number of children of age group 14 and 15 years attending school as a percentage of total number of children in the same age group. If the students were going to other states for higher education, the total students available in the state would go down and the net attendance ratio would not be so low. The low net attendance ratio is indicative of students dropping out of elementary school. Hence, A is true and Reason given for it is not correct.

19. **(d)** Both skilled and semi-skilled workers are employed in the tertiary sector. Service sector in India employs two different kinds of people. These are:
    (i) Highly skilled and educated workers but in less number e.g., advocates, teachers, technicians etc.
    (ii) Unskilled workers but in large number e.g., small shopkeepers, repair persons, transport persons, peddlers, hawkers, footpath vendors etc.

20. **(b)** Under Fair globalisation all the countries reap equally the benefits of foreign trades equally. Fair Globalization is about harnessing the benefits of globalization while promoting sustainable economic and social development.

21. Alluri Sitaram Raju is best remembered for leading the Rampa Rebellion against the British in which he organised the tribal people of Visakhapatnam and East Godavari districts to revolt against the foreigners. He was inspired by the revolutionaries of Bengal to fight against the British government.

    OR

    Simon Commission arrived in India in 1928.
    It was greeted with black flags and slogans like
    'Simon Go Back Both Congress and Muslim League protested against it. This Commission was boycotted by the Indian people as it did not include any Indian member in it. The Commission didn't give any hope of Swaraj for the Indians.

22. **Local Government before 1992:**
    (i) It was directly under the control of the State Government.
    (ii) Elections were not held regularly.
    (iii) Elections were controlled by the State Governments.
    Local Government after 1992:
    (i) Local Governments have got some powers of their own. ii Elections are held regularly.
    (iii) An independent state election commission is responsible to conduct the elections.

23. Secondary economic activities include construction, manufacturing, and utilities. Secondary sector industries make use of raw materials to produce something of a higher value.
    Examples of secondary activities include small potteries, handicraft manufacture, Factories that manufacture steel, chemicals, plastic, and automobiles, Textile mills, Food producing facilities such as breweries and food processing industries.

24. Industries that use minerals and metals as raw materials are called mineral based industries. Four examples of mineral based industries are
    (i) The Iron and Steel Industry
    (i) Chemical Industry
    (iii) Fertiliser Industry
    (iv) Cement Industry

25. Language Policy of India-
    The 'Language policy' was the second test for Indian federation. No language was given the status of national language by our Constitution. Hindi was identified as the official language. But only about 40 per cent of Indians has Hindi as their mother tongue.
    Therefore, 21 other languages besides Hindi, are recognised as Scheduled Languages by the Constitution. A candidate in an examination conducted for the Central Government positions may opt to take the examination in any of these languages.
    States have their own official languages. Much of the government work takes place in the official language of the concerned State. The flexibility shown by Indian political leaders helped our country avoid any conflict based on languages.

26. In situations where credit is taken to repay the earlier loans then it will increase the burden of repayment
    In high risk situations when the future is uncertain, their credit plays a negative role. For example, farmers take credit before sowing but their harvest may not be good and they may not be able to repay their loans.
    Rural borrowers normally depend on informal sources of credit who charge a high rate of interest. This repayment of larger amounts may sometimes be larger than their income. In that case, credit plays a negative role.

    OR

    Banks and cooperatives are needed to increase their lending facilities in rural. sareas because
    (i) People in rural areas take credit from moneylenders and traders who charge a very high rate of interest. These people must be aware about the role of banks and cooperatives so that they can be provided by cheap credit facilities.
    (ii) Rural people are explained by using unfair means thus, leading them to debt traps. To reduce the dependence of the informal sector in rural areas, there is a need for setting up more banks.
    (iii) Formal sources of credit provide cheap and affordable credit in rural areas without any under exploitation. These formal sources will serve as a building block for rural households. This will help the people to start up their small business or trade in certain goods.

27. This statement states the fact that the European conquest of colonies in Africa and South America was not just a result of superior, modern, sophisticated firepower. It was because of the germs such as those of smallpox that

they carried with them. Smallpox in particular proved to be a fatal disease. Once, it reached the continent, it started spreading deep into the continent and also before reaching any European there. It killed and destroyed a large portion of the community and paved the way for conquest. Thus, the global transfer of disease became instrumental in colonisation of Africa and South America.

28.

Red soil	Lateite soil
1. Red soil develops on crystlline igneous rocks in areas of low rainfall.	1. Laterite soil develops in areas with high temperature and heavy rainfall.
2. Red soil is found in parts of Odisha and Chhattisgarh, southern parts of the middle of ganga plain and along the piedmont zone of the Western ghats.	2. Laterite soil is mainly found in karnataka, kerala and the hilly areas of Odisha and Assam.
3. Red soil develops a reddish colour due to diffusion of iron in crystalline and metamorphic rocks.	3. In laterite soil, humus content is very low.

29. Difference between public sector and private sector are-

Public Sector	Private Sector
The main aim of this sector is public welfare.	The main aim of this sector is to earn maximum profit.
It is controlled and managed by the government.	It is controlled and managed by an individual or a group of individuals.
This sector provides basic facilities like education, health, food and security to the people, eg. Indian Railways, Indian Post office, BSNL	This sector provides consumer goods to the people, eg - Reliance, TISCO.

30. It is true that foreign collaboration give rise to monopolies and entry of MNCs in a domestic market may prove harmful for small-scale producers who are not able to compete with them.

- The most common route for MNCs investment is to buy up local companies and then to expand production. MNCs with huge wealth can quite easily do so.
- The large MNCs have tremendous power to determine price, quality and labour conditions for the small producers of other countries.
- The small industries in India employ the largest number of workers in the country next only to agriculture. Several of these units have shut down due to tough competition by MNCs. As a result, many workers became jobless.

- These days most employers prefers to employ workers flexibly. So, the workers' jobs are no longer secure.
- Thus, it can be concluded that MNCs often open for foreign collaborations to expand and diversify.

OR

We can feel the impact of globalisation on our daily life in following ways-

(i) It has provided huge market where we can buy and sell things produced in any part of the world. For example, there are many international brands operating worldwide. These include McDonald's, Nestle, Gillete, Toyota, etc.

(ii) With wide use of internet and other kinds of information technology, it has become much easier and faster to share information worldwide.

(ii) The growth rate of the economy h has gone up with the increase in foreign investment and foreign technology in India.

(iv) Globalisation in some ways has provided very high salary benefits to skilled people. However, in other ways, it has made the provision of flexible employment also.

(v) The quality of certain products and the availability of certain services have improved due to globalisation like electronic goods and customer care service.

31. Calling Off the Civil Disobedience Movement-
During the Civil Disobedience Movement, peaceful Satyagrahis were attacked, women and children were beaten and about 1,00,000 people were arrested. When Abdul Gaffar Khan was arrested in April 1930,several violent incidents took place in Peshawar.
In this situation, Mahatma Gandhi called off the movement and signed a pact with Lord Irwin on 5th March, 1931. This was called the Gandhi- Irwin Pact.
Relaunching of Civil Disobedience Movement-
In December 1931, Gandhiji went to London for the Second Round Table Conference but he returned disappointed as the British government refused to release the prisoners. When Gandhiji came back to India, he found that Congress had been declared illegal and Abdul Ghaffar Khan and Jawaharlal Nehru were imprisoned.

OR

Meaning of Swaraj was different for different social groups. These were-
In the countryside, rich peasant communities like the Patidars of Gujarat and the Jats of Uttar Pradesh were supporters of the Civil Disobedience Movement. They organised their communities to participate in boycott programmes. For them, the fight for Swaraj was a struggle against high revenues.
The poor peasantry found it difficult to pay their rent to the landlords as the depression continued. They joined a variety of radical movements often led by Socialists and Communists in the hope that they would not have to pay the rent any further.

Association like Indian Industrial and Commercial Congress and Federation of the Indian Chamber of Commerce and Industries under the leadership of GD Birla, Purushottam Thakur Das, etc supported the Civil Disobedience in the hope that business restrictions would be lifted. The Indian merchants and industrialists formed the Indian Industrial and Commerce Congress in 1920 and the Federation of the Indian Chamber of Commerce and Industries (FICCI) in 1927.

The industrial working classes did not participate in the Civil Disobedience Movement in large numbers, except in the Nagpur region. An important feature of this movement was the

large-scale participation of women. In urban areas, women came from high-caste families. In rural areas, women came from rich peasant households. Women were inspired by Gandhi ji's call and they began to see service to the nation as their sacred duty.

32. Multi-purpose projects and large dams have also been the cause of many environmental movements. In recent years, multi-purpose projects and large dams face several resentment and opposition from public as well as Civil Society because of their multiple adverse effects.

Some incidents are given below

Narmada Bachao Andolan or Save Narmada Movement is an NGO. It originally focused on the environmental issues related to trees that would be submerged under the dam water.

The NGO came forward with many environmentalists, tribal people, farmers and social activists demanding poor rehabilitation and ecological protections.

Inter-state water disputes are also common with regard to sharing the costs and benefits of the multi-purpose projects. For example, Krishna-Godavari water dispute between Karnataka and Andhra Pradesh Governments. It is regarding the diversion of more water at Koyna Dam by the Maharashtra Government for a multipurpose project. This diversion would reduce downstream flow in their states with adverse consequences for agriculture and industry. Thus, it leads to an inter-state water dispute.

OR

Multi-purpose projects also have many adverse effects and limitations. Due to these effects these projects have come under great opposition.

The adverse effects are as follows Effect on Soil Fertility The reservoirs that are created on the flood plains submerge the existing vegetation and soil

leading to its decomposition over a period of time.

Impact on Society

Large river projects cause large-scale displacement of local communities alongwith destruction of their livelihood and culture. Impact on Aquatic Life Dams break up rivers making it difficult for aquatic fauna like fishes to migrate especially for spawning (release or deposit eggs).

- Change in Cropping Pattern Irrigation has changed the cropping pattern in many regions with farmers shifting to water intensive methods and commercial crops. This has a great ecological consequences like salinisation of soil.
- Excessive Sedimentation at the Bottom of the Reservoir
Regulating and damming of rivers affect their natural flow. This causes poor sediment flow and excessive collection of sediments at the bottom of the reservoir.

-Excessive Use of Water

It has been observed that the multi-purpose projects induced earthquakes, caused water-borne diseases and pests and pollution resulting from excessive use of water.

33. In order to face the challenges, political parties need to be reformed. Some of the recent efforts and suggestions in our country to reform the political parties are

- Anti-Defection Law According to this law, MLAs or MPs cannot change the party after the election. If any MLA or MP changes parties, he or she will lose the seat in the Legislature. This was done because many elected representatives were involved in defection' in order to become ministers or for cash rewards.
- Details of Property and Criminal Cases In order to reduce the influence of money and criminals, the Supreme Court of our country passed an order. Now, it becomes mandatory for every candidate who contest elections to file an Affidavit giving details of his property and criminal cases pending against him. But there is no system to check if the information given by the candidate is true or not.
- File an Income Tax Return The Election Commission passed an order making it necessary for political parties to hold their organisational elections and file their income tax returns. The parties have started doing so, but sometimes, it is only formality.

Besides these suggestions, many other suggestions are often made to reform political parties.

These are as follows

A law should be made to regulate the internal affairs of political parties. It should be made compulsory for political parties to maintain a register of its members, to follow its own Constitution, to have an independent authority, to act as a judge in case of party disputes and to hold elections to the highest posts.

OR

India adopted a multi-party system for the following reasons

(i) India being a vast and diverse country, the multi-party system was needed to accommodate the vast population.

(ii) The social and geographical diversity of India could not be represented by two or three parties.

(iii) The multi-party system in India evolved over a long time, depending on the nature of society, its social, regional division, its history of politics and its system of elections.

(iv) Multi-party system ensures a healthy competition between different parties and prevents dictatorship of a single party. The Indian Constitution declares India as a democratic country. Multi-party system fulfils this criteria and provides a chance for proper growth of the nation.

34.(1) Democracy is a rule of majority and it is based on equality. Thus, it is expected that it will reduce the economic disparity among its citizens.

34.(2) Economic development of a country depends on several factors like country's population size, global situation, economic priorities, cooperation from other countries etc. Democracy can not control all these factors. In reality democracy is not successful to control the economic disparity between ultra-rich and the poor sections of people. Thus, democracy is unable to achieve higher economic development.

34.(3) As democratically elected government'is not interested to remove the disparity between the rich and poor in the society, people in poor countries depends on the grants of rich countries. Sometimes the find it difficult to poor meet their basic needs, like, food, clothing, house, etc. Poor people in some countries are even dependent on the rich countries for food supplies.

35.(1) Yes, I agree that farmers are also responsible for salinisation of soil. It is because they switched to water intensive commercial crops which need more irrigation and cause salinisation of soil.

35.(2) It is true that multi-purpose projects fail to achieve their aim for which they were built.

The dams were constructed to control floods but have triggered floods due to sedimentation in the reservoir. Moreover, the big dams have mostly been unsuccessful in controlling floods at the time of excessive rainfall. For e.g. the release of water from dams during heavy rains aggravated the flood situation in Maharashtra and Gujarat in 2006.

35.(3) It is true that dams create conflicts between people. As from the same water resources, different people want different uses and benefits. Two examples of this are as follows

(a) The Krishna Godavari dispute is due to the objections raised by Karnataka and Andhra Pradesh governments. It is regarding the diversion of more water of Koyna by the Maharashtra government for a multi-purpose project. This reduces downstream flow in their states with adverse consequences for agriculture and industry.

36.(1) The IMF was set up to promote International Monetary Cooperation. Q2- What was the Bretton Woods system?

36.(2) The Bretton Woods System was based on fixed exchange rates. In this system, national currencies viz.

The Indian rupees were pegged to the dollar at a fixed exchange rate. The dollar itself was anchored to gold at a fixed price of $35 per ounce of gold.

36.(3) In Bretton Woods Conference New Hampshire USA, decision were taken for establishing World Bank and International Monetary Fund (IMF) to preserve Global economical stability and full employment in the industrial world.

These institutions would also deal with surplus and deficit of member nations and finance post war reconstruction.

37.(a)   A.   Kheda

        B.   Amritsar

(b)

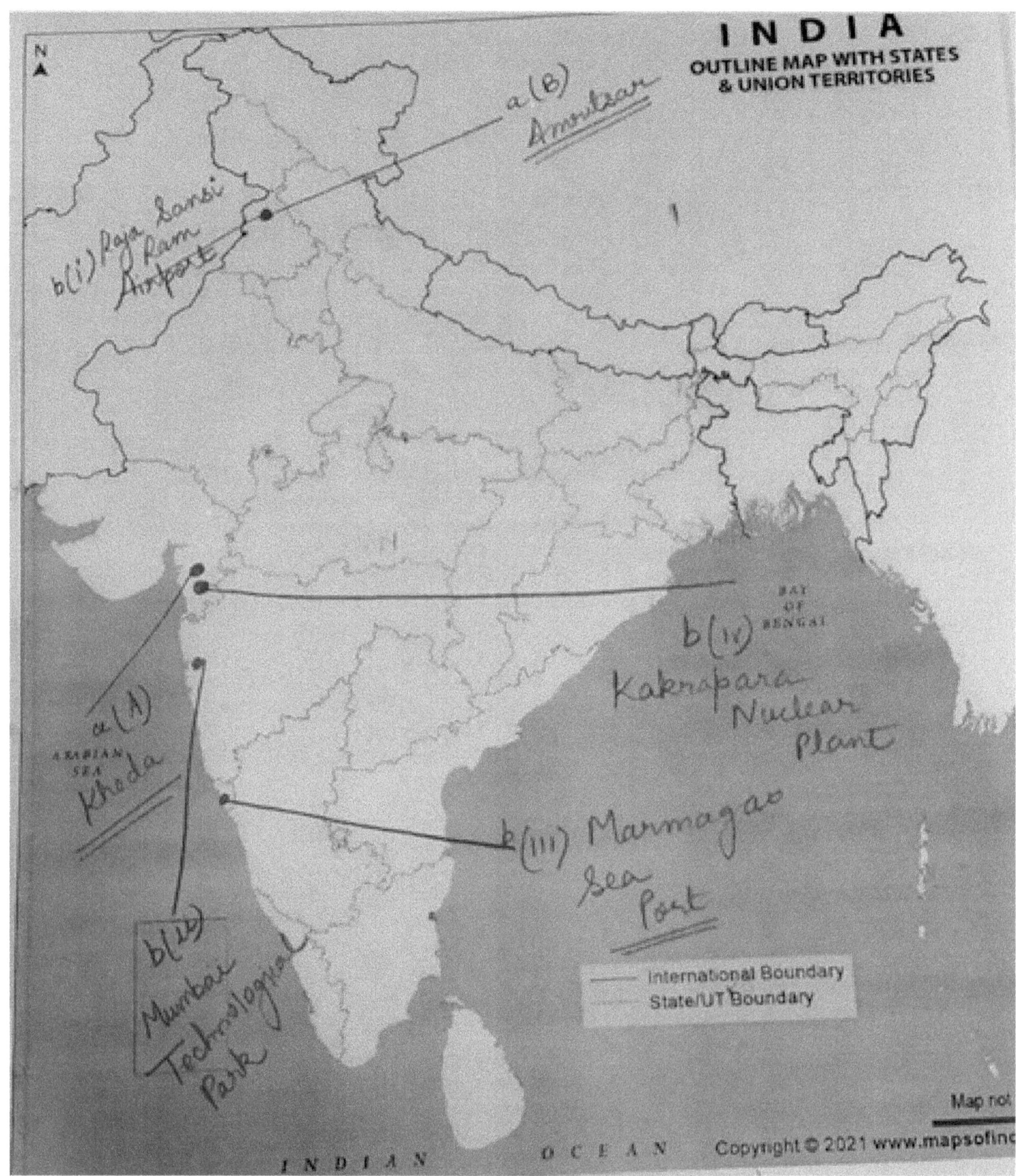

SAMPLE PAPER-8

1. **(a)** Customs barrier is any implementation of fees, rules, or regulations designed with the intention to limit international trade. Restrictions can come in the form of tariffs, levies, duties, trade embargoes, and even currency manipulation.

2. **(c)** Events arranged in a chronological order is as follows

   Gandhiji travelled to Champaran in 1917.

   The Rowlatt Act was passed in 1919.

   The Depressed Class Association was formed in 1930.

   Poona Pact was signed in 1932

3. **(c)** The image given above is a Postage Stamp with a picture. Marianne is a symbol of Republican France. A Marianne is a bust of a proud and determined woman wearing a Phrygian cap. She symbolises the attachment of the common citizens of the revolution to the Republic- Marianne is liberty, egality and fraternity.

4. **(a)** In 1848, population of Paris revolted due to food shortage and wide spread unemployment. Barricades were erected and Louis Philippe was forced to flee. As a result, various developments took place in the wake of the fleeing of Louis Philippe that are:

   A National Assembly was proclaimed a republic and granted suffrage to the adult males above 21 years and guaranteed them the right to work.

   National Work shop were setup to provide employment.

5. **(c)** The red shirts were started by Giuseppe Garibaldi. During his years of exile, Garibaldi was involved in a military action in Uruguay, where, in 1843, he originally used red shirts from a stock destined for slaughter house workers in Buenos Aires.

6. **(d)** West Bengal is the largest producer of rice in India..

   Kerala is the highest producer of Rubber in India

   Madhya Pradesh is the highest producer of pulses in India

   Maharashtra is the highest producer of jowar in India

7. **(d)** Forests that are owned by both the government and private individual sor communities. Unclassed forests are owned by both the government and private individuals or communities. North-eastern states and parts of Gujarat have a very high percentage of unclassed forests.

8. **(b)** Karnataka is the major Producer of Coffee of India. 71% of India's coffee is produced in Karnataka. The largest coffee-producing region of Karnataka is Kodagu (Coorg) district. Kodagu district of Karnataka produces 33% of the total coffee produced in India.

9. **(b)** Sugarcane is highly grown in Uttar Pradesh and Andhra Pradesh.

   Rice is highly grown in Karnataka and Tamil Nadu.

   Millets are highly grown in Bihar and Punjab.

   Maize is highly grown in Uttar Pradesh and Bihar.

10. **(d)** All the statements are correct regarding reserved forests in India.

Reserved forests are owned by the government and all human activities are not allowed in these forests. These forests are regarded as the most valuable forests in terms of conservation of forests and wild life. These forests constitute about more than half of the total forest land in India.

11. **(a)** Statement A is correct. Powers in the federations are not concentrated in single hands but distributed among units.

    On the basis of relationship between the centre and the units, the governments may be classified as unitary and federal. In a unitary government, all the powers of government are vested in the central government whereas in a federal government, the powers of government are divided between the centre and the units.

12. **(d)** A Panchayat Samiti at the block level in India is only a coordinating and supervisory authority. Panchayati Raj Institutions (PRI) is a system of rural local government in India. PRI was constitutionalised in 1992 to build democracy at the grass roots level and was entrusted with the task of rural development in the country.

13. **(d)** Political parties can be amended by following ways-

    Reducing the role of muscle power.

    Reducing the role of money

    State funding of election.

14. **(b)** Prudential reasons of Power sharing stress that power sharing will bring out better outcomes. Prudential reason for power sharing is that power sharing is good because it helps to reduce the possibility of conflict between social groups. Since social conflict often leads to violence and political instability, power sharing is a good way to ensure the stability of political order. Imposing the will of majority community over others may look like an attractive option in the short run, but in the long run it undermines the unity of the nation.

15. **(d)** The Union of State is headed by the prime minister of India.

    The Municipal Corporation is headed by the mayor. The Mayor is the political head of the Municipal Corporation. He acts as the city bureaucrat who is generally a state-appointed officer. He is usually chosen through direct vote for a term of 5 years. He is the first citizen of the city.

17. **(c)** In India, not the entire service sector is growing equally well. Service sector in India employs many different kinds of people. At one end there are a limited number of services that employ highly skilled and educated workers.

    At the other end, there are a very large number of workers engaged in services such as small shopkeepers, repair persons, transport persons, etc. These people rarely manage to earn a living and yet they perform these services because no alternative opportunities for work are available to them.

18. **(a)** Country A has a more equitable distribution of income. Equitable distribution of income means that income is distributed in a way that ensures fairness and allows everyone to have the same opportunities. Equitable distribution of income doesn't mean that income is distributed equally; it just means that income is distributed in a fair way.

19. **(d)** Raman can be placed in the obesity category. BMI of Raman is 33.3. If BMI is more than 25 then a person would be considered as overweight.

20. **(b)** This employment is an example of Seasonal Employment. The term seasonal employment refers to the practice of workers and professionals finding work during specific months of the year and being idle during the other months in which they do not have any concrete job.

21. Consequences of abolition of corn laws-
(i) The abolition of Corn Laws in England contributed to cheaper grain imports in Britain.
(ii) British farming was unable to cope with inexpensive imports and vast land was left uncultivated, leaving thousands of men and women unemployed.

22. Difference between International trade and Local trade

International trade	Local trade
International trade is carried out between two or more countries.	Local trade is carried out within a country between states or between cities, towns and villages in the same state.
Foreign currency is required for this type of trade.	National currency required for this trade.

23. The use of religion in politics, where one religion is shown as superior to other religions is called communal politics. Here, one religious group is against the other religious group and the demands of one religious group are against the demands of the other religious group.

24. The objectives of implementing the NREGA 2005 are
(i) This scheme targets the poor people of rural areas who suffer from poverty.
(ii) To provide livelihood to the people below the poverty line, this scheme guarantees 100 days of wage employment in a year to every rural/household in the country.

OR

Yes, workers are exploited in the unorganised sector because
(i) There are no fixed number of working hours. The workers normally work 10-12 hours without being paid overtime.
(ii) They do not get other allowances apart from daily wages.

25. Historians agree that print culture created the conditions within which the French Revolution occurred.
This is because of the following reasons.
(i) First Print popularised the ideas of the enlightened thinkers. Their writings provided a critical commentary on tradition, superstition and despotism.

(ii) Second Print created a new culture of dialogue and debate. All values, norms and institutions were re-evaluated and discussed by the public.
(iii) Third By the 1780s, there was a flow of literature, especially cartoon and caricatures 15 that mocked or insulted the royalty and criticised their morality.

26. The main difference between a federal form of government and a unitary are
(i) In the federal form of government like in India, the powers are divided between the Central Government and State Governments. Both levels have their areas of jurisdiction. On the other hand, in a unitary form of government, the National Government has all the powers. Any constitutional power given to the states or regions of the country is dependent on the National Government, which can be withdrawn at any time. Sri Lanka is one such example.
(ii) In a federal system, a State Government has powers of its own for which it is not answerable to the Central Government. On the other hand, in a unitary system, the State Government does not have power of its own.

27. It is right that national development of a country depends on the availability of public facilities. Public facilities are those provided by the government. They may be either highly subsidised or totally free of cost for the people.
They are important because poor people do not have enough income to be able to avail facilities provided by the private sector, resulting in difficulties faced like inadequate healthcare, poor nutrition, lack of education etc. The utility of two public facilities available in India are:
(i) The Public Distribution System (PDS) which provides fair average quality of foodgrains and other essential items to the weaker sections of the population at subsidised price.
(ii) Healthcare in government hospitals and which is provided to all at subsidised rates. This includes outpatient as well as hospitalisation facilities.

28. Yes, I agree with the statement that in India, there are regions which are rich in certain types of resources, but are deficient in some other resources. There are some regions which can be considered self-sufficient in terms of the availability of resources, while some regions have acute shortage of vital resources.
Some examples are as follows
States like Jharkhand, Chhattisgarh and Madhya Pradesh are rich in coal and minerals, but lack technological and institutional support.
- Arunachal Pradesh has abundant water resources, but lacks in infrastructure development. Rajasthan is well endowed with wind and solar energy, but lacks water resources.
- The cold desert of Ladakh lacks natural resources, although it has a rich cultural heritage.

OR

India has land under a variety of relief features. In India, 30 per cent area are mountainous, 27 per cent are plateaus and 43 per cent are plains, all of these have specific advantages to be utilised. Main advantages of India's land

- Mountains are source to many streams and rivers, some of them are perennial. These regions have very high potential for hydro electricity productions, etc and are also good tourism destinations.
- Plateaus are mostly laden (heavily loaded) with minerals, fossil fuels and forest, etc so are economically very useful.

Plains are most important land resource for human beings. These are fertile and most of the food crops, etc are grown here. They are also useful for the development of factories, roads, etc.

29. It is correct that several services which cannot be provided by private sector can be provided by the public sector. It is due to following reasons

(i) Only the government can invest large sums of money on projects with a long gestation period such as the railways.

(ii) Only the public sector provides quality health services at economical rates, as it works for the welfare of the people, e.g. AIIMS.

(iii) Public sector provides electricity at a lower cost rate to protect and encourage the small scale industries, e.g. NTPC. Private sector cannot provide electricity at a reasonable rate.

30. Gandhiji launched the Civil Disobedience Movement because Lord Irwin ignored Gandhi's eleven demands including the abolition of the Salt tax. Gandhi's 'Salt March' marked the beginning of the Civil Disobedience Movement all over India. Thousands of people in different parts of the country broke the salt law by manufacturing salt and giving demonstrations in front of government salt factories.

The following points state how the Civil Disobedience Movement came into force in various parts of the country and united different groups in the country

(i) With the spread of the movement, foreign cloth was boycotted and liquor shops were picketed. Peasants refused to pay revenue and chaukidari taxes. Village officials resigned from their post. Forest people violated forest law.

(ii) In the countryside, rich peasant communities viz, Patidars of Gujarat and the Jats of Uttar Pradesh became the supporters of the Civil Disobedience Movement.

(iii) The poorer peasantry, often led by the socialist and the communist, joined a variety of radical movements for the remission of their unpaid rent to the landlords.

(iv) Industrialists led by Purshottamdas Thakurdas and GD Birla supported the Civil Disobedience Movement. Moreover railway workers, dock workers, mine workers from Chota Nagpur and large number of women from all over India participated in the Civil Disobedience Movement.

OR

Dalit participation was limited in the Civil Disobedience Movement.

It can understood through following points

(i) Dalits or untouchables belong to the lower strata of our society. The Congress party ignored the Dalits for fear of offending the conservative high caste Hindus, i.e. Sanatanis. Gandhiji first realised that Swaraj would not come for a hundred years if untouchability was not eliminated. But many Dalit leaders believed in a different political solution to the problem of their community.

(ii) Dalits thought that only political empowerment would resolve their problem of social disabilities

(iii) They began organising themselves, demanding reserve seats in educational institutions and a separate electorate that would choose their Dalit.members for Legislative Councils.

(iv) Dr Ambedkar demanded a separate electorate for Dalits which was denied by Gandhiji.

(v) Dalit movement continued to be apprehensive of the Congress led national movement and their participation was limited.

Thus, it can be concluded that Dalit participation was limited in the Civil Disobedience Movement.

31. The following are the steps that can be taken to curb the pollution in freshwater sources caused by industries

(i) Minimising water usage by reusing and recycling waste water in two or more successive stages.

(ii) Rainwater harvesting to meet water requirements.

(iii) Treating hot water and industrial wastes before releasing them in rivers and ponds.

This can be done in three phases

(i) Primary treatment by mechanical means (ie. screening, grinding, flocculation and sedimentation.)

(ii) Secondary treatment by biological processes. Such as planting trees, rain water harvesting. iii) Tertiary treatment by chemical, physical and biological processes like recycling of waste water, in sewage treatment plants.

OR

The following are some of the general measures to minimise environmental pollution:

Overdrawing of groundwater reserves by industries need to be regulated legally.

Generators and other machinery should be tied with silencers and other noise absorbing materials to reduce their sound.

Particulate matter in the air can be reduced by fitting smoke stacks to factories with electrostatic precipitators, fabric filters, scrubbers and inertial separators.

Use of oil or gas instead of coal to reduce smoke emission from factories Redesigning machinery to increase their efficiency in using energy Promote sustainable development by integrating economic development goals with environmental construction.

32. The Human Development Index (HDI) is a single index measure that aims to record the three key dimensions

of human development: access to knowledge, a decent standard of living, and long and healthy life. In other words, the Human Development Index is practiced to measure how development has improved human life.

Indicators of the Human Development Index

The three indicators or factors that represent the different aspects of life include the following

Life expectancy: The human's longevity is measured by life expectancy at birth. The life expectancy at birth means how many years a newly born person is expected to survive in this world. This indicated the element of health in the Human Development Index.

Education: It is measured by the expected years of schooling life of a child at the school entry age and the mean years of schooling of the adult population.

Standard of Living: The standard of living of people is measured by Gross National Income per capita adjusted for the price level of the country.

OR

Sustainable development is referred to as the idea that human beings should sustain by meeting their basic needs, while also making sure that the future generations are able to meet their basic needs.

Emphasis of Sustainable Development

1. **Economic Growth:** For creating an economy that is sustainable and growing in the right direction.

2. **Protecting the Environment:** This objective focuses on contribution by humans towards protecting and enhancing the natural environment, by minimising pollution and waste, also working towards reducing the global carbon footprint..

3. **Social Inclusion:** This objective focuses on providing the facility of housing for future generations and assisting in creating healthy, strong and vibrant global communities.

Importance of sustainable development:

1. Using the available resources judiciously and working towards maintaining the ecological balance.

2. To prevent degradation of the environment and lay emphasis on protecting the environment.

3. To prevent overexploitation of resources.

4. Is it justified to state that it is not politics that gets caste ridden, but it is the caste that gets politicised? Explain.

33 It is correct to say that it is not politics that gets caste ridden, but it is the caste that gets politicised. Caste can take various forms in politics

(i) Each caste group tries to become bigger by incorporating within it neighbouring castes or sub-castes which were earlier excluded from it.

(ii) Various caste groups are required to enter a coalition with other castes or communities and thus enter a dialogue and negotiation.

(iii) New kinds of caste groups have come up in the political arena like 'backward' and 'forward' caste groups.

(iv) Caste plays different kinds of roles in politics. In some cases, politics gives many disadvantaged communities the opportunity to demand their share of power.

(v) Politics has helped people from OBC and Dalit castes to gain better access to decision-making.

(vi) But sometimes exclusive attention to caste can produce negative results like tensions, conflicts and violence in our society.

OR

In India women still lag behind men despite some improvements since independence.

This can be analysed in the following ways

(i) As India is still dominated by Patriarchal society,gender discrimination is prevalent at present. Parents prefer to spend money for a boy's education, thus dropout among girl child is high in schools.

(ii) Girls perform as well as boys in school, but the literacy rate among women is only 54 percent compared with 76 percent among men.

(iii) The proportion of women among the highly paid and valued jobs is still very little. Much of her work is not paid and therefore not valued.

(iv) In almost all areas of work, women are paid less than the men, even when both works exactly the same.

(v) Women still face harassment, exploitation and violence in our society.

34.(1) When state power is used to establish domination of one religious group over the rest of the groups and the demands of one religious group are formed in opposition to another, communalism happens at that time.

34.(2) If the followers of different religions have some commonalities then these will be superficial and immaterial from the stand point of communalism. Their interests should be differ according to the believers of communal politics

34.(3) People of the same religion do not have the same interests and aspirations. They have different views and identities. Thus any attempt to bring all followers of the same religion together is to suppress many voices within the same community.

35.(1) Punjab and Haryana of India produce rice commercially

35.(2) Rice is considered a subsistence crop in Odisha because it is grown on small patches of land with very little agricultural inputs. Productivity is also less.

35.(3) Farmers buy agricultural inputs like fertilisers, pesticides, HYV seeds and provide irrigation facilities in their limited land to take maximum output from it.

36.(1) The non-cooperation movement was launched in 1920 with the aim of obtaining self-governance and ultimately getting the British colonial authorities to grant full independence to India.

36.(2) The non cooperation movement had a great impact on Indian textile. Swadeshi goods got a great impetus. It led to the increase in Swadeshi goods providing a relief to the vanishing textile industry of India. The import of foreign goods halved between 1921 and 1922.

36.(3) Workers had their own understanding of Mahatma Gandhi and the notion of swaraj. For plantation workers in Assam, freedom meant the right to move freely in and out of the confined space in which they were enclosed, and it meant retaining a link with the village from which they had come.

37.(a)   A. Champaran

        B. Madras

(b)

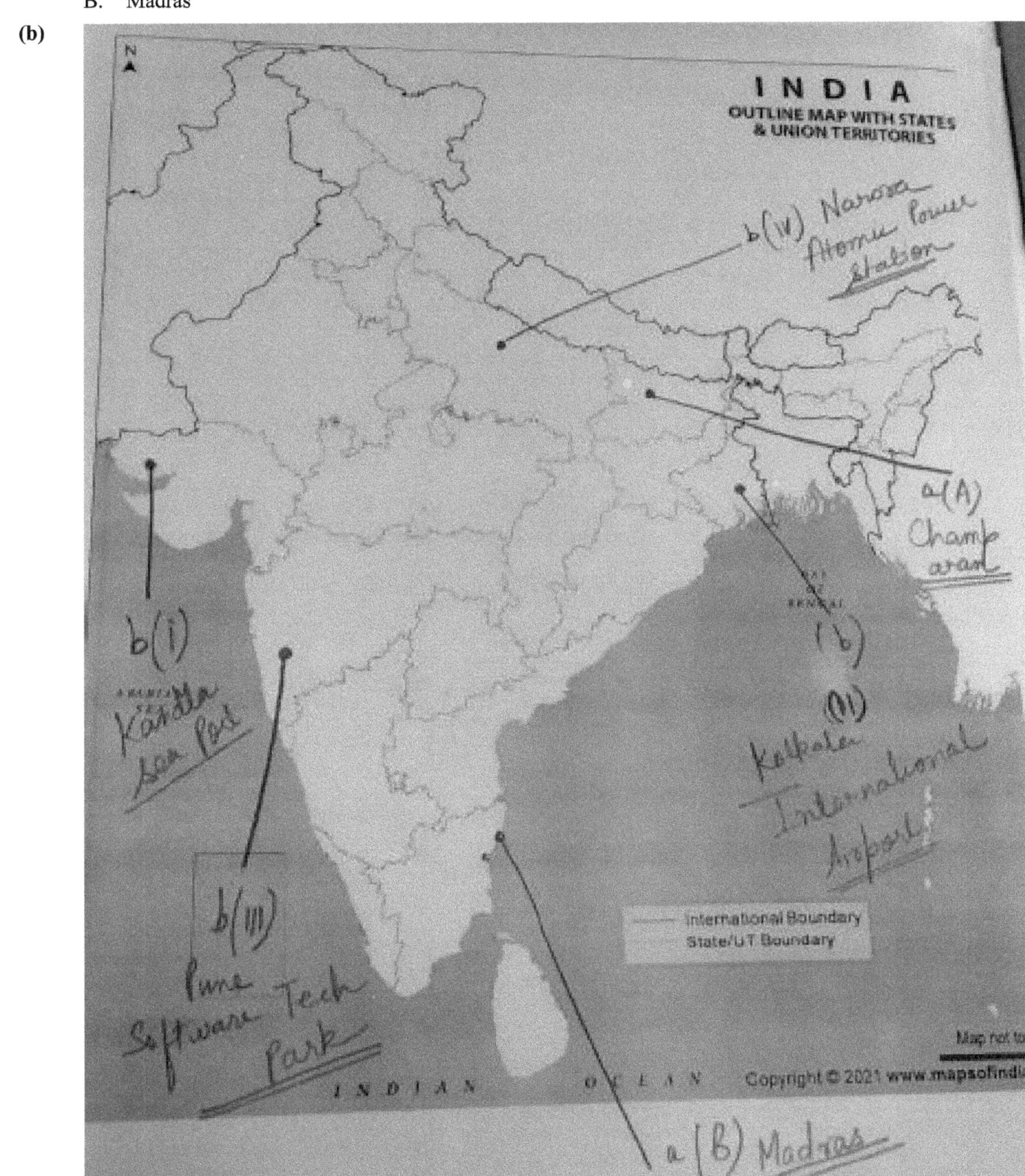

SAMPLE PAPER-9

1. **(c)** It was a Custom Union at the initiative of Prussia. The Zolloverein was a German customs union that was founded in 1834 during the Prussian rule. It formulated many rules for free trade and economic cooperation among the German states. It abolished the tariff barriers and reduced the number of currencies from over thirty to only two.

2. **(b)** Austria, Denmark and France
Austria, Denmark and France were involved in the Three Wars with Prussia and ended with victory and unification of Germa
The three wars were the War with Denmark, the Austro-Prussian War, and the Franco-Prussian war. These wars led to the unification of Germany. The Austro-Prussian War was essential for the more extensive contention among Austria and Prussia and brought about Prussian predominance over the German states.

3. **(a)** The Balkan was region of geographical and ethnic variations (Greeks, Serbs, Montenegro etc). A large part of Balkans was under the control of the Ottoman empire, so the disintegration of the Ottoman empire made this region explosive. Thus, statements I and II are correct.
Balkan states were fiercely jealous about each other and all hoped to gain more power. So, statement III is not correct.

4. **(b)** The Parliament through a bloodless revolution seized power from the monarchy.
The formation of the nation-state in Britain was not the result of a sudden upheaval or revolution. It was the result of a long-drawn-out process where the English Parliament had seized power from the monarchy in 1688.

5. **(c)** Events arranged in a chronological order is as follows-Agreement on Vienna peace settlement in 1815
Greek struggle for independence initiated in 1821
Integration of Italy took place in 1861
Unification of Germany took place in 1871

6. **(c)** Germania became the allegory (abstract idea which is expressed through a person) of the German nation.

7. **(d)** Option (d) is correct: It is one of the processes of land utilisation. Land is left uncultivated due to the following.reasons
(i) To allow it to store organic matter and recover the fertility of the soil. When land is leftuncultivated, the nutrients in the soil are allowed to accumulate.
(ii) To serve the purpose of disrupting the life cycle of the pests and insects that harm theplants by removing the host plants for a period of time.

8. **(d)** Laterite soil develops under tropical and sub-tropical climate with alternate wet and dry season and this humus rich soil is particularly found in the hilly areas of Karnataka, Kerala and Tamil Nadu.

9. **(c)** Rio de Janeiro Earth Summit convened to discuss environmental protection and socio economic development at the global level in 1992. In June 1992, more than 100 heads of different cour tries met in Rio de Janeiro in Brazil for the first International Earth Summit.

10. **(c)** India is known for its good quality of coffee, i.e. Arabic variety of Yemen. Its cultivation is confined to the Nilgiri in Karnataka, Kerala and Tamil Nadu.

11. **(a)** Social conflict often leads to violence and political instability. Power sharing is a good way to ensure the stability of political order and it reduces socio-economic conflicts.

12. **(a)** Power sharing reduces the possibility of conflict between social groups and ensures the stability of political order.
Hence, power sharing is necessary for maintaining social harmony and peace among different groups. It brings transparency in the government by making it good for democracy.

13. **(a)** By adopting the majoritarian policy (a belief that the majority community should be able to rule a country in whichever way it wants by disregarding the wishes and needs of the minority), Sri Lanka passed an Act in 1956 which recognised Sinhala as official language by disregarding Tamil. It followed the preferential policies to foster their culture, language and religion. Thus, both Assertion and Reason statements justify each other.

14. **(c)** There are 22 Languages in the Eighth Schedule of the Indian Constitution. Thus, Anita can opt any of the twenty-two languages for her examination.

15. **(a)** The constitution declared India as a Union of States as States are sovereign in their prescribed legislative field and their executive power is co-extensive with their legislative powers. Thus, it is clear that the power of the states are not coordinate with the Union.
The sharing of power between the Union government and the State Government is basic to the structure of our constitution. It is not easy to make changes to this power sharing arrangement. The Parliament cannot on its own change the arrangement. Thus, the statements I and II are correct and the statement III and IV are incorrect.

16. **(a)** Union List It includes subjects of national importance such as defence, foreign affairs, banking, communications and currency.
State List It contains subjects of state and local importance such as information technology, police, trade commerce, agriculture and irrigation.
Concurrent List It includes subjects of common interest to both the Union Government as well as the State Governments, such as education, forest, trade unions, marriage, adoption and succession.

17 **(a)** The Body Mass Index (BMI) can be calculated by dividing the weight in Kg by the square of the height.

18 **(b)** Has the most equitable distribution of income
Equitable distribution of income ensures distributing

welfare to ensure fairness and allowing members of the economy to have the same opportunity to accumulate wealth. Here, Rita found that country A has most equitable distribution of income, thus, she has chosen this country.

19. **(a)** Workers in the Primary Sector are underemployed
In India, more than half of the workers are working in the primary sector, mainly in agriculture, producing only a quarter of the GDP. There are more people in agriculture than required. So, even if we move a few people out, the production will not be affected Hence, in other words, we can say that workers in primary sector are underemployed.

20. **(c)** A is true, but R is false

21. The British government built these new canals for the following reasons
(i) They built a network of irrigation canals in West Punjab to transform semi-desert land into fertile agricultural lands.
(ii) The Britishers wanted to export wheat and cotton. So people from other parts of Punjab were called and settled to grow wheat and cotton canal colonies.

22. Casteism and communalism are bad as they usually divide the society and enhanceinequality. These two are major challenges to our democracy. Our constitution makers were aware of these challenges. That is why they chose the model of a secular state. On the other hand, feminism is a good thing as it believes in equal rights and opportunities for men and women. It aimed at defining, establishing and defending equal political, economic and social rights for women.

23.

Agro based industries	Mineral based industries
Industries which are dependent on agriculture to obtain their raw material are called agro-based industries.	Industries which are e dependent on mineral resources to obtain their raw material are called mineral-based industries.

Or

Negative impacts of waste from the nuclear plants are stated in the points below
(1) Waste from nuclear plants have radioactive properties and may cause cancers, birth defects and miscarriages.

24. Rupees in Indian currency is backed by the RBI, so it is accepted as a medium of exchange and cannot be refused as a form of payment.

25. Government attracts foreign investment in the followings ways
(i) Special Economic Zones have been set up to have world-class facilities such as cheap electricity, roads, transport, storage, etc.
(ii) The companies setting their units in SEZs are exempted to pay tax for initial period of fiveyears which increases their profit.
(iii) Labour laws are made flexible in SEZs. This has attracted foreign investment.

26. The highest tier of the Panchayati Raj System in rural areas is the Zilla Parishad. The Zilla Parishad coordinates the activities of all the Block Samitis in the whole district. The composition of Zilla Parishad is
(1) All the Panchayat Samitis or Mandals in a district together constitute the Zilla Parishad.
(2) Members of the Lok Sabha and MLAs of the district and some other officials of otherdistrict level bodies are also its members.
(3) Zilla Parishad Chairperson is the political head of the Zilla Parishad.

27. Weavers lived hard lives who produced coarse cloth in the 20th century. Amongst weavers some produced coarse cloth while others wove finer qualities.
The position of weavers who produced only coarse cloth can be explained in the following ways
(1) The coarse cloth was purchased by the poor. Its demand fluctuated violently.
(ii) In times of bad harvest and famines, poor people could not buy cloth as they had little to eat and their cash income disappeared.

Or

The conditions of workers in Europe after the Industrial revolution were as follows
(i) In most of the industries, the demand for labour was seasonal. The actual possibility of getting a job depended on existing networks of friendship and relations.
(ii) The workers were getting very low wages.
(iii) Factories employed a large number of women. With technological development womengradually lost their industrial jobs.

28. Important features of telecom network are mentioned below
(1) India has one of the largest telecom networks in Asia.
(ii) More than two-thirds of the villages in India have already been covered with SubscriberTrunk Dialing (STD) and this facility is to be extended 24 hours in every village of the country.
(iii) There is a uniform rate of STD facilities all over bas lo India.

29. The Per Capita Income of a country is the total Income of the country divided by its total population. It is used to compare the development of countries by the World Bank. The country with a higher Per Capita Income implies that its people are earning more on an average and this is considered the indicator of higher development. However, this hides the fact that there may be wide differences in the earnings of people, which implies inadequate social development.

30. By the first decade of the 20th century, a series of changes affected the pattern of industrialisation in India.

These are explained in the following points

(i) Effect of Swadeshi and Boycott

After the partition of Bengal, the Swadeshi Movement was developed. It has two sides i.e. positive and negative. On the positive side, nationalists urged people to use only swadeshi goods and on the negative side they mobilised people to boycott foreign goods. This movement had an immense effect on the economy. There was an increase in the demand for Indian goods, especially clothes.

(ii) Aim of Industrial Groups

Industrial groups organised themselves to protect their collective interests. They pressured the government to increase tariff protection and grant other concessions.

(iii) Decline of Exports to China

From 1906, the export of Indian yarn to China declined as produce from Chinese and Japanese mills flooded the Chinese markets. Thus, industrialists in India began shifting from yarn to cloth production. Cotton goods production in India doubled between 1900 and 1912.

(iv) Result of the First World War,

Until the First World War, industrial growth was slow. British mills became busy with war production, thus Manchester imports to India declined. Suddenly, Indian mills got a vast home market to supply. As the war prolonged, Indian factories had to supply different war needs. This led to set up new

Or

From the very beginning of the industrial age, advertisements played a vital role in expanding the markets for products. The role of advertisement was as follows

The Manchester industrialists began selling their cloth in India by putting labels on the cloth bundles. When buyers saw such labels on the cloth like 'Made In Manchester', they felt confident about buying the cloth.

- The manufacturers also used images of Indian Gods, Goddesses and importantpersonalities on these labels. These images helped to make the foreign products somehow familiar to Indian people.
- In the late 19th century, the British manufacturers used calendars to popularise their products. Unlike newspapers and magazines, calendars were being used even by illiterate people.
- Indian manufacturers even advertised the nationalist message which was clear andspecific. For example, if you care for the nation then buy products that Indians produce'. Advertisement became a medium of the message of Swadeshi.

31. It is true that minerals are an integral part of our lives. This can be understood through the following examples: Almost everything that we use in our daily life, from a tiny pin to a towering building or a big ship, are all made from minerals.

The railway lines and the paving of the roads, machinery, implements and tools too are made from minerals.

Minerals form the basis of all industries.

Our food contains various minerals that are essential for our body. They are absorbed by the body.

In conclusion, we can say that in all stages of development, human beings have used minerals for their livelihood, decoration, festivities, religious and ceremonial rites.

Or

Biogas can solve the energy problem in the rural areas due to the reasons mentioned below

(i) It produces gas having higher thermal efficiency than charcoal and kerosene.

(ii) It provides a way for optimum utilisation ofanimal and plant waste.

(iii) It produces enriched organic manure that can supplement or even replace chemicalfertilisers.

(iv) It burns smoothly and does not leave much residue behind.

(v) It is easy to produce and store.

Some suggestions to improve the biogas energy production in rural areas are given below

(i) Government should provide monetary assistance to people in the rural areas to set up biogas plants.

(ii) Awareness must be created for using this alternative sources of energy.

32. Two groups may have different notions of development. For example, The local community's notion of development on the case of construction of a dam was that they areas in which they live will be submerged and their will be greater environmental degradation.

However, the government's notion of development in this case would be that by raising the height of the dam, they would be able to provide more water to the people of Saurashtra region of Gujarat, which always suffers from water scarcity. In addition, more electricity would be generated with this measure, which would benefit all the people living in that area.

Or

Body Mass Index (BMI)

Body Mass Index (BMI) is an international standard used to determine whether an adult person is undernourished or not. If we divide the weight of a person by the square of his/her height, we get a ratio which is called BMI. The BMI is an important way to understand the level of nutrition a person takes.

BMI = Weight in kg/height in metres^2 For example, if a girl student is 14 years and 8 month old and the BMI is 15.2, then she is undernourished. Similarly, if the BMI of a boy aged 15 years and 6 months is 28, then he is overweight.

Human Development Report

Human Development Report published by UNDP (United Nations Development Programme) is one of the best methods to measure development.

The report compares countries based on three criterias namely

Living standard (Per Capita Income)

Health status (Life expectancy)

Educational levels of the people (Literacy rate and years of schooling).

India occupies 129th rank in HDI 2019. The Human Development Index (HDI) considers public health, education, poverty level, inequality and environmental aspects to measure human development.

33. Secularism refers to the separation of religion from the state. It means that the state should not discriminate among its citizens on the basis of religion. It should neither encourage nor discourage the followers of any religion. In India main features of secularism are

(i) There is no official religion for the Indian states, i.e. unlike Sri Lanka (Buddhism), Pakistan (Islam) and England (Christianity).

(ii) All individuals and communities have thefreedom to profess, practice and propagate any Religion or not to follow any religion.

(iii) It prohibits discrimination on grounds of religion.

(iv) It allows the state to intervene in the matters of religion in order to ensure equality withinreligious communities, viz. it bans untouchability.

Or

Caste inequalities are still prevalent in India. This statement can be explained in this way

(1) In India hereditary occupational division was sanctioned by rituals. Members of the samecaste group form a social community. Often they maintain the same or similar occupation.

(2) In India most of the marriages are held in the same caste group. Intercaste marriage isnot welcomed by all.

(3) Sometimes people do not eat with members from other caste groups.

(4) Untouchability has not ended completely, although it is prohibited by our constitution.Discrimination against the 'outcaste group' is still prevalent in our society.

34.(1) The main motive of the Non -cooperation movement was the achievement of Swaraj. Its motive was to grant self-government and another motive was the restoration of the old status of the Caliph.

34.(2) Gandhi's idea of swaraj did not simply mean political independence from the foreign rule; it also implied the idea of cultural and moral independence.

34. (3) • As per the Emigration Act, plantation workers were not permitted to leave the garden without permission, or they were rarely given such permission.

• As per plantation workers in Assam, freedom means right to move freely in and out of the places in which they were enclosed and it also meant extending or keeping a link with the village from which they had come.

• When they heard of the non-cooperation movement, thousands of workers defied the authorities, left the plantation and headed home.

35.(1) Formal Sources of Credit or Loans are those that come from banks, non-government establishments and financial institutions. These are typically recognized as credible lenders by other business enterprises, making their products and services appealing to investors.

35.(2) Difference between formal and informal source of credit

Formal sources typically charge lower interest rates whereas Informal sources of credit charge much higher interest rates for informal sources.

35.(3) Three functions of RBI are-

It promotes the integrity, efficiency, inclusiveness and competitiveness of the financial and payments system.

It ensures efficient management of currency as well as banking services to the Government and banks.

It supports the balanced, equitable and sustainable economic development of the country.

36.(1) Commercial farming is a farming method that involves growing crops, raising livestock, selling produce on the market, and making money. Commercial agriculture mainly produces high-demand crops.

36.(2) Rubber trees require moist and humid climates with heavy rainfall of more than 200cm.

It grows well in equatorial climate and temperature above 25-degree Celsius Q3- Evaluate the merits of commercial farming.

36.(3) Two merits of commercial farming are

1. Commercial farming boosts the power supply to areas in the suburbs of farmed land since it uses machinery and electricity.

2. It contributes to the improvement of local infrastructure. Roads are paved to facilitate the transit of goods and equipment quickly and comfortably.

37 (a)   A. Champaran
          B. Dandi

(b)

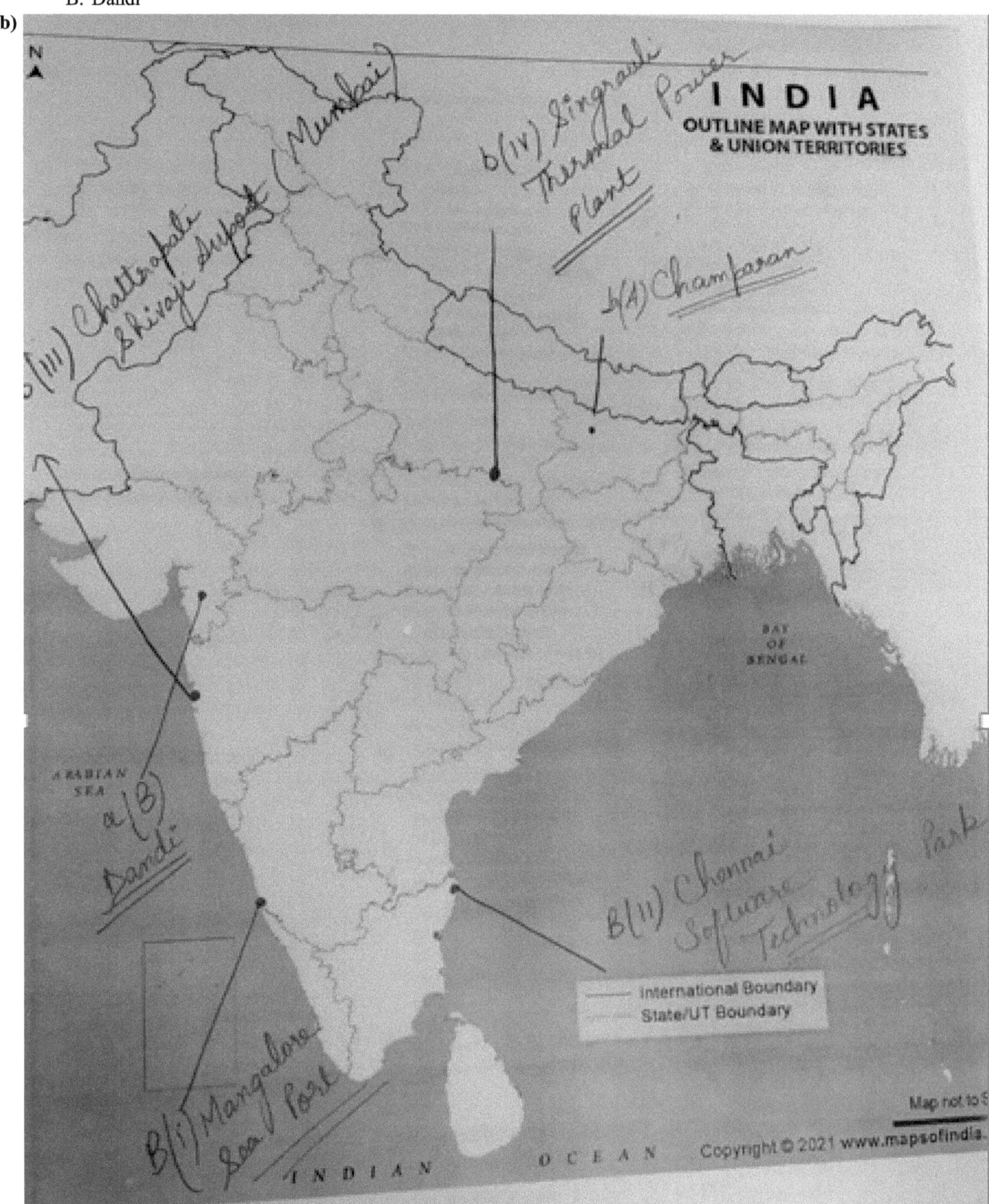

SAMPLE PAPER-10

1. **(a)** During the election of the Assembly, women were denied suffrage rights. Women were admitted only as observers to stand in the visitors' gallery, when the Frankfurt parliament convened in the Church of St Paul.

2. **(c)** Fall of Napoleon in 1814-15. The Continental Blockade, the Peninsular War, the Russian Campaign, and the direct role of Britain led to the decline of Napoleon.

3. **(c)** The image of baby Krishna was most commonly used to popularise baby products.

4. **(b)** Both A and R are true, but R is not the correct explanation of A. The Chauri Chaura incident occurred at Chauri Chaura in the Gorakhpur district of the United Province, (modern Uttar Pradesh) in British India on 4 February 1922, when a large group of protesters, participating in the Non-cooperation movement, clashed with police, who opened fire. In retaliation the demonstrators attacked and set fire to a police station, killing all of its occupants. The incident led to the deaths of three civilians and 23 policemen. Mahatma Gandhi, who was strictly against violence, halted the Non-cooperation Movement on the national level on 12 February 1922, as a direct result of this incident.

5. **(a)** Events arranged in a chronological order is as follows-
   French Revolution - 1789
   Napoleon invaded Italy - 1796
   Unification of Italy- 1861
   Unification of Germany - 1871

6. **(b)** Laterite soil develops in areas with high temperature and heavy rainfall. Humus content of the soil is low because most of the microorganisms, particularly the decomposer like bacteria, get destroyed due to high temperature. Laterite soils are suitable for cultivation with adequate doses of manures and fertilizers.Main reason for laterite soils formation is due to intense leaching. Leaching happens due to high tropical rains and high temperature.

7. **(a)** Monazite sands of Kerala are rich in thorium. Monazite sands comprise phosphate minerals of elements such as cerium which occur as small brown crystals in the Kerala sands. These monazite sands are mined for both cerium and radioactive thorium oxide

8. **(a)** The correct answer is Madhya Pradesh, Odisha, Andhra Pradesh and Rajasthan. India has the second-largest manganese ore reserves in the world after Zimbabwe.
   The main reserves are found in Karnataka, followed by Madhya Pradesh, Orissa, Maharashtra and Goa.
   Minor occurrences of manganese ore in
   Andhra Pradesh, Jharkhand, Gujarat, Rajasthan and West Bengal.

9. **(a)** Kandla in Kuchchh was the first port developed soon after Independence to ease the volume of trade on the Mumbai port, in the wake of loss of Karachi port to Pakistan after the Partition.

10. **(c)** Statement 3 is incorrect because the National Highways are maintained by the Central Public Works Department (CPWD).

11. **(d)** Democracy is a best form of government because of the following reasons:
    (i) A democratic government is a better government because it is an accountable form of government.
    (ii) Democracy improves the quality of decision making.
    (iii) Democracy provides a method to deal with differences and conflicts. Democracy enhances the dignity of citizens.

12. **(a)** India has adopted the policy of Secularism. Secularism is an ideology that says religion should not be involved with the ordinary social and political activities of a country. It dictates that there is no official religion of the state. Secularism abolishes communalism and ensures harmony and unity among the countrymen.

13. **(a)** A major step towards decentralisation was taken in 1992. The Constitution was amended to make the third-tier of democracy more powerful and effective.

14. **(c)** Dravida Munnetra Kazhagam (DMK)is a regional party. A regional party is a recognised political party whose influence is limited to a particular state of the nation.
    Except option c, all are national political parties.

15. **(b)** The Sri Lanka has Unitary Form of Government in which states are in subjugation to the center. It has semi presidential government system where two executives are present i.e. President along side with the Prime Minister and the Cabinet.

16. **(b)** When it comes to income , the World Bank divides the world's economies into four income groups: high, upper-middle, lower-middle, and low. The income classification is based on a measure of national income per person i.e per capita income

17. **(d)** $4000 + 7000 + 3000 + x / 4 = 5000$
    $14000 + x / 4 = 5000$
    $X = 20000 - 14000$
    $= 6000$

18. **(c)** BMI of Rahul
    150 cm into meter
    1.5 m
    $40/1.5 \times 1.5$
    $40/2.25$
    18.5
    BMI of Rahul is 18.5

19. **(b)** Share of sectors in GDP for 2000 Total GDP of three sectors

$= (52000 + 48,500 + 1,33,500)$

$= 2,34,000$ crore

Share of Primary sector

$= 52000/(2,34000) \times 100 = 22.22 \%$

Share of Secondary sector

$= (48,500) / (2,34000) \times 100$

$= 20.72 \%$

Share of Tertiary sector

$= (1,33,500)/(2,34000) \times 100 = 57\%$

20. **(c)** Money is called medium of exchange because money is a widely accepted token that can be used for exchange of any good or service.

21. **State Highways**

These are roads linking a state capital with its district headquarters. They are constructed and maintained by the State Public Works Department (SPWD) in States and Union Territories.

District Roads

These roads connect the district headquarters with other places of the district. These roads are maintained by the Zila Parishad of the district.

OR

Road transport is growing in importance as compared to railways because of the following reasons .

(i) Construction cost of roads is much lower than that of railway lines.

(ii) Roads can be built in uneven surfaces like hills and mountains.

22. Being producers of commercial crops, they were very hard hit by the trade depression and falling prices due to which the rich peasant communities took active participation in the Civil Disobedience Movement

23. Democracy is based on consultation and discussion. A democratic decision always involves many people, discussions and meetings. When a number of people put their heads together, they are able to point out possible mistakes in any decision. Even though this takes time, taking time over important decisions is a must. This reduces the chances of rash or irresponsible decisions. Thus, democracy enhances the quality of decision making.

24. The public sector contributes to the economic development of a nation by:

Improving Infrastructure -Economic development depends upon the creation of basic infrastructure such at powe transportation, communications, irrigation, education etc. As only public sector enterprises can arrange the larg investment necessary for such infrastructure, they contribute greatly to economic development

25. **(i) Per Capita Income**

The Per Capita Income is the total income of the country divided by its total population. It is also called average income.

(ii) Net Attendance Ratio

Net Attendance Ratio is the total number of children of age-group 14-15 attending school as a percentage of the number of children in the same age group.

OR

It can be said that Nisha's nutritional condition is much better than Sunita. Nisha is taking proper nutrition due to which her weight is normal but Sunita is underweight. This is known by finding out the BMI.

Sunita's BMI $= 36/1.45 \times 1.45 = 17.21$

Nisha's BMI $= 48/1.45 \times 1.45 = 22.82$

Sunita's BMI is 17.12 which is less than 18.5, hence she is not healthy. Nisha's BMI is 22.82 which is between 18.5 and 25, so she is healthy and hence taking proper nutrition.

26. The effects of non-cooperation on the economic front were dramatic. Foreign goods were boycotted, liquor shops picketed, and foreign cloth burnt in huge bonfires. The import of foreign cloth halved between 1921 and 1922, its value dropping from Rs 102 crore to Rs 57 crore. In many places merchants and traders refused to trade in foreign goods or finance foreign trade. As the boycott movement spread, and people began discarding imported clothes and wearing only Indian ones, production of Indian textile mills and handlooms went up. As a result of the boycott of British goods, Indian merchants and mill owners made a lot of money during this time. Khadi was given a raise.During this time, sugar imports from the United Kingdom fell dramatically.

27. The procedure or working of roof top rain water is a typical method. The rainwater falling on the roof is collected through a PVC pipe and filtered using sand and bricks. Then, it is collected in the sump for immediate use. Excess water from the sump is transferred to a well, which recharges the groundwater. Any further requirement of water can be taken from the well. Sometimes, a hand pump is attached to the pipe that connects the sump. With the use of a hand pump, the collected rain water can then be drained out and used.

28. Dictatorship is defined as an autocratic or authoritarian form of government in which a government is ruled by either an individual or an authoritarian party.

In dictatorship, a particular individual has power in the government and exercises his own will while taking the decisions. Here, masses are ignored while taking the decisions. great

The dictator or a few powerful individuals have all the economic, social, intellectual and moral powers to take decisions.

Such regimes justify, that it is better for the power to be concentrated in few hands, so that some goals can be achieved at a quicker speed.

29. (i) **Union List -** It includes subjects of national importance like defence, foreign affairs, banking and currency as we need uniform policies on these matters throughout the country. The Union Government alone can make laws relating to the subjects mentioned in the Union list.

(iii) **Concurrent List -** It includes subjects of common interest to both the Union and the State Government like education, forest, trade unions, marriage, adoption and succession. Both the Union and the State Government can make laws on these subjects

30. Gross Domestic Product (GDP) is the total sum of the value of all final goods and services of all the sectors of the economy of a country produced during a year. The counting of the

various goods and services for calculating GDP can be understood by the following example.

Wheat and flour are intermediate goods used for making final products like bread and biscuits. Intermediate products should not be counted in GDP. Biscuits and breads are the final products prepared using flour and other ingredients like sugar, salt, oil, etc.

Only the final products are reaching the actual consumer. The value of the intermediate products are already counted in the final products and if this is again counted, it will lead to double counting, causing an error in the estimation of GDP.

OR

The history of developed countries reveals a general pattern of development in their economic structure.

First, primary sectors predominantly contributed to GDP and held most of the employment. Then when agricultural activities increased, there was a need for industrialisation and gradually industrial sectors dominated the economy. Much of the workers shifted to the industrial sector, but agriculture productivity did not hamper as the industrial sector produced farm equipment, fertilisers etc that increased the productivity.

After a hundred years, the service sector increased and most of the workers shifted to service sector. Now, the service sector contributes maximum to the share of the economy.

The service sector has now become the most important sector in terms of total production and employment generation without disturbing the production and productivity of other two sectors.

So, it is seen that the economic structure had been shifting from primary to secondary and finally to the tertiary sector in developed countries. Similarly, almost all the developing countries are following the same path but may be at a different pace.

31. Political parties are rightly called the government in disguise. The four arguments in reference to the statement are

(i) In most democracies, elections are fought among the candidates put up by political parties. The party which wins the majority, forms the government. In a parliamentary system, the leader of the party in power becomes the Prime Minister and he appoints the other ministers.

(ii) In a democracy, a large number of similar opinions have to be grouped together to provide a direction in which policies can be formulated by the government. Political party reduces a vast multitude of opinions into a few basic positions and if it is ruling party, government accepts the line taken by it

(iii) Political parties raise and highlight issues. Often they shape public opinion. There are always some socio-economic and political issues at the domestic and international level. Political parties always try to tackle the issues.

(iv) The parties which play the role of opposition in the government always criticise the government for its wrong policies. Opposition parties mobilise opposition to the government.

OR

Lack of internal democracy is a challenge to the efficient functioning of political parties.

The following points justify the statements

(i) All over the world, there is a tendency in political parties towards the concentration of power in one or few leaders at the top.

(ii) Parties do not keep membership registers, do not hold organisational meetings and do not conduct internal elections regularly.

(iii) Ordinary members of the party do not get sufficient information on what happens inside the party. They do not have the means or the connection needed to influence the decisions. As a result, the leaders assume greater power to make decisions in the name of the party.

(iv) Since one or few leaders exercise the power in the party, those who disagree with the leadership find it difficult to continue in the party.

32. The cultivation of fruits and vegetables is known as horticulture. India ranked second after China (2015) in the production of fruits and vegetables in the world. It produces both tropical as well as temperate fruits. Fruits are grown in orchards and plantation. Some of the important fruits produced in India are mango, banana, orange, pineapple, grape, apple, apricot, walnut, litchi and guava. India produces around 13% of the world's vegetables. Some of the important Vegetables produced in large quantities in India are peas, cauliflower, onion, cabbage, tomato, brinjal and potato.

States that are famous for the production of oranges and apricots are Orange Maharashtra (Nagpur), Meghalaya(Cherrapunji) Apricot Himachal Pradesh, Jammu and Kashmir.

OR

Jute is called golden fibre for its colour and high cash value in India. Geographical conditions

(i) It grows well in well-drained fertile soils in the floodplain where soil is renewed every year.

(ii) It requires a high temperature during growth, so a hot and humid climate is required. Among major regions of jute production, West Bengal, Assam, Bihar, Odisha and Meghalaya are important.

Uses of Jute

(i) Jute is used in making carry bags, carpets, ropes, yarn and other artefacts.

(ii) Its stem is also used for fuel in rural belt.

(iii) After refining and proper treatment, used for clothes. it can be used for clothes

(iv) It is cropped for commercial purposes which earns a livelihood for farmers.

(v) It is used to replace polythene bags in India to promote a pollution free environment.

33. Many women contributed to print culture. Prominent among them were :

Rashsundari Debi

In East Bengal, Rashsundari Debi, a young married girl in a very orthodox family, learnt to read in the secrecy of her kitchen. She wrote her autobiography Amar Jiban' in 1876.

Kailashbashini Debi

From the 1860s, some Bengali women like Kailashbashini Debi, highlighted the experiences of women i.e. how they were imprisoned at home, kept in ignorance, forced to do hard domestic work and treated unjustly.

Tarabai Shinde and Pandita Ramabai

In the 1880s,women writers like Tarabai Shinde and Pandita Ramabai both from Maharashtra, wrote about the miserable lives of upper caste Hindu women, especially widows.

Begum Rokeya Sakhawat Hossein

In 1926, famous educationist and literary figure, Begum Rokeya Sakhawat Hossein disapproved of men for withholding education from women in the name of religion.

OR

China was one of the countries where the earliest kind of print technology was developed.

The different stages of development of printing technology in China are

(i) From AD 594 onwards, books in China were printed by rubbing paper against the inked surface of woodblocks. These papers were also invented in China. The imperial state of China was the major

producer of printed material for a very longtime. At that time, China possessed a huge bureaucratic system which recruited its personnel through civil service examination. From the 16th century, the number of candidates for the examination increased, so the number of books also increased.

(ii) By the 17th century, urban culture developed in China and merchants, rich women, wives of scholar-officials not only started reading different books like, fictions, poetry, autobiographies, anthologies of literary masterpieces, romantic plays, they also began to write.

(iii) In the late 19th century, Shanghai became the hub of the new print culture by importing Western printing techniques and mechanical presses. From hand printing, there was a gradual shift to mechanical printing in China.

34.(1) Three sectors of an economy are Primary sector, secondary sector and tertiary sector.

34.(2) In the 'Secondary Sector', the natural products are changed into several useful forms through manufacturing for example: making sugar from sugarcane or making cement from limestone and then constructing a house. All the industries of this type are kept in the secondary sector.

34.(3) The primary sector includes the basic industries for providing basic materials to other industries.

The secondary sector includes industries that use basic materials to form new and improved materials.

The tertiary sector includes industries that supply the materials made by the secondary industries to the consumers.

35.(1) The Congress of Vienna ensure peace in Europe by laying out a balance of power between all the great powers in Europe.

35.(2) Conservatives believed in traditional and cultural values. They were the people who supported monarchy and nobility. They believed that privileges of the monarchy and nobility should exist. After the French Revolution, they contended that gradual changes should be brought in the society.

35.(3) Main features of Napoleonic Code

• It removed all privileges based on birth, established equality before the law and secured the right to property.

• It simplified administrative divisions in Dutch Republic, Switzerland, Italy and Germany.

• It abolished the Feudal system and freed peasants from serfdom' and manorial dues[1].

36.(1) The laterite soil is formed under conditions of high temperature and heavy rainfall with alternate wet and dry periods.

36.(2) Features of laterite soil

All laterites are of rusty-red coloration, because of high iron oxide content.

Laterite soil is a rock type soil rich in iron and aluminium, and is commonly considered to have formed in hot and wet tropical areas.

36.(3) **Red Soil**

(i) Red soil develops on crystalline igneous rocks in areas of low rainfall.

(ii). Red soil is found in parts of Odisha and Chhattisgarh southern parts of the middle of Ganga plain and along the piedmont zone of the Western ghats.

(iii) Red soil develops a reddish colour due to diffusion of iron in crystalline and metamorphic rocks.

Laterite soil

(i) Laterite soil develops in areas with high temperature and heavy rainfall

(ii) Laterite soil is mainly found in Karnataka Kerala and the hilly areas of Odisha and Assam.

(iii) In laterite soil humus content is very low.

37.(a) A. Nagpur
  B. Amritsar

(b)

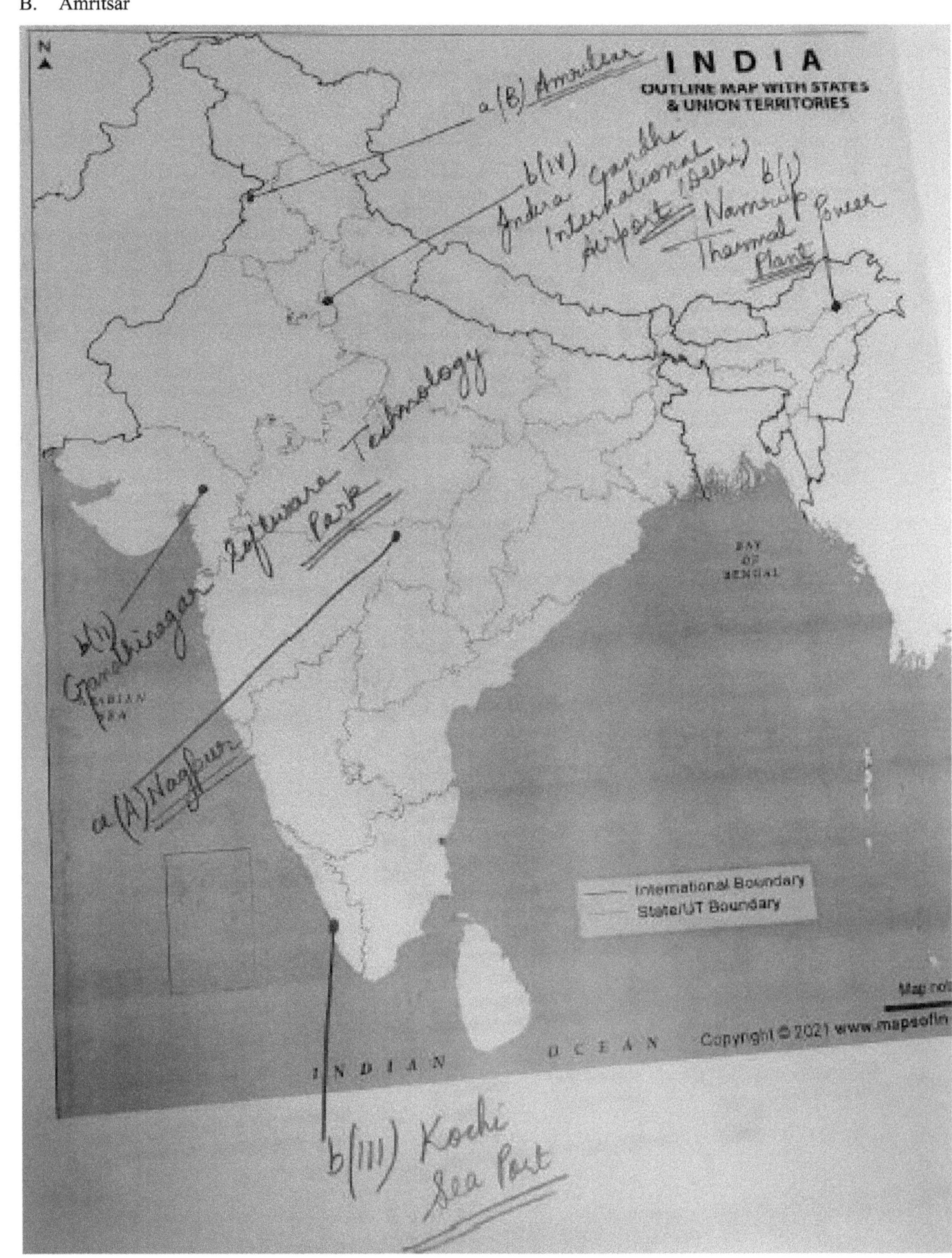